FROM MAINFRAMES
TO SMARTPHONES

MARTIN CAMPBELL-KELLY
DANIEL D. GARCIA-SWARTZ

From Mainframes
to Smartphones

A History of the International
Computer Industry

HARVARD UNIVERSITY PRESS   Cambridge, Massachusetts, and London, England   2015

First printing

Library of Congress Cataloging-in-Publication Data

Campbell-Kelly, Martin.
   From mainframes to smartphones : a history of the international
computer industry / Martin Campbell-Kelly and Daniel D. Garcia-Swartz.
       pages cm
   Includes bibliographical references and index.
   ISBN 978-0-674-72906-3 (alk. paper)
   1. Computer industry—History. 2. Computer industry—United
States—History. I. Garcia-Swartz, Daniel D., 1962– II. Title.
   HD9696.2.A2C36 2015
   338.4'7004—dc23   2014039385

Contents

PART IV   THE INTERNET ERA, 1995–2010

FROM MAINFRAMES
TO SMARTPHONES

Introduction

The aim of this book is to provide a compact and up-to-date business and economic history of the computer industry. The reader we have in mind is someone who wants to make a "quick study" of the computer industry. There is, in fact, no shortage of histories of the computer industry, and they fall into two broad classes. First, there are deeply researched and lengthy scholarly works dealing typically with a relatively narrow facet of the industry. Second, there are shorter and livelier treatments, but generally these are lightly documented or cover just a sliver of the industry. Because we know of no reasonably comprehensive treatment of the recent developments in the computer industry, we seek to fill what we and our editors view as a gap in the market: a book that is short, reliable, and includes an analysis of the industry through 2010 or so.[1] In our quest for brevity, we have assumed that our readers are themselves information-technology users and are familiar with the everyday vocabulary of computing (such as "operating systems," "disk drives," and "broadband"), and that they are aware of recent gadgetry such as tablet computers and smartphones.[2]

Although this book is primarily a business and economic history, the development of the computer industry is also a social and technical story that features many agents of change: human actors, corporations, and technologies. Among the human actors were the professional scientists, engineers, and mathematicians—and college kids—who made the key innovations, and the entrepreneurs who turned them into products. The computer industry was created by myriad firms of wildly distinct characters: from the staid office machine giants such as IBM and Remington Rand to college-dorm start-ups such as Dell Computer Corporation and Facebook. Above all, the relentless pace of technological improvement has transformed the industry, resulting not only in the "revolution in miniature" that saw the cost and power of electronics improve by multiple orders of magnitude but also in the development of complementary technologies such as storage devices, software, and telecommunications. We try to bring some of this background to our narrative, although our twin foci are primarily business and economic.

PERIODIZATION AND THEMES

There are many possible ways to organize the telling of the 60-year history of the computer industry, but we have opted for the most straightforward: a strictly chronological narrative. We have divided our story into four parts, each encompassing 15 years, beginning in 1950 and ending in 2010. By fortuitous historical accident, each one of these four periods constitutes a largely self-contained epoch in the evolution of the computer industry. The first period, from 1950 to 1965, saw the beginning of the commercial exploitation of the computer and the emergence of the first major players in the industry. The second period, spanning from 1965 to 1980, saw the arrival of the IBM System/360 computer family, which created the first information-technology standard and transformed the industry. The third period, from 1980 to 1995, saw the emergence of the personal computer, which led to another industry transformation. The final period we consider, covering the years 1995 to 2010, saw the industry transformed yet again, this time by the commercial development of the Internet. Although our periodization highlights these major transformations, we use the trends, themes, and continuities that defined the industry over time to thread our narrative. We detail these below.

One major theme in the development of the computer industry is the unstoppable miniaturization of computer platforms, a trend driven primarily by technological change in the field of electronics. The early mainframes were massive machines typically housed in dedicated spaces with powerful air-conditioning equipment. The first step toward making computers more compact came with the introduction of minicomputers and small business computers in the 1970s. Another step came with the dawn of the personal computer in the 1980s. In recent years further miniaturization has resulted in the proliferation of smartphones, which are in essence general-purpose computers with telephone capabilities.

A second theme in our book is the shifting core of the computer industry from hardware to software and services. Computer hardware has tended to become a commodity; only those firms able to successfully diversify into other markets have managed to remain significant players in the industry. No company provides a better example of this transformation than IBM, the firm that has stayed at the top of the industry for decades. Although by 1995 IBM may have been perceived as a computer hardware company, it was already obtaining almost half of its revenues from computer software and services. At the time of this writing, IBM derived just 17 percent of its revenues from hardware.

A third theme in the industry is the evolution of "computers as systems." Information systems are collections of interconnected hardware and software components that work well with one another. In the early days of the industry, computer vendors supplied bundles of hardware, software, and services. During the 1960s independent firms entered the market to compete with computer manufacturers by supplying complements for computer processors. "Plug-compatible" manufacturers of peripherals, for example, thrived by supplying components that could be connected to IBM mainframes and beat IBM's peripherals in price-performance ratio. Later that decade, IBM started unbundling software from hardware, a decision that facilitated the development of a software market populated by numerous independent providers.

Manufacturers of computer processors have traditionally faced the choice of either supplying all the components of the system themselves or relying on third-party suppliers for at least some components. In the early days of System/360, IBM implemented a fully integrated model: it supplied all-inclusive systems designed and manufactured in-house. With the IBM PC, the company changed its approach radically: the PC's components were sourced from a variety of third-party vendors. In recent decades the process of vertical disintegration of PC production, driven by its modular nature, has deepened even further along geographic dimensions, with manufacturing of components shifting first to Asian countries such as Taiwan and later to China.

Computers are often described as both "systems" and "platforms." System- or platform-type products are characterized by "network effects," a topic that comes up often in our book. Network effects generally happen when additional users generate benefits for existing users. System- or platform-type products with just one type of user can only derive benefits from *direct network effects:* early adopters of computer mainframes, for example, benefited from a growing user base because, among other things, a growing base led to the formation of user groups that facilitated the exchange of technical information and software, which reduced costs for all participants. *Indirect network effects* happen in platforms where there are users of different types— computer owners and commercial software developers, say—and an increase in the number of one brings about benefits for the other. A growing user base for the IBM PC, for example, generated strong incentives for developers to create software for IBM-compatible PCs, and the rising availability of IBM-compatible software further attracted users. Platforms such as these, with multiple user types and indirect network effects, are usually known as multisided platforms.

A fourth theme covered in this book is the rise and fall of standards: sets of technical specifications that, because of their pervasiveness, dictated the competitive dynamics of the industry for a significant period of time.[3] The IBM System/360, introduced in the mid-1960s, was such a standard, perhaps the first in the history of the computer industry. A second was the IBM-compatible PC standard, introduced in the early 1980s. Some standards were owned or sponsored by a single firm—IBM's ownership of the System/360 standard is the quintessential example. Other standards, including that of the IBM-compatible PC, were owned or sponsored by more than one firm— Intel and Microsoft were the principal beneficiaries in this case. Newly introduced standards reshape the competitive dynamics of the industry because firms that do not own or sponsor the standard are usually forced to resort to one of three strategies: competing by supplying systems that are incompatible with the standard; competing by marketing systems that are compatible with the standard but better in price-performance; or competing in a niche market poorly covered by the computers embedding the standard. These competitive patterns appear time and again in our narrative.

A fifth and related theme is the competition between proprietary and open standards. Proprietary standards are ones in which one or more firms own the key components of the standard and profit from that ownership. For example, Intel owned the microprocessor and Microsoft owned the operating system at the core of the IBM-compatible PC standard, which brought both companies immense financial rewards. The 1980s, however, witnessed the rise of open standards, such as the UNIX operating system, which were available to all comers. Many companies exploited the UNIX standard to compete with previously dominant proprietary standards. The rise of open standards in the 1980s was perhaps as disruptive to the computer industry as the arrival of the personal computer.

A sixth theme relates to how various national governments fostered their domestic computer industries. In its early years, the American computer industry, highly entrepreneurial as it was, did not develop in isolation from the U.S. government. Indeed, the government was one of the main sources of demand for computers at least through the mid-1950s. But it is also the case that the U.S. government never implemented the kinds of economic policies in favor of the domestic computer industry that governments in several Western European countries and Japan put into practice. For example, in 1952 the U.S. Justice Department launched an antitrust suit against IBM regarding the way it marketed its electromechanical equipment. The 1956 Consent Decree, which emerged from the lawsuit, had an impact on IBM's subsequent behavior in both the electromechanical and the computer equipment markets.

The governments of Britain, France, and West Germany anointed national champions in the computer industry and invested resources to try to fend off the American penetration of their domestic markets. The government of Japan implemented a somewhat different policy: rather than promoting a national champion, it erected barriers to trade that protected its domestic market from foreign competitors, while facilitating both competition and R&D cooperation among several Japanese companies. Among these different approaches to industrial policy in computers—no national champion in the United States, national champions in Western Europe, a protected market for several competitors that cooperated with one another in Japan—some turned out to be more successful than others.

A final theme in our book is the coexistence of persistence and change in the computer industry.[4] On the one hand, the history of the computer industry has been one of constant change: changes in technology, in the key sources of revenue, in the geographic location of production, and in the industry segment that dictated the pace of change of the industry as a whole (from mainframes to personal computers and most recently to mobile computing devices). On the other hand, there has been a remarkable degree of persistence in the industry. Standards have persisted for many years, sometimes decades. The mainframes used in organizations as of this writing in 2014 are still compatible with the System/360 standard that IBM created in the 1960s. The IBM-compatible PC (or Intel-Microsoft) standard introduced in the early 1980s remains dominant in the personal computer market.

The persistence of companies is perhaps even more remarkable than the persistence of standards. Some of them—including IBM, Microsoft, Apple, Hewlett-Packard, Automatic Data Processing, and the Computer Sciences Corporation—have succeeded as major players for several decades by regularly "reinventing themselves." Others, including Digital Equipment Corporation, Compaq, and Electronic Data Systems, no longer exist as independent companies but were major players in their markets for a long time. Persistence in an industry is driven by complex factors that are often poorly understood. We hope that our interpretation of the evolution of the computer industry will contribute some insights toward the growing literature explaining long-run corporate success.

STRUCTURE OF THE BOOK

As explained above, this book is divided into four parts, each part covering a 15-year period in the 60-year history of the computer industry.

Part I (Chapters 1–3) analyzes the events of 1950 to 1965, which we call the "era of no standards," since no computer model (or family of models) was dominant enough to dictate the dynamics of the industry. This was the period in which the early computer industry developed, at a differential pace, in the United States and in a number of other (mostly Western European) countries. We analyze computer demand at the dawn of the industry, the computer start-ups, the early entrants and their entry strategies, and the supply of "complements" (mainly software and services) for computer processors. We raise and attempt to answer two fundamental questions: What were the factors that propelled IBM to the top of the American and international computer industry? And why did a domestic computer industry develop in the United States at a much faster pace than anywhere else?

Part II (Chapters 4–6) covers 1965 to 1980, the "era of the IBM System/360 standard." This period extends roughly from the unveiling of IBM's System/360 to the introduction of the IBM-compatible PC. We start by focusing on the structural shakeup that IBM generated with the introduction of System/360 and the competitive responses to it not only in the United States but also in several European countries and Japan. In addition, we explore the rise of minicomputers and small business computers in the 1970s, software companies' transformation from software contractors to producers of corporate software products, and the rise of new computer-services sectors such as the computer time-sharing industry. We maintain an international and comparative perspective by analyzing the strategies that national governments in Western Europe and Japan implemented to foster the development of their own computer industries.

Part III (Chapters 7–9) examines the period from 1980 to 1995, the "era of the IBM PC standard," starting with the introduction of the IBM PC up to the advent of the commercial Internet. We examine the diffusion of personal computers and the approaches that personal computer makers adopted to compete in the marketplace. We also track the growth of the personal computer software industry, highlighting the rise and fall of software leaders in various product categories, including operating systems and applications. The rise of open systems, including the UNIX operating system, is also explored, along with what it meant for companies that had thrived on the basis of proprietary designs. Additionally, we provide an international and comparative perspective by gauging the extent to which the rise of the personal computer (and the relative decline of mainframes and minicomputers) affected the computer industry in countries other than the United States.

Part IV (Chapters 10–12) closes the book, tracing events in the industry from 1995 to 2010—the "era of multiple standards"—from the rise of the commercial Internet to the present time. These years witness the (sometimes peaceful and sometimes conflictive) coexistence of standards in different layers of the industry: the System/360 standard for mainframes, the Intel-Microsoft standard for personal computers, the open standards of the Internet, the UNIX open standard for server operating systems, and the more recent smartphone standards—Apple's proprietary iOS standard and Google's open Android standard, among others. We highlight how the Internet has transformed the industry, including the declining significance of computer hardware as a revenue source, the rise of the open-source software movement, the development of software-as-a-service (SaaS) platforms, and the metamorphosis of traditional computer companies such as IBM into computer-services companies. A notable feature of this most recent phase in the history of the computer industry is the shifting of computer production to new geographic locations and the rise of new players on the international software scene.

PART I

Origins of the Computer Industry
1950–1965

CHAPTER ONE

The Mainframe Computer Industry

C hapters 1, 2, and 3 focus on the period from 1950 to 1965, the first 15 years in the life of the international computer industry. One could characterize this as an era without standards, because no computer model (or family of models) became dominant enough to dictate the competitive dynamics of the industry as a whole.

In the United States, this time frame witnessed the rise of the first computer start-ups in the late 1940s and early 1950s, the computer forays of a variety of incumbent firms from the office-equipment and electronics-control industries, and also the irruption, in the late 1950s and early 1960s, of a few firms dedicated exclusively to computer design and production for specific market niches. Computer developments in other countries, including Britain, France, Germany, and Japan, occurred during this period as well, but they took place somewhat later than in the United States and at a more leisurely pace. American computer manufacturers—IBM especially—penetrated foreign markets, but foreign producers failed to establish a presence in the American market.[1]

The first "mainframe" computers were large, room-sized systems that were housed in air-conditioned environments. The images of computers shown in films such as *Desk Set* (1957) and *Billion Dollar Brain* (1967) give a good impression of what early computers looked like.

The first computers were serviced by a staff of operators and programmers numbering at least a dozen, and often many more. Computer users spent as much in computer-staff compensation as they paid for the computer rental itself—typically $15,000 per month in the 1950s.[2] Despite the enormous cost, computers were expected to have long-term benefits for corporations and government organizations. In any case, there was a need for enterprises to be seen as modernizers, even if the cost-benefit analysis of computers was hard to implement in a rigorous manner.

The modern computer—technically known as a stored-program computer—was invented by the mathematician John von Neumann and others as a mathematical instrument toward the end of World War II at the Moore School of Electrical Engineering at the University of Pennsylvania. In the first two or three years of peace that followed war's end, several entrepreneurs saw a market opportunity for scientific computers and began manufacturing them in small numbers.

By the beginning of the 1950s, however, the traditional office-machine companies (notably IBM and Remington Rand) had started considering the possibility that a volume market for business data-processing computers might develop; they decided to take steps to hedge their bets. These firms were shortly joined by their principal business-machine rivals, Burroughs and National Cash Register (NCR). A number of major control engineering and electrical engineering firms also saw a market opportunity for computers, of which Honeywell, the Radio Corporation of America (RCA), and General Electric (GE) were the most prominent. Because of its superior execution in almost every respect, IBM soon dominated the industry—which journalists began to describe as "IBM and the seven dwarfs."

The motivations for entering the computer industry varied, and there were conflicting opinions within each one of these companies as to the costs and benefits of entering. For the office-equipment companies, the risk of staying on the sidelines was that the development of a volume market for commercial computers might cause a collapse in the demand for traditional data-processing equipment. This was more of a problem for companies that were narrowly focused on punched-card equipment, such as IBM, than it was for diversified conglomerates such as Remington Rand (later Sperry Rand), and this fact probably goes a long way toward explaining why IBM entered computers more decidedly. For the electronics-control firms, entering the computer business was simply moving into an adjacent market, one for which they already had—or at least thought they had—most of the required capabilities.

COMPUTER START-UPS: ERA, EMCC, CRC, AND ELECTRODATA

The first commercial computer companies—such as Engineering Research Associates (ERA), the Eckert-Mauchly Computer Corporation (EMCC), Computer Research Corporation (CRC), and Electrodata—were founded by small groups of physicists and engineers who had come to understand computer technology through their involvement in military projects. All of the start-ups discussed here were later acquired either by one of the traditional data-processing companies or by one of the electronics-control conglomerates that entered the computer industry.

ERA was established by a group of engineers who had participated in the U.S. Navy's cryptanalytic activities during World War II and had accumulated substantial knowledge of cutting-edge computer technologies.[3] The navy promised them that, if they were able to find private capital to set up a company, the U.S. government would provide a steady flow of (classified) computer-related R&D contracts. In 1946, under the leadership of Howard Engstrom and William Norris and with financial backing from an investment banker, ERA was founded in St. Paul, Minnesota.

With funding from its first navy contract, ERA developed the Atlas, a stored-program computer. After obtaining the government's permission, ERA marketed the Atlas commercially as the 1101 system (1950). (Unless otherwise noted, we follow the convention of reporting between parentheses the year when a system was first installed.) The company later developed other computers within the same line, and by late 1952 it reportedly accounted for 80 percent of the value of electronic computers installed in the United States at the time.[4]

The company that eventually became the Eckert-Mauchly Computer Corporation was also established in 1946. John Mauchly had taught physics at Ursinus College in the 1930s and later joined the faculty of the University of Pennsylvania's Moore School of Electrical Engineering as an instructor. There he met J. Presper Eckert, who had graduated from the Moore School with a bachelor of science degree and a master's in electrical engineering. At the Moore School, Mauchly and Eckert developed a large-scale electronic digital computer, the ENIAC (an acronym for Electronic Numerical

Integrator and Computer), for the Ballistic Research Labs of the U.S. Army Ordnance Corps in Aberdeen, Maryland. Delivered in 1946, the ENIAC remained in use for about a decade. From 1944, von Neumann was a regular visitor to the group, and they jointly specified a far more efficient and general-purpose design (the stored-program computer), which is the ancestral blueprint for almost all subsequent computers.

In mid-1946, Eckert and Mauchly left the University of Pennsylvania and set up a partnership, the Electronic Control Company, in Philadelphia. Having attracted outside investors, the partnership became EMCC in late 1947. In its early days, the new venture relied mostly on one client—the U.S. Commerce Department's Bureau of the Census, which was interested in acquiring a digital computer for processing the census of 1950. While working on this Universal Automatic Computer (UNIVAC), EMCC also developed the one-of-a-kind Binary Automatic Computer (BINAC) for Northrop Aircraft, a West Coast defense contractor. Because it greatly underestimated development costs, by early 1950 EMCC found itself under strong financial pressure.

CRC had its roots in a group of Northrop engineers who worked on the design and manufacturing of a small computer, the digital differential analyzer or DIDA, for the Snark missile.[5] The device was completed in 1949 and von Neumann was commissioned to provide an evaluation. Then at the Institute for Advanced Study in Princeton, New Jersey, von Neumann assessed the DIDA computer in highly optimistic terms. Northrop, however, failed to grasp the technology's potential, which prompted the engineers to leave and set up CRC in the summer of 1950. The computers the company developed in the early 1950s were used primarily for scientific computing, including solving complex differential equations and determining the location of an airplane in flight.

Around the same time, Consolidated Engineering Corporation (CEC), a small company involved in data recording and the manufacturing of scientific instruments, established a computer division named Electrodata in Pasadena, California. CEC developed a digital data processor, the CEC 202/203, which later became the Datatron 203/204. Electrodata, which was spun off from CEC in early 1954, sold its first Datatron system to the Jet Propulsion Laboratory in mid-1954. Within a few months, several more systems were sold to the U.S. Navy Ordnance Laboratory, Purdue University, and All-

state Insurance. Although the Datatron was originally marketed as a scientifically oriented system, after securing the Allstate contract Electrodata
searched for further opportunities in the commercial market, where the Datatron competed mainly with the IBM 650 (discussed later).

REMINGTON RAND AND IBM

The skirmishes between two of the leading data-processing companies of the
time—Remington Rand (later Sperry Rand) and IBM—shaped the competitive dynamics of the American computer industry in the 1950s.[6]

Remington Rand was established in 1927 as a holding company whose
subsidiaries operated independently but cooperated in sales and manufacturing. The company marketed punched-card equipment, adding machines,
typewriters, and filing and record-keeping systems. In 1928, Remington Rand
had sales of roughly $60 million, about three times as much as IBM
recorded.[7]

During the Great Depression, business-equipment manufacturers saw their
sales decline by about 50 percent. IBM managed to weather the Depression
and prepare for the upturn better than Remington Rand. When the demand
for business equipment started recovering around 1935 with President
Franklin D. Roosevelt's New Deal, IBM was in an optimal position to take
advantage of the upsurge. By 1948, IBM ranked first in assets ($242 mil-
lion) and second in annual revenues (with $162 million versus NCR's $168
million) among the leading business-machine manufacturers, whereas Remington Rand ranked second and third respectively.[8] Remington Rand entered the computer industry by acquiring EMCC in 1950 and ERA in 1952.

International Business Machines (IBM) was established in 1896 as the
Tabulating Machine Company, which participated in a three-way merger
with the Computing Scale Company and the International Time Recording
Company in 1911; the resulting corporation was named the Computing-
Tabulating-Recording Company (C-T-R). Thomas J. Watson became its general manager in 1914. Watson had enjoyed a stellar career in sales at NCR
between 1895 and 1914, but he left the company after a confrontation with
John Patterson, NCR's founder. C-T-R, renamed IBM in 1924, manufactured and sold card punches, readers, sorters, tabulators, and (from 1935)
electric typewriters.

Whereas Remington Rand entered the computer industry via acquisition, IBM established relationships with some of the organizations and institutions that developed computer know-how in the 1940s and early 1950s, and then used that knowledge as the foundation to enter the computer business. Between 1937 and 1943, working with the Harvard University researcher Howard Aiken, IBM constructed a large electromechanical computer, the Automatic Sequence Controlled Calculator (ASCC) or Harvard Mark I, for the university. After that project was completed, the company built the Selective Sequence Electronic Calculator (SSEC) in collaboration with Wallace Eckert of Columbia University. A one-of-a-kind, partially electronic and partially electromechanical digital computer, the SSEC took three years to develop and was finally shown to the public in 1948. Although both machines were specified by academic scientists, they were designed and constructed by IBM, giving its engineers early expertise in large-scale computing-machine development.

Some of IBM's engineers acquired direct exposure to the navy's cryptanalytic activities. Ralph Palmer, an electrical engineering graduate from Union College, joined IBM's Endicott Laboratory in 1932, rising to head of the electrical department in 1940. Three years later, Palmer joined the U.S. Navy and spent some time at the Naval Computing Machinery Laboratory, located at an NCR plant in Dayton, Ohio. It was there that he became familiar with electronic cryptanalytic devices. After returning to IBM in 1945, Palmer formed an electronics group in the Poughkeepsie laboratory, which designed a sequence of products that led the firm directly into electronic digital computers.

IBM gained extensive experience with protocomputers in the 1940s and early 1950s, introducing the IBM 603 Electronic Multiplier, the first commercial product to incorporate electronic arithmetic circuits, in 1946. It decided to limit production of the device to 100 units and replace it with a better product, the IBM 604 Electronic Calculating Punch in 1948, which became a major commercial success.

In 1949, the IBM 604 morphed into the IBM Card-Programmed Electronic Calculator (CPC) after Northrop prompted IBM to combine the electronic calculator with other equipment for improved computational functionality. Northrop was particularly interested in interconnecting pieces of equipment for calculating guided-missile trajectories. The CPC, which combined an IBM 604 Electronic Calculating Punch with an accounting machine and an electromechanical storage unit, sold extremely well—about 700 machines—in the first half of the 1950s.[9] Even though the CPC was not technically a stored-program computer, it satisfied a swath of computer demand before stored-program computers became commercially available.

One of IBM's most important external relations was with von Neumann. The design choices made for his computer under construction at the Institute for Advanced Study, which became public in 1946–1948, inspired the architecture of IBM's first mainframe, the 701. Von Neumann himself was hired as an IBM consultant in 1952.

In the 1950s, IBM also established an extremely fruitful working relationship with MIT in the context of the SAGE (an acronym for Semi-Automatic Ground Environment) air defense system. After the Soviet Union demonstrated its first nuclear weapon in 1949, the U.S. Air Force decided to fund the development of an early-warning defense system, and IBM was selected to work with MIT from a group of candidates that also included RCA, Raytheon, Remington Rand, and Sylvania. The SAGE project grew out of work on an earlier Air Force project led by Jay Forrester at MIT's Lincoln Laboratory in the second half of the 1940s. Forrester and his associates designed the Whirlwind, a one-of-a-kind digital computer system for which they invented a novel form of memory based on a matrix of magnetic ceramic toroids known as "cores." Core memory was vastly superior to previous forms of main memory and would dominate memory technology until the 1970s. First tested in 1951, Whirlwind was conceived as a "real-time" digital computer, able to receive information from multiple sources, process it, and present the results instantaneously on visual display screens.

IBM was responsible for building the SAGE computers, installing and maintaining them, and training Air Force staff to use them. Although the firm had to divert substantial human resources from its immediate commercial projects (the 701, the 702, and the 650, discussed later), it reaped phenomenal benefits from its involvement with SAGE. Thousands of IBM engineers and programmers acquired direct exposure to state-of-the-art computer technologies. The company also developed considerable expertise in the commercial manufacturing of magnetic-core memory, which turned out to be particularly valuable for IBM in competing with Remington Rand in the mid-1950s.

REMINGTON RAND VERSUS IBM

Between 1951 and 1955, IBM and Remington Rand introduced their first large-scale vacuum-tube computers. Remington Rand was the earliest player in the market with the UNIVAC in 1951; IBM's model 701 was delivered in 1953. Measured by the number of installed computers, IBM surpassed Remington Rand sometime between 1955 and 1957; by 1959, IBM solidified its lead, and over the next five years both companies introduced transistorized computers, with IBM clearly ahead.

In 1951, after investing about $12 million on computer-related R&D on top of what it paid for EMCC, Remington Rand sold the first UNIVAC to the Census Bureau for $1 million. The firm entered the computer industry with a product that no other competitor was able to match for some years, making the terms "computer" and "UNIVAC" synonymous for a while. Remington Rand sold the first five UNIVACs to governmental organizations (the Bureau of the Census, the U.S. Air Force, the U.S. Army, the U.S. Navy, and the Atomic Energy Commission's Lawrence Livermore Laboratory). GE became the first nongovernmental customer to acquire a UNIVAC computer in 1954, and Remington Rand ended up installing about 40 of them in total.[10] Technically, the Achilles' heel of the UNIVAC was that its primary memory was based on mercury delay lines, an obsolescent technology derived from wartime radar research.

IBM responded to the UNIVAC with the first two machines of what became the 700 line: the IBM 701 for scientific computing in 1953 and the IBM 702 for commercial data processing two years later. Taking advantage of the expertise acquired through its involvement with SAGE, in 1954 IBM announced the 704 and the 705 models, the first a replacement for the 701 and the second a successor to the 702. These were the first large-scale, commercially available computers with magnetic-core primary memory.

The introduction of these models—and the 705 especially—enabled IBM to become the leading vendor in the American market ahead of Remington Rand. In price-performance, the IBM 705 ranked higher than the UNIVAC, mainly because ferrite-core memory allowed much faster access to data than mercury delay line storage. Remington Rand's response to the IBM 705 came too late—although UNIVAC II (1957) was better than the 705, perhaps by a factor of two, the same year that UNIVAC II was first installed IBM introduced the IBM 705 III, a considerably better model.[11] This constant leapfrogging in price-performance, as new models took advantage of improved technology, became a permanent characteristic of the industry.

The 709, first delivered in 1958, was the last IBM vacuum-tube computer. It was compatible with the 704 and could be used both in large-scale scientific and business applications. Although it represented a substantial improvement over the 704 in price-performance, it quickly became obsolete as IBM started introducing its first transistorized computers in 1959.

While Remington Rand's UNIVAC computer line competed with the commercially oriented members of IBM's 700 series, Remington Rand's 1103 series—derived from ERA's 1103 model—competed with the scientifically oriented IBM mainframes. The 1103 was first delivered in 1953. Just as it took Remington Rand six years to deliver UNIVAC II, the successor to the original UNIVAC, it took the firm about five years to install the 1105 as a successor to the 1103. Although many users considered Remington Rand's 1103 series to be superior to the scientifically oriented models in IBM's 700 series, the machines developed a reputation for late delivery and poor support, which contributed to their limited installed base.

Whereas its involvement with SAGE helped IBM develop considerable expertise in magnetic-core memories, the company's work on the STRETCH project gave it the opportunity to build know-how in transistor-based computer systems. Two of the Atomic Energy Commission's labs (Lawrence Livermore and Los Alamos) solicited bids to build a high-speed computer in the mid-1950s. IBM lost the 1954 Lawrence Livermore bid to Remington Rand, which ended up building the LARC (Livermore Advanced Research Computer), but it won the 1955 Los Alamos bid and developed the STRETCH computer. Although STRETCH failed to meet its stated goal of being 100 times faster than the 704 and generated multimillion-dollar losses for IBM, the machine brought important benefits to the firm; through its involvement in the project, IBM acquired advanced knowledge of computer architecture, component manufacturing, and the use of transistors in electronic digital computers.

STRETCH was IBM's first transistor-based machine, but the company installed only a few of them. The first two transistorized computers marketed by IBM to a large number of customers were the 709-compatible 7090, a scientifically oriented model, and the 7070, a business-oriented model. In a joint development project with IBM, American Airlines used the 7090 in a pathbreaking application known as SABRE, the first real-time, online passenger-reservation system. (SABRE was a contrived acronym for Semi-Automatic Business Environment Research, indicating that it was a spin-off from the expertise IBM acquired as a contractor in the SAGE project.) In the early 1960s, IBM introduced new transistor-based models at a steady pace, both for scientific computation and commercial data processing.

Remington Rand delivered its LARC computer in 1960, approximately 27 months behind schedule and at a loss of several million dollars. That same year, the firm also announced three large (and mutually incompatible) computers, but none was delivered until 1962.

By the early 1960s, both Remington Rand and IBM were beginning to face a product proliferation problem—many product lines that were mutually incompatible and overlapped one another. IBM, however, was clearly ahead in many ways—it attempted to keep the new transistorized models software compatible with their vacuum-tube-based predecessors, introduced new products at a much faster pace, and had amassed a considerably larger market share than Remington Rand.

Both IBM and Remington Rand introduced small- to medium-sized computers in the 1950s and early 1960s, and these models sold in far greater volumes than the much larger mainframes. For IBM, the two best sellers were the IBM 650 in the mid-1950s and the IBM 1401 in the early 1960s. Remington Rand competed in this segment first with the UNIVAC File Computer and later with the so-called Solid State computers (the SS80 and the SS90). These computer developments are analyzed in more detail in the next chapter.

BURROUGHS AND NCR

Developed in the late nineteenth century through the efforts of William Burroughs, a former bank clerk, to create a mechanical aid to calculation, the Burroughs Adding Machine Company played a key role as a supplier of office-machine equipment in the first half of the twentieth century. By the late 1930s, Burroughs manufactured adding machines, accounting and bookkeeping machines, and cash registers. The firm's forays into computers started in the 1940s, when the director of research at the University of Pennsylvania's Moore School, Irwin Travis, moved to Burroughs to start a computer research group.

The company entered the commercial market in 1955 with the E-101, a small computer designed for both business and scientific applications that failed to take off. Burroughs acquired Electrodata in 1956. As discussed earlier, Electrodata had introduced the Datatron computer, which had some innovative architectural features and competed with the IBM 650 in the mid-1950s. After the acquisition by Burroughs, the Electrodata division began working on the Datatron 220, a large-scale mainframe, for delivery in late 1958. The 220, the last U.S. vacuum-tube computer, was quickly made obsolete by the introduction of transistorized models.

In 1959, several companies—including NCR, RCA, and IBM—started introducing transistorized, medium-sized, business-oriented systems, a market segment that came to be dominated by the IBM 7070 and the IBM 1400 series. Burroughs entered this segment in 1962 with the B5000, which had advanced architectural features but was late in delivery and too slow to develop a large installed base. The firm also introduced a series of small transistorized computers that competed with similar offerings from RCA, NCR, Honeywell, and GE.

NCR, established in 1884, owed its success to its proprietor, John Patterson, a brilliant salesperson and later the mentor of IBM's Thomas Watson, Sr. For the first four decades of its existence, the company focused on the manufacturing and marketing of one product, the cash register, which enabled retailers to keep track of sales and prevent thievery by salesclerks; it diversified into the accounting machine market in the 1920s.

NCR participated actively in the military-related protocomputer research of the 1930s and 1940s. When World War II ended, the U.S. Navy attempted to convince NCR to keep its electronics lab involved in the design and manufacturing of cryptanalytic machines, but NCR chose to refocus the entirety of its business on its traditional office equipment. Thus, the navy took a different path and made the (previously described) arrangements with ERA.

In 1952, the same year that Remington Rand delivered its first computer, NCR decided to enter the industry by acquiring the start-up CRC; soon after the acquisition, NCR introduced a small, scientifically oriented computer based on CRC technology, but chose not to develop it into a product line in order to continue focusing on its traditional customers (retail stores, banks, and department stores).

Although in the mid-1950s NCR started working on a tube-based computer, it discontinued development after recognizing that the introduction of transistorized computers would make it immediately obsolete. NCR abandoned the vacuum-tube computer market and announced that it would return with a transistorized model; first delivered in 1959, the model 304 was a medium-sized, business-oriented system, which NCR designed and GE manufactured. The 315 model, an improved successor to the 304, arrived in 1962. NCR then developed the 315 into a family of computer models marketed mainly to its traditional customers in retail and banking in conjunction with its traditional office-machine equipment.

HONEYWELL, RCA, AND GE

Both Honeywell and RCA entered the industry with large machines, failed in their first attempt, and did not try again until the end of the 1950s. GE did not venture into the industry until the late 1950s.

The Minneapolis-Honeywell Regulator Company was created in 1927 by the merger of the Minneapolis Heat Regulator Company, a thermostat manufacturer, and Honeywell Heating Specialty, a heat generator business that the engineer Mark Honeywell had founded in Wabash, Indiana. Later, Minneapolis-Honeywell expanded its portfolio of products to include an array of heat-regulating devices and instruments. Honeywell partnered with the Raytheon Corporation in 1955 to set up Datamatic, a joint computer venture.

Raytheon, an East-Coast defense contractor, had developed expertise in electronic digital computers in the 1940s and early 1950s. With funding from the Office of Naval Research, it had designed and manufactured the Hurricane computer, later renamed the Raydac. Although it incorporated a number of novel features, the Raydac was outmoded by the time Raytheon first installed it in 1953. The IBM 701, for example, beat the Raydac by a factor of 12 in price-performance.

The stated goal of the Datamatic venture was to produce large-scale dataprocessing computers for businesses. The venture, which Honeywell interpreted as a natural extension of its automation business, entered the market in 1957 with the D-1000, a large-scale vacuum-tube computer that sold for about $2 million.[12] Although it had an innovative magnetic tape system, the D-1000 could not compete with the IBM 705, much less with the IBM 705 III, which beat the D-1000 by a factor of five in price-performance.

Honeywell abandoned the vacuum-tube market and reentered the computer industry in 1960 with an outstanding transistorized machine, the Honeywell 800. The H-800 competed in the segment of medium-priced, business-oriented systems and surpassed all other computers in its price range, including the IBM 7070. The company later introduced several transistorized models compatible with the H-800 to cover a broad section of the performance spectrum.

Having introduced a series of successful products, Honeywell established itself as a significant competitor to IBM and proceeded to confront it directly. In 1964, Honeywell launched the H-200, compatible with the best-selling IBM computer of the time, the IBM 1401. In price-performance, the H-200 beat the IBM 1401 by a factor of five. Although the installed base of the H-200 grew quickly, it never managed to displace more than about 10 percent of 1401 installations; nonetheless, this represented a major success for Honeywell's computer division.[13]

RCA was founded in 1919 with the purpose of administering radio stations that had previously belonged to American Marconi. It also served as a repository for all the radio-related patents owned by AT&T, GE, Westinghouse, and the United Fruit Company. David Sarnoff, who had been commercial manager at American Marconi, transferred to the newly created RCA, where he became commercial manager and then general manager.[14] RCA developed considerable electronic skills, which it used—with Sarnoff at the helm—to venture into radio, and later TV, manufacturing.

In the 1940s and early 1950s, RCA invested resources in R&D of computer-related products in three different areas: computing devices, vacuum tubes and transistors, and core memories. In 1947, the company delivered its first computer, the Typhoon, a large analog device for simulation studies requested by the U.S. Navy, and within three years it was conducting research on digital computers for commercial applications. Since it was in the radio- and TV-set business, it was a large manufacturer of vacuum tubes, and understood the potential benefits of substituting tubes with transistors in electronic digital computers. By 1953, it had developed an early form of ferrite-core memory.[15]

Despite this impressive background, RCA's first computer, the Bizmac (1956), turned out to be a major disappointment. A large system designed for business use, the Bizmac could not compete with any of the machines that IBM had on the market at the time. The IBM 705, for example, beat the Bizmac by a factor of five in price-performance.

Not unlike Honeywell after its D-1000 failure, after the Bizmac debacle RCA suspended computer production for a number of years, reentering the industry in 1959 with the transistorized 501 model. The RCA 501 was comparatively slow among medium-sized, business-oriented systems, and it did not come equipped with good peripherals; RCA was forced to discount it heavily in order to increase sales.

Despite this sequence of false steps, the company continued to introduce computer models. In 1960, RCA announced two new systems, the 301 and the 601. The RCA 301 competed in the small- to medium-sized market, while the RCA 601 targeted the high end of the performance spectrum. Although some of its peripherals were not up to par, the RCA 301 sold reasonably well. The RCA 601, on the other hand, flopped, plagued by cost overruns, late deliveries, and deficient wiring.

The history of GE predates that of Honeywell and RCA. GE was the result of the 1892 merger between the Edison General Electric Company and Thomson-Houston. In the first half of the twentieth century, it grew into a vast corporation that produced a spectrum of electrical goods from generating plants to domestic electrical appliances. During the 1950s, its main involvement with computers was its participation in the Electronic Recording Machine, Accounting—or ERMA—project, through which the company built a check-processing computer for Bank of America.

Although ERMA gave GE a platform to expand its electronic computing presence in the banking industry, the company failed to capitalize on the opportunity because banks did not belong to the group of core customers it was used to targeting. In the late 1950s, the company developed the GE 312, a process-control computer designed for the engineering customers it knew best, and used it as the foundation to build the GE 225, a small, scientifically oriented machine that sold rather poorly. In 1963 it introduced the smaller and larger models in the line, the 215 and the 235; it also announced the DATANET-30, a computer that targeted communication systems and, with the model 235, would play an important role in the company's later success in computer time-sharing (see Chapter 4).

COMPUTER DEMAND

If early on the demand for electronic digital computers came mainly from the military establishment, civilian users (and uses) ultimately played a dominant role in driving the computer industry's growth. In the 1940s and early 1950s, computers were frequently used to carry out scientific calculations with military-related goals. The search for quick and reliable solutions to a number of computational problems—in areas as diverse as ballistics, crypt-analysis, flight simulation, command and control, and missile guidance—transformed the military into heavy users of computers. Scientists also used computers to tackle problems such as weather prediction, which required intensive and rapid calculations.

During the 1950s, academics in universities started using computers to enhance their teaching and research. The number of colleges and universities with at least one computer installed grew slowly in the 1950s and at a considerably faster pace after 1960. About 83 institutions had computer facilities in 1960, and this number more than tripled by 1964. By 1970, about 23 percent of the 2,556 institutions of higher education in America had a computer installation.[16] Computers supported teaching and research in a variety of areas, including mathematics, statistics, physics, biology, economics, business, education, and sociology.

Federal, state, and local government facilities used computers for various data-processing tasks. Slightly over 71,000 computer installations existed in the United States by 1971, and almost 8 percent of them (6,310) were in government offices (federal, state, and local).[17] By the mid-1960s, all municipal government offices in cities with at least 100,000 people relied on either punched-card equipment or electronic digital computers, as did three out of every five cities with populations between 50,000 and 100,000.[18]

Although various governmental organizations and branches of the military establishment accounted for most computer installations in the late 1940s and early 1950s, the industry would not have taken off as it did without the boost of corporate demand. Businesses did not come to computers out of the blue. Starting in the late nineteenth century, a powerful industry developed in the United States to serve the information-processing needs of government agencies and corporations. By the 1920s, the office-equipment business included typewriters, adding machines, cash registers, and tabulating equipment. The main vendors at the time were Burroughs, IBM, NCR, Remington Rand, and Underwood Elliott Fisher. By certain measures, computers did not surpass the more traditional office equipment until well into the 1950s—the value of total U.S. computer shipments reached $155 million in 1956, still $50 million less than the value of punched-card machinery, adding machines, calculators, and cash registers produced in America in that year.[19]

By incorporating computers into their business processes, American corporations expected to achieve cost savings and "control." A small- to medium-sized

Table 1.1. Percentage of all U.S. Mainframe Installations Accounted for by Each Sector, 1953, 1959, and 1966

SIC code	Sector	1953	1959	1966
01–09	Agriculture	0.00	0.00	0.20
10–14	Mining	0.00	0.30	2.00
15–17	Construction	0.00	0.40	0.40
19–39	Manufacturing	18.70	42.40	36.80
40–49	Transportation, communications & utilities	3.30	8.20	7.90
50–59	Wholesale and retail trade	0.00	1.30	6.90
60–67	Finance, insurance & real estate	1.10	9.90	17.30
70–89	Services	23.10	14.60	14.50
91–94	Government	53.80	22.90	13.40
99	Other	0.00	0.00	0.60
	Total	100.00	100.00	100.00
	Total installations	91	3,110	28,300

Source: M. Phister, *Data Processing Technology and Economics* (Bedford, MA: Digital Press, 1979), 444.

computer, which rented for $3,000–$7,000 per month in the late 1950s, substituted for roughly 20 clerical jobs—which cost the company a total of $100,000 per year—and, after accounting for installation and programming, generated some nontrivial savings for a small- to medium-size business.[20] A larger corporation could afford a more expensive and considerably more powerful computer, with the extra twist that a monthly rental twice as high bought much more than twice the performance—a phenomenon which came to be known in the industry as Grosch's Law. "Control" involved the potential to make optimal decisions regarding production, sales, inventories, and investments. The computer, many believed, helped corporations optimize their decisions because it allowed them to track market trends in real time.

The structure of demand changed quickly during the first decade and a half of the industry's history. Table 1.1, based on various censuses and surveys of installed computers in the United States, shows the proportion of the total stock of computer installations accounted for by each sector of the American economy in 1953, 1959, and 1966.

Three facts stand out. First, in the late 1940s and early 1950s, government agencies accounted for more than half of all computer installations. Second, by the end of the 1950s, the manufacturing sector had taken over the leading role. Third, by the mid-1960s, manufacturing still accounted for most computer installations in the United States, but banking and insurance had increased their share considerably.

It became clear in the mid-1960s that corporations, rather than the government or academia, would account for the bulk of computer demand in the future. By the end of the decade, corporate computer installations outnumbered those at government offices by a factor of about 5.5, and those in colleges and universities by a factor of about 35, even though at the time a tiny fraction of all business plants in the country had a computer installation.[21]

CHAPTER TWO

Production Differentiation, Software, and Services

The market for large-scale mainframes in the 1950s was relatively small because their high cost proved prohibitive for all but the largest firms and government organizations. By the early 1960s, however, as the technology matured and decreased in price, the market broadened in two directions: first, to small- and medium-sized computers, and second, to giant machines.

Most of the mainframe incumbents had begun to manufacture smaller computers by the early 1960s in order to expand the market and provide a transition point for users of traditional accounting machinery. With the advent of transistorized electronics, a new wave of entrepreneurial start-ups began making small- and medium-sized computers, the Digital Equipment Corporation (DEC) and Scientific Data Systems (SDS) being the most prominent and successful. Giant computers were a niche product that sold in very small numbers; they lay at the other end of the performance spectrum and targeted the scientific market, particularly the laboratories of the Atomic Energy Commission and the nuclear products industry. The incumbents made few attempts to enter this market. As the computer population grew, the scarcity of software increasingly became the biggest single factor inhibiting the growth of the industry. This led, on the one hand, to computer manufacturers easing the constraint by developing software for their customers,

and on the other, to the development of firms specializing in software contracting. In a parallel development, computer-services firms evolved to help
user firms establish and manage complex computer systems.

COMPUTERS AS DIFFERENTIATED PRODUCTS

Early computers quickly became highly differentiated products. In the early
1960s, the trade journal *Computers and Automation* started publishing a
monthly census of computer installations and an annual description of computers and their core characteristics. Among the computer features discussed
were the size of the primary memory, the type of memory (e.g., drum, core,
or delay line), the time required to retrieve information from main memory,
the time required to fetch and complete one instruction, and information
about the peripherals that came with each model (e.g., the number of
magnetic-tape units, tape density, and tape speed).[1]

Since computer models varied widely in price and specifications, customers
tended to choose a model not only on the basis of price but also on the basis
of what a model could deliver for their particular workload for a given price. A
survey of 69 installations drawn randomly from the readers of *Datamation,* a
trade publication, found that, apart from reading hardware and software evaluation reports, most customers relied on assessments of how well each model
performed when completing a set of benchmark tasks.[2] Auerbach, a consulting
group, published an extensive set of estimates of the total time it took each
computer model to carry out a set of six benchmark jobs (updating sequen-
tial files, updating files on random-access storage, sorting, inverting matrices,
evaluating complex equations, and carrying out statistical computations).

SMALL- AND MEDIUM-SIZED COMPUTER SYSTEMS

A number of companies entered the industry in the 1950s to supply models
both cheaper and less powerful than the UNIVAC or the IBM 700-series
computers. Most of these electronic tube-based machines relied on a magnetic drum for their primary memory, which was slow but reliable and relatively inexpensive. Many of the companies that built these machines were
located on the West Coast, and two of them (CRC and Electrodata) were
described in Chapter 1. Two other companies that marketed popular small

computers were the Librascope division of General Precision, which built the LGP-30, and the computer division of Bendix Aviation, which manufactured the Bendix G-15.

Most of these machines were designed for engineering and scientific computation. In the market for small, commercial data-processing computers, IBM established itself as the leader with the remarkably popular IBM 650 (1954). The success of this model caught everyone by surprise, including IBM. The company expected to produce about 50 of them but ended up selling 20 times as many.[3] The IBM 650—which rented for between $3,250 per month and $3,750 per month, depending on storage capacity—represented a considerably smaller investment for customers than, say, the IBM 701 (at $15,000 per month), and thus offered customers a much easier transition from traditional punched-card equipment to electronic digital computers.[4]

The UNIVAC Division of Sperry Rand also ventured into the small computer segment with its File Computer in 1956. Developed by the ERA group in Minneapolis-St. Paul as an alternative to the IBM 650, the File Computer never challenged the 650. In price-performance, the 650 beat the ERA model by a factor of 15, and the company managed to secure only about 100 installations of its small computer.[5] Remington Rand's Philadelphia group also developed a more powerful small machine, the transistorized Solid State computer, which was marketed in Europe starting in 1957–1958. This computer beat the IBM 650 in price-performance but was not installed in the United States until 1960. By this time, the Solid State machine had to confront the IBM 1401, with which it could not compete.

The transistorized IBM 1401, announced in 1959, transformed the segment of small- to medium-sized systems. Its success has often been attributed to the Type 1403 chain printer, which was usually rented with the 1401 processor and provided good print quality at 600 lines per minute, about four times the speed provided by the average printer or accounting machine at the time. With almost 2,000 installations by late 1961, and a total installed base that peaked at over 10,000 in the mid-1960s, the IBM 1401 quickly became the best-selling computer of the early 1960s.[6]

CDC, DEC, AND SDS

Companies such as Remington Rand, Honeywell, and RCA covered wide portions of the performance range in direct confrontation with IBM. In the late 1950s and early 1960s, three new companies entered the industry with a radically different approach: they competed by avoiding direct confrontations with the big industry players. Initially, all of them targeted the scientific and engineering segments of the market. DEC and SDS focused on producing small, cheap, powerful systems, whereas Control Data Corporation (CDC) consistently stretched the upper limit of the performance spectrum. All of them benefited from the fact that their scientific and engineering customers required relatively little support and software.

The origins of CDC go back to the navy's cryptanalytic tradition.[7] Some of the ERA engineers that had joined Remington Rand in 1952 decided to leave the company in 1957 to launch their own venture, CDC. Seymour Cray, who eventually became the company's star computer designer, was hired from Remington Rand shortly thereafter.

In 1958, CDC announced its first computer, the 1604. The first transistorized, large-scale system ever announced, it was conceived for government laboratories and customers conducting military, space, and nuclear research. The 1604 started shipping in 1960 and competed mainly with IBM's scientifically oriented, second-generation mainframes. In late 1959, the company announced its second system, the 160, a small machine for engineering computation. CDC's business model relied on the fact that scientific customers tended to have more heterogeneous requirements than business users, which allowed the company to deliver high-performance hardware with little software. This strategy worked well: CDC quickly developed a relatively large installed base in the education, aerospace, and government laboratory sectors.

CDC diversified its product portfolio via acquisition. Soon after its founding it purchased Cedar Engineering, a large machine shop that manufactured products for the aircraft industry and would soon come to play an important role in CDC's entry into the computer-peripheral business. In 1960, it bought Control Corporation, through which it entered the market for computers for automatic control. It also acquired seven additional companies in 1963, including the Bendix computer operations.

In mid-1962, CDC announced the 6600 model, a very powerful computer that none of the IBM scientific models could match in price-performance. The first 6600 was sold to the Lawrence Livermore lab for about $7 million in 1964.[8] The process of building the 6600 turned out to be longer and more difficult than the company anticipated; in order to fend off the competition from IBM's scientifically oriented computers while the 6600 was under construction, CDC first delivered a less advanced high-performance system, the 3600, in 1963. Leaving aside the small 160 model, CDC's first computers—the 1604, the 3600, and the 6600—were "bet the company" endeavors that succeeded and consolidated the firm's position as an important player in the industry, especially in the upper reaches of the performance spectrum.

DEC and SDS both focused on producing cheap and powerful computers for real-time and scientific applications.[9] Kenneth Olsen and Harlan Anderson, who in 1957 founded DEC in Maynard, Massachusetts, had both worked at MIT's Lincoln Lab and had participated in the SAGE project. DEC received its initial funding from the American Research and Development Corporation (ARD), which was headed by General Georges Doriot, a pioneer of venture-capital financing in the United States. In its early years, DEC designed and manufactured system modules—the building blocks of computers, memory testers, and other logic systems. It entered the computer business in 1960 with the PDP-1, followed two years later by the PDP-4. From then on, it introduced improved models almost every year, each new computer achieving dramatic gains in price-performance.

The PDP computers became a commercial success because they delivered outstanding performance at a low price. DEC's computers sold cheaply because the company's main customers—scientists and engineers—required less software and support services than corporate customers. DEC's sophisticated customers also valued the real-time interactive capabilities that the DEC computers delivered.

SDS followed a similar approach. Max Palevsky and Robert Beck, who had worked together in computer design at Packard Bell, founded SDS in Santa Monica, California, in 1961 and introduced the company's first computer, the SDS 910, in 1962. Just like DEC, SDS designed a sequence of computers that delivered consistently better price-performance combinations year after year, and, on the basis of these offerings, it quickly developed a large and loyal following among scientific users.

COMPUTER MANUFACTURERS AS SUPPLIERS OF PERIPHERALS, SOFTWARE, AND SERVICES

Computer customers needed a variety of complementary products and services to make computing machines fully productive. Three types of players supplied complements in the early days: computer manufacturers, users, and independent companies. Since only a few businesses in America were able to afford a computer at the start of the industry, companies were also founded to offer services that substituted for the purchase or rental of a computer.

Computer manufacturers understood early on that the availability of a wide assortment of high-quality complements for computer processors played as important a role in selling a computer as delivering good performance for any given rental level. No company understood that fact as well or as quickly as IBM.

Few technology areas reveal IBM's commitment to providing good complementary products and services better than its development of magnetic-disk storage. Punched cards served information storage purposes well so long as the time required for the automatic analysis of information remained roughly in balance with that required to handle the cards. The introduction of digital electronics in the 1940s, however, created a radical imbalance, since it allowed for computation and analysis to be carried out considerably faster than data could be read from cards. Over time, magnetic tapes replaced cards because tapes were both faster and less bulky. Magnetic-disk storage was invented primarily to address the problem of immediate access for real-time data processing.

In early 1952, IBM set up a laboratory in San Jose, California, to explore the development of advanced technologies. The project that led to the invention of disk storage was launched later that year, with the goal of finding a better method for organizing, storing, and retrieving information. By visiting customer installations, IBM's researchers realized that magnetic tape worked well when random access to data was not necessary. The five-million-character IBM 350 Disk Storage Unit, designed at the San Jose lab and publicly demonstrated in mid-1955, became a hit in the market because it made random access at real-time speeds feasible. The main competition for the 350 Disk Storage Unit, which was originally coupled with the IBM 305 RAMAC computer, came from UNIVAC's File Computer, which used magnetic-drum storage with a considerably smaller capacity.

In the early 1960s, IBM introduced two new disk drives, the 1301 and the 1311, with its transistorized computer systems. The 1301 (1961) beat the RAMAC by a factor of four in access speed and by a factor of 10 in total storage capacity.[10] The 1311, announced in late 1962, was a relatively small disk-drive product that became a commercial success because it was affordable, provided fast random access to data, and featured a removable disk pack that enabled information to be moved from system to system and to be stored off-line.

At first, IBM proved better at providing peripherals than at supplying programs (or *software,* a term that became prevalent in the mid-1960s). Computers required both "systems" and "applications" programs. The former were of little direct concern to the user: they included operating systems and programming aids that enabled the machine to function as a system. Applications programs, on the other hand, allowed the machine to perform functions required by the user—functions such as payroll processing and inventory management. When IBM delivered its first model 701 in 1953, it provided no applications programs for the computer and only a few rudimentary systems programs, the total amounting probably to less than a thousand lines of code.[11] Since customers participated actively in the process of modifying the computer code to suit their needs and in many cases wrote their own applications, IBM delivered both the binary and the symbolic forms of computer programs to its customers.[12]

Throughout the 1950s, IBM developed a competence in basic operating systems, language processors, and utilities. Among the programming languages, Fortran made an impact like no other. The mathematician John Backus, the creator of Fortran, had joined IBM in 1950 and programmed the SSEC and the CPC before working on the 701. He concluded that programming and debugging accounted for as much as three-quarters of the cost of operating a computer. In order to simplify the task of programming and cut costs, Backus designed Fortran, a mathematically oriented programming language. The Fortran translator, which IBM made freely available, became an instant hit with customers, who used it not only for scientific computing but also for a variety of business-oriented applications, including payroll and accounts receivable. Fortran dramatically reduced the cost of programming and increased the number of people who dared to venture into computer programming.

By the time IBM first installed the 1401 in 1960, it was able to supply a comprehensive suite of systems software for the machine, including a simple operating system, utilities, and language processors (Assembler, Fortran, COBOL, and RPG). COBOL was a language designed for data-processing, complementary to Fortran for scientific applications. The RPG processor enabled IBM's accounting machine customers to upgrade to the 1401 and de-velop applications for the 1401 using the concepts and nomenclature of IBM's punched-card equipment.

IBM also delivered some applications software in the early 1960s through its Program Applications Library. In 1962, for example, the company released one of the best-known applications suites of the early days, the so-called '62 CFO package (Consolidated Functions Ordinary, 1962) for the insurance industry.[13] Unlike systems programs, applications targeted specific industries and required substantial customization.

Most computer manufacturers also established their own service bureaus. In fact, some of the office-machine companies, IBM and Remington Rand among them, began operating service bureaus in the 1930s, so this repre-sented a change of technology rather than a new line of business. Offices were equipped with medium- and large-sized computers in major cities to process corporate data usually delivered by messenger. The bureau was the best route to serve those companies that were large enough to benefit from the services of a computer but not large enough to rent or acquire their own.

USERS AS SUPPLIERS OF SOFTWARE

Customers incurred most of the direct costs of developing software well into the 1970s. Users participated in two ways in the production of soft-ware. First, they invested considerable resources in modifying the systems and applications software that came bundled with the computer hardware and in writing their own applications programs. Second, customers set up user groups to share their experiences with, and knowledge of, a specific computing machine (or group of machines). The experiences of the IBM-sponsored SHARE user group provide many examples of users' contributions to the soft-ware stock at the dawn of the industry.[14]

A group of sophisticated users, primarily West Coast aerospace compa-nies, set up SHARE to address the problem of the scarcity of programs in the early days. Users of the first IBM digital computer, the IBM 701, report-edly invested the equivalent of the first year's rental, around $150,000, in individually creating software for the machine.[15] SHARE's main goal was avoiding duplicative development efforts while supplying code that adhered to strict programming standards. At its second meeting, in September 1955, the SHARE committee recommended the adoption of the SHARE Assembly Program (SAP), developed by United Aircraft, in place of IBM's own AP1 assembler, reportedly saving members around $1.5 million.

INDEPENDENT COMPANIES AS SUPPLIERS OF
SOFTWARE AND SERVICES

From annual industry surveys conducted for the software and services industries' Association of Data Processing Service Organizations (ADAPSO), we know that the number of computer-services firms rose from about 24 in the mid-1950s to 210 in 1960 and further to 665 in 1965.[16]

Many of the early software entrepreneurs developed their skills by working either at one of the main computer manufacturers or at a computer installation of a large customer. Computer Sciences Corporation (CSC), the Computer Usage Company (CUC), Advanced Computer Techniques (ACT), Applied Data Research (ADR), and Informatics—all of them founded between 1955 and 1962 either on the East Coast or in California—provide good examples of this evolution.[17]

The early development of CSC gives us a glimpse into the life of a typical independent software company. Fletcher Jones and Roy Nutt founded the company in 1959 in Los Angeles, California. Jones had been the head of North American Aviation's computer operation and a founder of SHARE, and Nutt had worked at the United Aircraft Research Computation Laboratory.

The types of projects that CSC undertook in the early years reveal the way in which the early independent software companies operated—as contractors working on one-of-a-kind software projects and charging on a time-and-materials basis. Many of the jobs that CSC carried out at the beginning involved creating systems software for some of the main hardware manufacturers. For example, the company developed the FACT translator for Honeywell and the operating system for the UNIVAC 1107. By 1963, CSC had annual revenues of $4 million and 230 employees, making it the largest independent computer software and services firm in the world.[18] In 1964, CSC decided to expand its market beyond computer hardware manufacturers and government agencies, and started focusing on computer users as well. At the time of this writing, it remained one of the leading players in the computer-services market.

The service bureaus represented the bulk of the computer-services industry in the early years. Automatic Data Processing (ADP), still a major name today in the industry, is the prime example of a service bureau that successfully adapted to the changing technology of data processing. In 1949, Henry Taub, who had a background in accounting, founded Automatic Payrolls, Inc., in Patterson, New Jersey. The company processed the payroll for large firms, managing payments to employees, taxes, and deductibles. By 1956, the firm had over 200 clients, mostly in northern New Jersey and New York City.[19] That same year Taub started a second business, Automatic Tabulating, which carried out various types of data processing for customers in the area, and Automatic Payrolls made the transition from manual bookkeeping machines to automated punched-card accounting. In 1958, the two businesses merged into a new company, Automatic Data Processing, which became a publicly held corporation in September 1961, also the year in which the firm acquired its first computer.

In some cases, service bureaus entered into facilities management agreements with customers. In this model, the corporate customer bought or rented a computer, but the service bureau took over management of the customer's computer installation. Ross Perot, who had been a superstar computer salesman for IBM, founded Electronic Data Systems (EDS) in Dallas, Texas, in 1962.[20] Like all the early entrants, at the starting point EDS did not own its computer and served its customers by buying unused time on Southwestern Life Insurance's IBM 7070 mainframe. EDS entered into the industry's first facilities management agreement—a five-year contract with Frito Lay—in 1963. This business model, based on a long-term, fixed-price arrangement, had its appeal in that it provided EDS with a predictable revenue flow while freeing the customer from the need to manage an unfamiliar technology. EDS acquired its first computer, an IBM 1401, in 1965.

THE U.S. COMPUTER MARKET, 1950–1965: TAKING STOCK

Between 1956 and 1964, the total stock of computer installations in the U.S. economy grew from an estimated 750 to 19,200. Mainframes represented almost 100 percent of the 1956 installations, but small computers—the ones produced by firms such as DEC and SDS—already accounted for about 13 percent of the total stock by volume as of 1964. Table 2.1 tracks computer shipments and installations in the American market between the mid-1950s and the mid-1960s.

Table 2.1.   Number and Value (in USD Billion) of Computers Shipped and Installed in the
United States, 1955–1965

Year	Mainframes				Small Computers			
	Number shipped	Number in use	Value shipped	Value in use	Number shipped	Number in use	Value shipped	Value in use
1955	150	240	0.063	0.180				
1956	500	700	0.152	0.320	50	50	0.003	0.003
1957	660	1,260	0.235	0.540	190	240	0.010	0.012
1958	970	2,100	0.381	0.900	210	450	0.014	0.025
1959	1,150	3,110	0.475	1.340	250	700	0.020	0.045
1960	1,500	4,400	0.560	1.865	300	1,000	0.030	0.075
1961	2,300	6,150	0.850	2.605	400	1,400	0.030	0.105
1962	3,100	8,100	1.060	3.485	400	1,800	0.030	0.135
1963	3,800	11,700	1.220	4.550	400	2,100	0.080	0.210
1964	5,100	16,700	1.570	6.000	500	2,500	0.100	0.300
1965	5,300	21,600	1.910	7.800	800	3,100	0.150	0.434

Source: M. Phister, *Data Processing Technology and Economics* (Bedford, MA: Digital Press, 1979), 251.

IBM took the lead from Remington Rand in the mid-1950s and main-tained a market share in mainframes of about 80 percent by volume through the early 1960s, when it faced new challenges.[21] As explained in Chapter 1, some of the companies that had disappointed with their computer offerings in the 1950s, such as Honeywell and RCA, came back with renewed strength. Others, such as NCR and Burroughs, expanded their computer portfolio. Whereas DEC and SDS made inroads in the small-machine segment, CDC delivered computers that outperformed IBM's most powerful scientific machines.

Figure 2.1 tracks computer mainframe installations in the United States through the mid-1960s—the figure shows the quick displacement of IBM first-generation by IBM second-generation machines starting in 1960, and then a slight decline of IBM's relative share starting around 1963.

Why was it that IBM, rather than any other company, came to dominate the computer industry almost from the beginning?[22] More abundant finan-cial resources do not explain IBM's dominance of the industry. Although

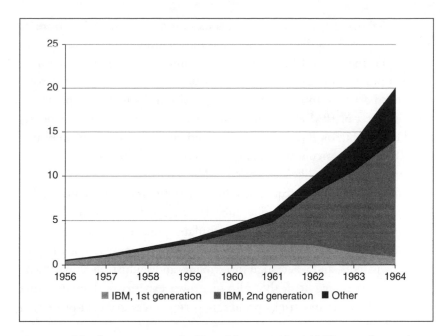

Figure 2.1. Mainframes in use in the United States, 1956–1964. Units in thousands.
Source: M. Phister, *Data Processing Technology and Economics* (Bedford, MA: Digital Press, 1979), 253.

by the late 1940s IBM was the largest vendor of traditional data-processing equipment (by assets), competitors such as NCR and Remington Rand were of comparable size in annual revenues. Some of the electronics-control conglomerates, such as RCA and GE, had considerably higher yearly revenues than IBM in the early 1950s. IBM was not competing against a collection of underfunded start-ups; in fact, with their limited resources, the computer start-ups did better against IBM than the established conglomerates.

What organizational capabilities enabled IBM to dominate the industry? More generally, which ones mattered in the incipient computer industry? An analysis of the early years of the industry in the United States suggests the importance of: a tradition of technical innovation; expertise in electromechanical manufacturing; a high-quality sales force; well-developed service operations; a tradition of employee and customer training; electronics know-how; and experience with integrated data-processing installations. Although IBM may not have been the absolute best company in each of these areas, it did well in all of them.

Although patents are an imperfect proxy for innovative ability, from its earliest days IBM was heavily committed to patenting, and it remains so to this day. Furthermore, IBM excelled in the manufacturing of electromechanical equipment. Since the 1930s, IBM's data-processing machines were considered superior to those of Remington Rand, its main competitor. A larger portion of IBM's machines were electric relative to those manufactured by Remington Rand, which still relied heavily on mechanical principles. IBM's sales force was legendary, considerably more effective than its competitors' with the likely exception of NCR's staff.

Firms producing office equipment in the late 1940s differed considerably from one another in their product mix. IBM tended to focus on, and was the market leader in, accounting and tabulating machines, the segment of the market where equipment was most complex and most frequently protected by patents, and where high investments and sophisticated marketing and services were required. IBM also had more experience than any other firm in the industry in setting up and supporting integrated data-processing installations.

IBM was ahead of its competitors in the incorporation of electronics into traditional office equipment. It is usually argued that Remington Rand pioneered electronic computers with UNIVAC, and IBM came from behind. One often overlooked factor, however, is that while Remington Rand managed to secure about 40 UNIVAC installations in the early 1950s, in the same years IBM sold or rented several hundred installations of the CPC protocomputer. Despite the fact that it was considerably less powerful than UNIVAC, the CPC nevertheless served the needs of many customers who were not ready to spend the small fortune required to buy or rent a large mainframe. The large electronics-control vendors surely had electronic know-how at least as good as that of IBM but knew very little about how to incorporate that knowledge into data-processing applications.

IBM's phenomenal combination of capabilities manifested itself in two outcomes that help explain its rise to, and permanence at, the top. First, even though IBM may not have always manufactured the best processors, it consistently offered the best systems—the best bundles of processors, peripherals, software, and services. There are abundant examples of computer vendors that were competitive with IBM in processor quality but were far behind in their peripheral offerings, not to mention software and services. The fact that IBM offered the best combinations of processors, peripherals, software, and maintenance and training services—the best *systems*—was particularly valuable from the perspective of the early computer customers, who were dealing with the uncertainty of adopting an unproven technology.

Second, IBM introduced new and improved technology at a pace that Remington Rand was not able to match. Other companies were hesitant in their commitment to computers in the early days. Honeywell and RCA vanished from the computer market for several years after their first attempts failed; NCR and Burroughs did not have competitive offerings other than in the small-computer segment until the late 1950s or early 1960s; and GE did not even try to enter the market until the late 1950s.

CHAPTER THREE

The International Computer Industry

B etween 1950 and 1965, an incipient computer industry emerged outside the United States, especially in Britain, France, West Germany, and Japan.[1] Computer developments in all of them were considerable but lagged behind those in the States. In all regions, the introduction of the IBM 1401 in the early 1960s caused a shakeup for which domestic companies were unprepared.

BRITAIN

By 1946, computers were under development in three leading research institutions in Britain: Cambridge University, Manchester University, and the National Physical Laboratory (NPL, the national standards-setting organization, comparable to the National Bureau of Standards in the United States, or NBS, now the National Institute of Standards and Technology, or NIST).[2] The Manchester University researchers demonstrated a "baby machine" in 1948 and a full-scale computer, the Mark I, the following year. At Cambridge University, a group led by Maurice Wilkes demonstrated the Electronic Delay Storage Automatic Calculator (EDSAC) in 1949, the first practical stored-program computer in the world. At the NPL, the now-famous mathematician Alan Turing designed the ACE computer; a smaller version of this machine, the Pilot ACE, was completed in 1950. All of these machines were conceived as tools for mathematical computing, with little regard for business applications.

Two of the large electrical manufacturers—English Electric and Ferranti—entered the computer industry with machines derived from those built in academic settings: Ferranti built the Mark I, based on the Manchester computer, and English Electric the DEUCE, based on NPL's Pilot ACE. Meanwhile, in one of the most intriguing episodes in the history of computing, the J. Lyons bakery company decided to pioneer the use of digital computers in commercial applications. In 1947, it assembled its own team to build a computer, LEO (Lyons Electronic Office), which became available for use in 1951, based on the Cambridge University EDSAC.

For much of the 1950s, the British punched-card machine vendors, British Tabulating Machine (BTM) and Powers-Samas, did not view electronic digital computers as a fundamental threat to their business. The firms had originated as licensees of IBM and Remington Rand, respectively. After these agreements were terminated in the late 1940s, they faced competition from the U.S. companies in their territories for the first time. This competition, however, was mostly in traditional office equipment rather than computers. Although both BTM and Powers-Samas recruited electronic engineers in the early 1950s, their R&D resources continued to be split among mechanical, electromechanical, and electronic projects throughout the 1950s. Both companies incorporated electronics in punched-card machines, but traditional products continued to account for most of their revenues through the early 1960s.

The early computer industry in Britain was encouraged by the National Research Development Corporation (NRDC), an institution created in 1949 with the goal of fostering the patenting and commercial exploitation of British inventions. The NRDC prodded BTM and Powers-Samas to form a consortium with Ferranti to develop a commercial computer as a joint venture. Although the joint-venture idea was soon abandoned, BTM decided to explore digital computers on its own while Powers-Samas remained on the sidelines. With the help of an academic consultant, A. D. Booth from Birkbeck College, University of London, the BTM computer development group built a small semi-scientific machine, the HEC (Hollerith Electronic

Computer), a prototype of which was ready in early 1953. A commercial version, the HEC 4, followed.

By 1957, several British companies had explored computer production (and several of them had designed and manufactured at least one model): the large electrical manufacturing firms (Ferranti, GEC, AEI, and English Electric), Elliott Brothers (scientific instruments), Leo Computers (established by the catering company J. Lyons), Electrical and Musical Industries Ltd. (EMI), Standard Telephones and Cables Ltd. (STC), Marconi, and the punched-card equipment vendors. BTM had probably developed the clearest business strategy—it was competitive at the low end of the market with the 1200 series, based on HEC 4; it was developing the mid-sized 1300 series in cooperation with GEC; and it was collaborating with an American electronics lab in the construction of the more powerful and expensive 1400 series.

BTM and Powers-Samas merged to form International Computers and Tabulators (ICT) in 1959. Its principal source of revenues at that time remained the traditional punched-card machine market, but the company was diversifying into small- and medium-sized data-processing computers as well. The introduction of the IBM 1401 completely altered the pace of change of the data-processing industry in Britain, as it had in the United States, because it led to the collapse of traditional punched-card equipment sales in late 1961 and early 1962.

The success of the 1401 in Britain forced domestic computer manufacturers to rethink their strategies. ICT engaged in negotiations with American companies (GE and RCA) and with the French Compagnie des Machines Bull, which in turn negotiated with GE and RCA on its own account as well. A process of mergers and acquisitions ensued. ICT acquired the computer operations of GEC, EMI, and Ferranti. Whereas most of the electrical manufacturers had decided to exit the computer market by the early 1960s, English Electric decided to stay for the long haul; it acquired Leo Computers and the Marconi computer group to become English Electric Leo Marconi (EELM). By 1964, only three British computer manufacturers remained—ICT, EELM, and the much smaller computer division of Elliott Brothers (Elliott-Automation). At this stage, the American computer manufacturers, of which IBM was by far the most important, had a 40 percent share of all computer installations in Britain.[3]

FRANCE

Developments in France between 1950 and 1965 included one computer start-up, one punched-card data-processing firm that moved slowly into computers, and two large electronics manufacturers that entered the industry late in the game.[4] The Société d' Electronique et d'Automatisme (SEA), a start-up not unlike the ones established in the United States in the late 1940s and early 1950s, delivered its first digital computers in 1955. A thriving data-processing company, Compagnie des Machines Bull (CMB), a firm comparable to BTM in Britain, made the transition from traditional punched-card equipment to electronic calculators in the first half of the 1950s, and then to stored-program digital computers in the second half. Finally, the large electronics manufacturers—the Compagnie Générale de Télégraphie sans Fil (CSF) and the Compagnie Générale de Electricité (CGE)—started producing computers in the early 1960s.

SEA was founded in Paris in 1948 as a consulting company and a manufacturer of electronic calculating equipment; it quickly developed a reputation for its analog computers, communications and automation products, and aeronautics simulators. In 1955, SEA installed the first digital computers in France, all of them for defense-related purposes. In 1960, it introduced a small scientific computer, the CAB 500, which became the company's best-selling machine, as well as a line of transistorized, business-oriented computers.

CMB, incorporated in Paris in the early 1930s, had by the late 1940s established itself as one of the main players in the French market for punched-card data processing equipment, where it competed mainly with IBM. CMB set up an electronics lab in 1948 to develop know-how for improving its traditional equipment. The lab built the Gamma 3 electronic calculator (1952) to compete with the IBM 604 punched-card calculator, which was first installed in France in late 1951. The Gamma 3, better than the 604 according to some assessments, turned out to be a remarkably successful product with more than 1,200 installations over a 10-year period.[5]

In 1956, after IBM introduced its drum-based 650 computer in France and SEA installed its first digital computers, CMB added a magnetic drum to the Gamma 3 and marketed the machine as the Gamma Extension-Tambour (ET, meaning "added drum"), its first stored-program computer. The following year, CMB announced the transistorized Gamma 60, designed to compete with the more powerful models of IBM's 700 line. By the turn of the decade, CMB was growing at a rapid pace. It was, after the British ICT, the second-largest European manufacturer of business machines, with more than 800 electronic machines in service (300 of them outside France) and almost 3,500 traditional data-processing installations (half of them overseas).[6]

The large electronics manufacturers, CSF and CGE, entered the industry in the early 1960s. The Compagnie Européenne d'Automatisme Électronique (CAE) was set up in 1960 as a joint venture involving CSF, Intertechnique, and the American corporation Thompson-Ramo-Wooldridge (TRW). Early on, CAE marketed computer models designed by TRW—one for controlling nuclear power plants and another for missile guidance systems—and developed a real-time scientific computer. It also took over the computer operations of CGE, which had established a licensing relationship with the American computer manufacturer SDS. In 1964, CAE announced a computer range based on the SDS 900 line.

In the meantime, CMB had started to falter. Its profits declined in 1962, and soon turned to losses. The development of the Gamma 60 supercomputer, on which CMB lost substantial amounts of money, was only one factor contributing to the crisis. In the 1950s and early 1960s, CMB expanded at a very fast pace but continued to be managed like a family business, focused on electromechanical punched-card equipment. In 1960, the IBM 1401 was first installed in France and caught CMB, and everybody else, by surprise. Like ICT in Britain, CMB had to scramble to survive. It licensed the 301 model from RCA and marketed it as the Gamma 30, but this was not enough; by 1963, the company was operating at a loss.

At this stage, the French government intervened and encouraged CSF and CGE to merge their computer operations with CMB's; the government's efforts were unsuccessful. At the end of a convoluted process of offers and counteroffers, GE, the American conglomerate, acquired a controlling stake in a new company created under the name Bull-GE, which owned CMB's network of commercial interests in France and abroad. GE's intervention was part of a process of expansion of its computer business in Europe that also included the purchase of a controlling interest in the computer operations of Olivetti, the Italian business-equipment firm. CMB became a holding company whose only assets were its minority participation in Bull-GE and a stake in another firm created by the operation. By this time, the American computer manufacturers, of which IBM was the largest, had a 50 percent share of all installations in the French market.[7]

WEST GERMANY

Leaving aside the United States and Britain, West Germany was the country most favorably positioned to take a lead in the development of electronic digital computers after World War II.[8] During the war, Konrad Zuse, an engineer who had worked in the car and aircraft industries, led the development of a series of mechanical, electrical, and electronic computing machines. Two factors, however, delayed the development of electronic stored-program computers in West Germany: the devastation caused by war and a ban imposed by the occupying forces on the commercial manufacturing of computers (not lifted until 1955).

In the mid-1950s, four domestic companies entered the computer industry: Siemens, Standard Elektrik Lorenz (SEL), Telefunken, and Zuse KG. Siemens, SEL, and Telefunken were established manufacturers of electrical and electronic equipment, whereas Zuse KG was a computer start-up that Konrad Zuse had founded in 1949. SEL introduced its first commercial computer in 1959 but withdrew from the industry in 1964. Telefunken was active in computers as an independent company only until 1967, when it was rescued by Allgemeine Elektrizitäts-Gesellschaft (AEG) to become AEG-Telefunken. Zuse KG grew rapidly from the mid-1950s onward but could not manage to raise enough funds to support its expansion and was acquired by Brown, Boveri & Co., an electrical plant manufacturer, in 1964.

Siemens, an electrical engineering powerhouse, established a data-processing division in 1954 and delivered its first computer—the transistorized, scientifically oriented 2002—in 1957. The company undertook a systematic effort to build fast peripherals and came out with its first high-speed printer in 1962. It developed a commercially oriented computer, the 3003, in 1964, the same year it absorbed the remnants of SEL's computer operations. By the mid-1960s, Siemens had become the leading domestic computer producer in the German market.

Siemens's main competitor in West Germany was not its domestic rival, Telefunken (AEG-Telefunken after 1967), but rather IBM, which had established a computer manufacturing plant in Stuttgart in 1956. As in Britain and France, the introduction of the IBM 1401 in West Germany transformed the market for computers—so much so that by1965, the 1401 had become the best-selling computer in the country. At this point, the American computer manufacturers, among which IBM was dominant, had achieved a 72 percent share of the German market.[9]

JAPAN

In Japan there were neither domestic data-processing companies nor entrepreneurial start-ups; the companies that eventually entered the computer industry in the 1950s were the large-scale manufacturers of telecommunications and heavy electrical equipment.[10]

Dominant among the firms that specialized in the production of telecommunications equipment were Nippon Electric (NEC), Fujitsu, Hitachi, and Oki. They formed the select group of companies that supplied equipment to Nippon Telephone and Telegraph (NTT), the state-owned communications monopoly established in 1952. (In some ways, NTT resembled the American AT&T but did not have a captive equipment producer like AT&T had in its Western Electric subsidiary.) The leading producers of heavy electrical equipment included Hitachi, Toshiba, and Mitsubishi Electric—Hitachi being the only firm that belonged to both groups.

In the late 1940s and early 1950s, the telecom and heavy electrical equipment makers in Japan were growing at a rapid pace thanks to government-supported reconstruction programs. These companies had no serious intentions of diversifying into a technology field—namely, computers—whose profitability was uncertain at best. Therefore, early computer developments originated in government research institutions and universities. The two key entities responsible for early computer research in Japan were the Electrotechnical Laboratory (ETL) of the Ministry of International Trade and Industry (MITI) and NTT's Electrical Communications Laboratory (ECL). Both had a mandate to conduct research in certain technology areas regardless of short-term profitability and thus were better positioned than the large private corporations to venture into computers; the same was true for some of the public universities.

ETL built relay-based computers in 1953 and 1954, and completed the development of its first transistorized computer by 1956. While ETL focused on developing transistor-based computers, ECL concentrated on building machines that relied on the parametron, a logic circuit invented at Tokyo

University in 1954. The first parametron-based computer was introduced by ECL in 1957. The technologies used by ETL and ECL in these early computers were subsequently transferred to the private corporations. In late 1957, ETL came out with a considerably more advanced transistorized model and again transferred the technology to private corporations such as NEC, Hitachi, and Matsushita, which applied it in their first second-generation computers.

By this time, it was becoming clear to government officials that, in spite of these technology transfers, the gap between American and Japanese computer manufacturers was growing at a rapid pace. A piece of legislation enacted in 1957, the Extraordinary Measures Law for Promotion of the Electronics Industry, identified the computer industry as a key target for government support in Japan. The law encouraged cooperation among firms and gave MITI, the agency in charge of developing and coordinating industrial policy, the authority to "advise" firms and even penalize them for noncompliance; for example, MITI would be able to encourage firms to cooperate and provide advice on how much each company should manufacture of what product. At the same time, the legislation exempted the computer industry from the antimonopoly law that was in force at the time.

The Extraordinary Measures Law for Promotion of the Electronics Industry, along with subsequent pieces of legislation, also provided the legal basis for policy measures that the Japanese government introduced to support the domestic computer industry. MITI started by raising tariffs on foreign computers from 15 to 25 percent and by negotiating with IBM so that the Japanese computer makers would have access to IBM's patents.[11] IBM had been selling traditional data-processing equipment in Japan since 1925; its assets, which had been confiscated during World War II, were returned to the company in 1949 during the American Occupation of Japan. In any case, IBM had been prevented by various laws—the Foreign Exchange Control Law of 1933, the Foreign Exchange and Foreign Trade Law of 1949, and the Foreign Capital Law of 1950—from manufacturing in Japan or repatriating earnings. In 1956, for example, IBM Japan applied to MITI for permission to receive from its parent company, the IBM World Trade Corporation, the technology and capital required to produce in Japan, but MITI denied the request.

IBM had something that MITI wanted, however—computer know-how. In a change of policy, in December 1960 MITI allowed IBM to start manufacturing computer equipment in Japan (and to start repatriating a portion of the revenues obtained from equipment sales) in exchange for broad access to IBM's patents. The agreement, which covered the period from 1961 to 1965, opened up the doors for seven companies—Fujitsu, Hitachi, NEC, Toshiba, Mitsubishi Electric, Oki, and Matsushita—to license the IBM technologies at a 5 percent royalty.[12]

Since it soon became clear that this mechanism was not sufficient to close the technology gap, under MITI's supervision the Japanese computer makers entered into technology agreements with their American peers. Between 1961 and 1964, deals were signed that linked Hitachi with RCA, Mitsubishi Electric with TRW, NEC with Honeywell, Oki with Sperry Rand, and Toshiba with GE. After negotiating unsuccessfully with IBM, Fujitsu opted for a go-it-alone strategy. MITI did not stop there: since anyone wishing to import a computer in Japan had to obtain a license from the government, the agency used its power to nudge companies and public organizations to buy Japanese.

The government also encouraged Japanese firms to enter the computer industry by providing subsidies, low-interest loans, tax benefits, and loan guarantees. In the 1960s, government subsidies and tax benefits to the computer industry reportedly amounted to almost $132 million, about 46 percent of what the computer companies themselves invested in R&D and manufacturing facilities. Government loans to the industry through the Japan Electronic Computer Co. (JECC), discussed below, exceeded $410 million in the 1960s alone.[13]

MITI and NTT sponsored a number of cooperative research projects linking Japanese computer manufacturers with one another. One of the main goals was to induce firms to avoid duplicative research—NEC, Fujitsu, and Hitachi tended to specialize in mainframes and memories, whereas Oki, Mitsubishi, and Toshiba concentrated on small machines and peripherals. The first such venture, the FONTAC project (1962–1964), which involved Fujitsu, NEC, and Oki, aimed at producing a system competitive with IBM's 1401, which was in high demand in Japan; in fact, MITI was monitoring the strength of this demand in real time because it was receiving numerous import applications from companies in the early 1960s. For this particular project, Fujitsu developed the main processor while NEC and Oki built the peripheral equipment. Although FONTAC did not produce the expected results, Fujitsu later relied on research conducted during FONTAC to develop its FACOM 230-50 second-generation computer.

Probably the single most important policy measure that MITI implemented to foster the development of the Japanese computer industry was the creation of JECC, a semiprivate computer rental firm through which the government granted about $2 billion in subsidized loans between 1961 and 1981. The company, owned by the computer manufacturers, used the loans to purchase computers up front from the Japanese makers and lease them to customers at competitive rates. In the 1960s, JECC reportedly accounted for 65 percent of all domestic computers leased or sold.[14]

The share of foreign computer installations in the Japanese market peaked at around 60 percent in the early 1960s and declined consistently thereafter. By 1965, Japanese computer companies had a larger market share than foreign manufacturers (roughly 52 percent versus 48 percent in value).[15]

INTERNATIONAL DEVELOPMENTS, 1950–1965: TAKING STOCK

As in the United States, three types of companies entered the computer industry in Britain, France, and West Germany: office-equipment firms, including BTM and Powers-Samas in Britain and CMB in France; electrical manufacturers such as Ferranti and English Electric in Britain, Siemens and SEL in Germany, and CSF and CGE in France; and start-ups such as Leo Computers in Britain, SEA in France, and Zuse KG in Germany. Many of them soon realized that the investments required to be successful in the computer industry were larger than they were willing or able to make. By the mid-1960s, three domestic computer producers remained in Britain and two in Germany, whereas in France CMB had been taken over by the American conglomerate GE.

Another similarity among the Western European countries is that in all of them the introduction of the IBM 1401 in the early 1960s considerably accelerated the pace of change—traditional data-processing sales plunged and the domestic players, many of which still had a lukewarm commitment to computers at that stage, were confronted with the reality that the old order was being replaced with a radically new one. The situation in Japan was somewhat unique: the 1401 did cause turbulence in the Japanese computer industry but the domestic producers received stronger support from their government than any of the Western European computer manufacturers, and received it earlier. Thus, by the mid-1960s, the domestic computer industry in

Table 3.1. Number of Computer Installations in the United Kingdom, France, West Germany, Western Europe, Japan, and the United States, 1955–1964

Year	United Kingdom	France	West Germany	All Western Europe	Japan	United States
1955	13	5	5	27		240
1956	24	10	10	63		750
1957	62	15	20	140		1,500
1958	116	35	85	340	9	2,550
1959	153	65	200	610	35	3,810
1960	217	165	300	1,000	85	5,400
1961	314	285	500	1,650	200	7,550
1962	502	460	690	2,620	440	9,900
1963	740	700	1,020	3,900	825	13,800
1964	1,120	1,050	1,650	6,000	1,350	19,200

Source: M. Phister, *Data Processing Technology and Economics* (Bedford, MA: Digital Press, 1979), 287–288.

Note: "All Western Europe" includes the following countries: France, the United Kingdom, West Germany, Belgium, Luxembourg, Denmark, Italy, the Netherlands, Spain, Sweden, Switzerland, Finland, Norway, Austria, Greece, Ireland, and Portugal.

Japan was stronger relative to the American invaders than it was in any Western European country. The British, French, German, and Japanese computer markets had one key factor in common with the American market: no single computer model became dominant enough to dictate the dynamics of the industry.

Computer diffusion proceeded faster and a commercial computer industry developed earlier in the United States than anywhere else. Table 3.1 tracks the number of computer installations in Britain, France, West Germany, all of Western Europe, Japan, and the United States. By 1960, more than 5,000 computers had been installed in the States, nearly 25 times as many as in Britain, the country that ranked second in the number of installations.

The American computer industry was ahead both in absolute terms and relative to the size of the economy. In 1958, the United States had 5.70 computer installations per billion dollars of GNP, about 3.2 times more than Britain, which ranked second by this criterion. Two years later, the United

States had almost 30 computer installations per million people, about 5.5 times more than West Germany, which ranked second by this measure.[16] Furthermore, whereas American computer manufacturers invaded foreign markets with a certain degree of success, no foreign computer producer was able to penetrate the American market. By 1964, U.S. computer companies accounted for about 50 percent of all installations in France, almost 40 percent in Britain, about 70 percent in West Germany, and about 45 percent in Japan. (They also accounted for 100 percent of installations in the United States.)

On both sides of the market, supply and demand, the United States had distinguishing features that helped it become the world leader in computers. On the supply side, the States had IBM. By the late 1940s, no other company in the world had developed a combination of the capabilities that mattered for success in electronic computers as comprehensive as those of IBM.

In Britain, firms such as Ferranti, English Electric, GEC, and AEI had abundant electronics know-how but lacked the kind of knowledge of the data-processing business that IBM had amassed for decades. The same applied to many of the key companies that entered the business early in France (CSF and CGE), West Germany (Siemens, Telefunken, and SEL), and Japan (all of them).

Although the non-U.S. data-processing equipment companies—BTM and Powers-Samas in Britain and CMB in France—had capabilities in the data-processing field that were comparable to IBM's, their defensive strategy toward electronic digital computers was far less effective. For all of them, IBM included, the 1950s were more about managing change than about embracing digital computers wholeheartedly. But IBM was more daring in its attempt to grapple with the challenges posed by digital computers. IBM was always one step ahead relative to its European peers, both in incorporating electronics into traditional data-processing equipment and in exploring the possibilities of digital computers.

If on the supply side the United States had IBM, on the demand side IBM (and its American competitors) had the United States. The unique strength of both government and civilian demand in the States helped IBM and the other American computer companies pull ahead of their foreign competitors. A large share of the early computer know-how was developed under government contracts. Although the U.S. government did not provide a direct subsidy for computer R&D in private corporations, it did invest heavily in military R&D contracts, and many of the technologies developed for military purposes later found their way into civilian uses. Thus, at a time when there was great uncertainty about the kinds of results that computers could deliver, the government became an important source of demand, both directly through its own military institutions and indirectly through the defense contractors.

The strength of civilian demand also distinguished the United States from Europe and the rest of the world. In 1950, Britain, France, and West Germany lagged considerably behind the United States in per-capita income and would have had to combine their populations to match the size of the U.S. market.[17] The American market provided enough breadth and depth to justify the investments required for competing successfully in the computer industry, to an extent that none of the individual domestic European markets did.

Finally, European businesses showed considerably less enthusiasm than their American counterparts for mechanizing their data-processing tasks. Since real wages tended to be higher in the United States than in any European country throughout most of the twentieth century, American businesses faced much stronger incentives than their European counterparts to replace labor with machinery.

PART II

THE IMPACT OF IBM'S SYSTEM/360
1965–1980

CHAPTER FOUR

IBM's System/360 in the American Market

C hapters 4, 5, and 6 cover the period from 1965 to 1980, the "era of the IBM System/360 standard." The System/360, a family of compatible models across the performance range, transformed the computer industry upon its release in the mid-1960s and forced IBM's competitors to respond in one of three possible ways:

1. producing a range of computers that were software compatible within the range but not compatible with IBM or any other manufacturer
2. producing a range of computers that were software compatible with IBM's
3. focusing on a niche area not (yet) occupied by IBM

Most of IBM's competitors opted for the first response: these were Honeywell, Burroughs, GE, NCR, and Sperry Rand in the United States, CII (later CII-HB) in France, and ICT (later ICL) in Britain. RCA in the United States and its licensees in Japan and Europe made the second response, while others, including SDS, DEC, and CDC in the States and Nixdorf in Europe, chose to exploit niche markets.

The System/360 computers were unique not only because they generated radical responses among competing computer vendors at home and abroad but also because they created an ecosystem of companies that supplied complements for the IBM machines (and, to some extent, for their competitors as well). Among these were the makers of plug-compatible peripheral equipment such as Memorex and Telex, and the creators of corporate software products such as Informatics and ADR. The number of companies that supplied substitutes for computer ownership—including service bureaus such as EDS and ADP and time-sharing companies such as Comshare and Tymshare—also rose at a fast pace in the late 1960s, as did mainframe leasing companies such as Greyhound and Leasco.

System/370 followed System/360, and the strategies that IBM's competitors implemented in the 1970s mirrored those taken in the prior decade. Most of the competing mainframe manufacturers responded with families of IBM-incompatible mainframes. A few—Amdahl in the United States, Siemens in Germany, and Fujitsu and Hitachi in Japan—tried a new version of the IBM-compatibility route, the plug-compatible mainframe (PCM). Others exploited niche strategies either at the top of the price spectrum (CDC and Cray Research in the States, for example) or at the bottom (the makers of minicomputers and small business computers in the United States and beyond).

Governments in Western Europe and Japan reacted to System/360 and System/370 as well. Several European countries anointed a "national champion"—ICL in Britain, Siemens in Germany, and CII in France—and supported it with what often turned out to be inadequate subsidies in the hope that the chosen company might be able to fend off the American threat. The Japanese government, however, took a radically different approach: rather than picking a winner, it used tariffs, quotas, and other means to create a protected domestic market, within the boundaries of which it encouraged both competition and cooperation among a number of domestic firms.

THE INDUSTRY BEFORE SYSTEM/360

At the end of 1962, almost 13,000 computers were installed in the United States.[1] Customers had the choice of either buying the computers upfront or renting them from one of the manufacturers, an option that resulted from the 1956 Consent Decree.

In 1952, the Justice Department's Antitrust Division launched an action against IBM in connection with various practices the company used in marketing its electromechanical equipment. Four years later, IBM consented to the entry of a final judgment in this case before a ruling was issued. This judgment became known as the 1956 Consent Decree and applied to IBM tabulating and electronic data-processing machines. It forced IBM to offer its machines for sale as well as for lease; in practice, however, computer rentals considerably outnumbered outright purchases. Between 1960 and 1964, for example, sales of IBM's data-processing equipment (including computers) accounted for about 30 percent of the company's total revenues, and service and rentals represented the remaining 70 percent.[2]

IBM charged customers a flat monthly rental rate for a total usage of 176 hours per month, the equivalent of eight hours of daily use over a 22-day period. If customers exceeded the 176-hour limit, they had to pay an "extra charge" (or "extra shift") that amounted to 40 percent of the hourly flat rate charge. For a computer that rented for $2,000 per month, the hourly rate equivalent was $11.36, and the extra charge about $4.50 per hour. High-utilization customers paid more (per month) than low-utilization ones, and academic customers paid considerably less than corporate ones. In the mid-1960s, educational discounts, which most manufacturers offered, ranged from as low as 10 percent to as high as 50 percent, depending on the manufacturer and the system.[3] Computer vendors subsidized educational markets because they believed that students using computers of a given brand would lead to businesses using them once those students moved to corporate jobs after graduation.

SYSTEM/360: INTERNAL CONFLICTS, ANNOUNCEMENT, AND LAUNCH

In the early 1960s, outside observers may have viewed IBM as sitting comfortably at the top of the industry and systematically following a centrally determined master plan; however, inside the company, three product development groups were vying to determine the key components of the next computer architecture. First, the Poughkeepsie, New York, faction—the creators of the IBM 700 and 7000 machines—started to design a new family of mainframes, the 8000 Series. Second, the Endicott, New York, group—the creators of the best-selling IBM 650 and IBM 1401—wanted to build upon the success of the 1401 with a set of compatible products. And third, the laboratories of IBM's World Trade subsidiary in Hursley Park, England, started working on various scientific- and business-oriented models, the SCAMP computers.

The year 1961 was a turning point for IBM in terms of defining its future computer identity. In the fall of that year, the company formed a special task force with the mission of outlining an overarching plan for its data-processing products. The SPREAD group—an acronym for systems programming, research, engineering, and development—completed its report in December 1961; it proposed that the company engage in the design and manufacturing of a family of machines, the New Product Line or SLT Series, later called IBM System/360.

The New Product Line would consist of a range of compatible machines, each supported by software, memories of various sizes, and an array of input-output devices. The SPREAD report recommended that each processor be capable of "operating correctly all valid machine-language programs of all processors with the same or smaller I/O and memory configurations."[4] This would facilitate customer migration from smaller to larger machines without massive losses of sunk software investments. It would also make IBM's sales and service operations more productive, because personnel would be supporting just one computer product.

Beginning in May 1962, IBM focused all of its resources on what would become System/360. Although it added a few more models to the line later on, in April 1964 the company announced what was then considered the full family of machines—a total of six processor models and almost 20 combinations of processor and memory size. The new range was described by IBM's marketers as a "third generation" because of its use of solid logic technology (SLT), an early form of integrated-circuit technology.

The demand for System/360 computers skyrocketed, and new models were introduced. By the end of 1966, IBM had installed nine different System/360 models, from the 360/20 at the bottom ($2,000 per month) to the 360/75 at the top ($78,000 per month). Table 4.1 shows the gamut of System/360 computers as of December 1966, with dates of first installation, monthly rental rates, number of installations, and number of pending orders.

By this point, the System/360 computers already accounted for about 13 percent of all installations in the American market (for all manufacturers) and also for a remarkable 57 percent of all pending orders (for all manufacturers). System/360 had a major impact on both IBM and the marketplace. In the process of conceiving and bringing to market the System/360 computer

Table 4.1. Computer Installations and Unfilled Orders in the American Market, December 1966: IBM System/360, All IBM, and All Manufacturers

System	Average monthly rental	Date of first installation	Number of installations	Number of unfilled orders
IBM 360/20	$2,000	Dec. 1965	1,200	6,400
IBM 360/30	$7,500	May 1965	2,500	4,400
IBM 360/40	$15,000	Apr. 1965	1,350	1,500
IBM 360/44	$10,000	July 1966	20	150
IBM 360/50	$26,000	Aug. 1965	140	600
IBM 360/62	$55,000	Nov. 1965	1	0
IBM 360/65	$50,000	Nov. 1965	28	215
IBM 360/67	$75,000	Oct. 1966	6	66
IBM 360/75	$78,000	Feb. 1966	16	32
System/360 Total			5,261	13,363
IBM Total			24,538	17,719
Total All Manufacturers			39,983	23,443

Source: "Monthly Computer Census," *Computers and Automation,* January 1967, 62–63.

models, IBM transformed itself as a company. It reportedly invested half a billion dollars in research and development for System/360 and budgeted an additional $4.5 billion for computer rentals, plant, and equipment. Between early 1964 and late 1967, it hired one-third of the 190,000 employees it had at the end of 1967 and built five new plants in the United States and abroad.[5]

The company became more integrated during this phase: the World Trade subsidiary abandoned its goal of developing its own computers and focused on designing, manufacturing, and marketing System/360. In fact, the World Trade Laboratories in Hursley Park designed one of the models, the 360/40. IBM also became a major manufacturer of computer components, setting up a components division in 1961 to manufacture the hybrid (SLT) integrated circuits that powered the System/360 computers. By 1966, IBM had become the largest producer of integrated circuits in the world.

Competitors reacted quickly to IBM's April 1964 announcement of the new computer line. System/360 represented a price cut of 30–50 percent for a given level of performance relative to the company's previous computer offerings. Competing vendors cut prices on existing products and reformulated their plans for future product lines in light of System/360.

Many of IBM's competitors responded to System/360 by either lowering or eliminating the extra charge on their machines—that is, the charge that users paid when they exceeded the 176-hour monthly limit. IBM counterattacked by reducing the extra charge first from 40 to 30 percent, and then to only 10 percent.[6]

STRATEGIC RESPONSES TO SYSTEM/360

It soon became obvious to IBM's competitors that a more fundamental response to System/360 was required. Most of the competition introduced one or more families of computers such that, at least in theory, customers who started by purchasing a model at the bottom of the range would be able to migrate upward within the range without having to rewrite all of their computer programs. Most of these computer families were incompatible with System/360—RCA's Spectra 70 was the exception. A few companies also attempted niche strategies, focusing on those segments of the market where System/360 was absent or weak. Table 4.2 presents the competitive responses to System/360 (and then to its successor, System/370) in the American market, highlighting the three strategies described.

The table shows the extent to which RCA was unique among IBM's competitors: it delivered a range of computers, the Spectra 70, such that customers starting at the bottom of the System/360 range would be able to migrate to one of the IBM-compatible Spectra 70 machines. Of course, migration could potentially take place from RCA to IBM as well, and RCA was perfectly aware of this fact. It expected, however, that it would be able to gain many more customers than it would lose to IBM.

RCA announced its Spectra 70 family—10 models in total—in December 1964. The company positioned each of its machines between a pair of System/360 models, with the RCA computer performing better than the less powerful IBM model. For example, RCA placed the Spectra 70 Model 45 between System/360 Model 40 and System/360 Model 50, with the goal of beating at least the 360 Model 40 in price-performance.

Whereas GE, UNIVAC, Honeywell, Burroughs, NCR, and RCA responded to System/360 with ranges of compatible computers that spanned most of the performance spectrum, CDC, DEC, and SDS chose to concentrate on either the low- or high-end of the performance range. As discussed in Chapter 2, all of these companies developed a powerful reputation

Table 4.2.   Competitive Responses to System/360 (Late 1960s) and System/370 (1970s)

Company	Late 1960s	1970s
I. IBM-Incompatible Family		
GE	400, 600, and 100 Series	Exited mainframe production but remained active in time-sharing
Sperry Rand UNIVAC	1108 and 1106 models, 9000 Series	Acquired RCA's customer base; 1110 and 90 Series
Honeywell	200 Series	Acquired GE's customer base; 6000 and 2000 Series
Burroughs	500 Series	700, 800, and 900 Series
NCR	Century 100 and 200	Additional Century models, Criterion 8000 Series
II. IBM-Compatible Family		
RCA	Spectra 70 Series	Exited the computer industry
Amdahl		Plug-Compatible Mainframes
III. Niche Strategies		
CDC	6000 and 3000 Series	Seymour Cray left and founded Cray Research in 1972; CDC focused on services and peripherals
SDS	Sigma Series	Acquired by Xerox in 1969
DEC	Additional PDP models	Joined by dozens of new minicomputer entrants

Source: F. Fisher, J. McKie, and R. Mancke, *IBM and the U.S. Data Processing Industry* (New York: Praeger, 1983), chapters 5, 6, 8–10, 13, 14, 16, and 17.

among scientific and technical users, and all of them chose the IBM-incompatible route.

INDEPENDENT PERIPHERALS COMPANIES

System/360 generated a wide variety of reactions not only among competing computer manufacturers but also among a heterogeneous assortment of smaller companies that were not in the business of producing computer processors. Among the firms in the latter group, many offered goods and services that functioned as complements for the System/360 machines (and the mainframe offerings of other computer manufacturers), whereas others marketed services that substituted for computer ownership.

In the second half of the 1960s, the term "peripherals" covered a wide variety of products—card readers and punches, printers, plotters, tape and disk drives, optical scanners, and remote entry devices (such as point-of-sale electronic cash registers). Mainframe manufacturers did not readily cede the peripheral business to the independents. By the late 1960s, IBM derived more revenues from peripherals (60 percent of the total) than from the processors themselves. IBM's peripherals also accounted for between 75 and 80 percent of all peripheral-related revenues in the United States at the time.[7]

The introduction of System/360 generated an explosion of entry into the computer peripherals business. The number of independent peripherals makers went up from about 100 in 1960 to about 250 in 1968.[8] The Computer Peripherals Manufacturers Association, a trade group founded in 1970, had around 650 member companies at its inception.[9]

The independent peripherals companies sprang to life in one of two ways: through innovation or imitation. Mohawk Data Sciences, founded in 1964 by the UNIVAC alumnus and self-taught engineer Virgil Johnson, was among the innovators. It created a "key-to-tape" system that allowed data-preparation operatives to enter data directly onto magnetic tape rather than punched cards. A version of the technology had existed since the early 1950s, but Mohawk updated it in such a way that it quickly started displacing punched-card equipment. By 1966, Mohawk had sold about 1,500 of its data recorders.

The so-called plug-compatible manufacturers took the imitation route: they manufactured peripherals that, when connected to the IBM mainframes, beat the IBM peripherals in price-performance. Telex and Memorex implemented this business model most successfully.

Between the 1930s and the late 1950s Telex was a family-owned company that marketed hearing aids and a few acoustic products. In the late 1950s and early 1960s, after a change in ownership, it broadened its portfolio of products to become a comprehensive electronics manufacturer. It sold its first IBM-compatible tape drives in 1966. Soon after, a host of small firms—Memorex among them—copied the approach and entered the disk-drive market with IBM-compatible devices.

Memorex was incorporated in 1961 by four former employees of Ampex, a firm that had been active in the tape-drive market since 1955 and was also one of the first to enter the plug-compatible peripheral business. In its early years. Memorex focused on marketing magnetic tape to mainframe users. In 1967, it started developing disk packs for systems made by IBM and other computer manufacturers, and then it moved to IBM plug-compatible disk drives. In order to give a credibility boost to its plug-compatible strategy, in the late 1960s it hired hundreds of former IBM employees, including engineers with experience in disk-drive design.[10]

By 1970, the plug-compatible peripheral manufacturers had reportedly displaced about 14 percent of IBM's tape drives and about 5 percent of its disk drives. In addition, plug-compatible manufacturers started to make some threatening inroads into the very heart of IBM's systems by replacing and augmenting main computer memory with IBM-compatible memory.

The relationships between the plug-compatible peripheral makers and IBM were complex. By creating complements for the IBM processors, the plug-compatible peripheral manufacturers enhanced the demand for the processors themselves, boosting IBM sales in the process. By creating substitutes for the IBM peripherals, however, they also harmed IBM; the demand for IBM's own tape and disk drives decreased. IBM quickly concluded that Memorex, Telex, and their peers caused the company more harm than good.

IBM responded to the plug-compatible manufacturers in a number of ways throughout the early 1970s. The company introduced a disk drive, code name Mallard, which, without being fundamentally different from the products that it had in the market at the time, sold for considerably less than the existing IBM drive products and the comparable plug-compatible products. Mallard was an interesting example of price discrimination at work: by introducing the disk drive camouflaged as a new product, IBM managed to cut the peripheral's price only to customers buying or leasing *new* systems, while maintaining the old (higher) price on the already installed disk drives. Telex responded by cutting the prices of its own products, and Mallard ultimately failed to fend off the plug-compatible disk-drive threat.

IBM also counterattacked by introducing long-term leasing plans on some of its tape drives, disk drives, and printers. Until May 1971, IBM tended to lease its mainframes for 90 days and its peripheral equipment for 30 days; customers usually renewed their contracts at the end of the term but had the option not to. But then the company announced the "fixed-term plan," offering discounts of 8 percent on some peripheral equipment for a one-year lease and 16 percent for a two-year lease. IBM also lowered the purchase price of the equipment by about 15 percent and offered customers a "technological discount" of 12 percent per year for up to two years.[11] Customers eagerly switched to the new plan; after a few months, about 40 percent of all tape drives, disk drives, and printers were covered by it. By the end of 1971, the plug-compatible manufacturers had started feeling the impact of IBM's new rental policies—their monthly tape-drive sales had collapsed by 62 percent and their monthly disk-drive sales had fallen by 48 percent.[12]

COMPUTER LEASING COMPANIES

Computer leasing companies can best be described as a peculiar species in the computer ecosystem: they increased demand for computer equipment from the original manufacturer and then competed with that manufacturer in the process of placing the equipment with customers. For IBM and the other computer makers, leasing firms acted as both customers and competitors. If, on the one hand, they increased the demand for IBM's equipment on the computer-sales side of the business, they put downward pressure on IBM's profit margins on the other, since they undercut the computer maker's monthly rental rates by as much as 20 percent. IBM, which reportedly made higher accounting profits from leasing than from selling, eventually took measures to counteract the leasing companies' influence.

The leasing companies' business model relied on the fact that nobody knew the real length of the average rental life of a computer. IBM (and other manufacturers) tended to assume that it was about five years; the leasing companies believed that it was closer to ten. If customers were willing to make long-term rental commitments, leasing firms offered them monthly rental rates well below those of IBM. By placing, say, a System/360 Model 40 with a customer at monthly rates about 20 percent lower than IBM's for a period of 10 years, leasing companies could—under admittedly optimistic assumptions—generate more than $500,000 in profits.

Companies that leased computer equipment at a discount, including Boothe, Leasco, and Greyhound, proliferated in the 1960s. Itel, one of the main players, incorporated in 1967, drafted its first lease in early 1968, and by the end of that year had a portfolio of contracts on computer equipment whose original cost was $130 million. It quickly diversified into other areas of the computer business by acquiring a specialized service bureau and a vendor of word processors and data terminals, and by creating an affiliate whose initial focus was the manufacturing of mass-memory devices.[13]

IBM reacted in stages to the threat posed by Itel and its peers. The leasing companies' profitability hinged on the ability to purchase secondhand equipment at relatively low prices, so the pricing structure derived from the 1956 Consent Decree benefited them considerably. The agreement required IBM to sell the equipment at a discount equivalent to 10 percent of the purchase price for each year the machine remained in use up to a maximum discount of 75 percent. A machine that sold for $100,000 when it was brand new could be purchased for $80,000 after two years and for $25,000 after eight years. Although the ruling established that IBM would have the burden of proof to show compliance if civil suits were launched against the company for non-compliance with this provision for up to 10 years after 1956, IBM started to eliminate this pricing structure in 1963: it reduced the discount from 10 percent a year to 5 percent a year, and also capped the discount at a maximum of 35 percent (down from 75 percent).[14]

Furthermore, after the announcement of System/360 in 1964, IBM changed the discount to 12 percent the first year with no further discounts in the following years. In practice, IBM prevented the leasing companies from purchasing third-generation computer equipment for less than 88 percent of the original price.

IBM further squeezed the leasing companies when it introduced System/370. In the IBM pricing strategy of the time, the "multiplier" played a key role. The multiplier was simply the ratio of the purchase price to the monthly rental—a computer that sold for $900,000 and rented for $19,550/month had a multiplier of about 46. The leasing companies, of course, loved low multipliers. With the introduction of System/370, IBM raised the average multiplier from about 42.5 to about 48, which dented the leasing companies' profit margins from 1970 on.

COMPUTER-SERVICES AND SOFTWARE COMPANIES

The number of computer-services firms, some of which were also software-products vendors, exploded after the introduction of System/360. Table 4.3 tracks the number of computer-services companies in the United States between the mid-1950s and 1973, and shows that the rate of (net) entry accelerated after 1965—it went from 37 firms annually for 1955–1960 to 147 annually for 1965–1970. Additionally, the revenues of the average company

Table 4.3. Computer Software and Services Firms in the United States, 1955–1973 (Revenues in USD Million)

Year	Number of firms	Total revenues	Software revenues
1955	24	15	
1956	31	20	
1957	31	25	
1958	70	40	
1959	150	90	
1960	210	125	
1961	310	180	
1962	370	220	
1963	440	270	5
1964	520	317	20
1965	665	410	50
1966	750	540	100
1967	900	735	175
1968	1,300	1,040	270
1969	1,300	1,460	360
1970	1,400	1,900	440
1971	1,500	2,350	450
1972	1,600	3,037	717
1973	1,700	3,618	868

Source: M. Phister, *Data Processing Technology and Economics* (Bedford, MA: Digital Press, 1979), 277.

more than doubled between 1965 and 1970, from slightly over $600,000 to about $1.36 million.

Many of the companies that entered after 1964 did so to create software products for System/360. Among companies that supplied software and services in 1970, more than 50 percent declared that they wrote code for System/360.[15]

The term "software" gained currency in the mid-1960s, highlighting its growing importance in the overall computer industry. System/360 itself represented an attempt at eliminating, or at least minimizing, the switching costs that customers had to bear when they migrated to a larger (incompatible) system; these costs arose from the fact that customers invested massive amounts of time and money in the creation and customization of computer software—and continued to do so well into the 1970s.

IBM made significant investments in the creation of software for System/360. The computer family came equipped with a comprehensive suite of systems software, including languages, operating systems, and utility programs. Since many sophisticated customers were interested in modifying the systems software that came with the IBM machines, the company provided its customers with access to the software's source code.

Measured by annual revenues, by 1970 the independent companies that supplied software and services in the United States were highly heterogeneous. CSC, one of the leading software companies in the country, grew rapidly in the second half of the 1960s. In 1965, it tripled its revenues by acquiring two ITT engineering divisions, which enabled it to become one of the top U.S. government contractors, particularly in the areas of command-and-control and communications. It then expanded successfully into Canada and Europe and, by 1970, with revenues of about $100 million, became the first software company to be listed on the New York Stock Exchange.[16]

The experiences of ADR, a much smaller company founded in Princeton, New Jersey, in 1959, are probably closer to those of the typical software firm of the 1960s. Established by a group of former UNIVAC employees, ADR functioned mainly as a "programming services" firm for a good portion of the decade, working on one-of-a-kind projects for hardware manufacturers and government agencies on fixed-price and competitively bid contracts.

ADR provides a good example of a transition that started taking place in the mid-1960s and consolidated during the 1970s—from a business model based on software contracting to one based on the creation of corporate software products. In 1963, RCA approached ADR with a request for a flow-charting program for its users. (The program automated the programmers' manual chore of documenting their code in a graphical form.) With a modest investment, ADR developed a prototype program, Autoflow, for the RCA 501. Although RCA lost interest in the product, ADR saw the potential for licensing Autoflow, suitably modified, to the much larger IBM 1401/1410 installed base. ADR drafted a patent for Autoflow—the first patent on computer software—and focused on marketing the product to the IBM 1401/1410 users. After sales of IBM's System/360 took off, ADR rewrote Autoflow and marketed the product to the System/360 installed base. Between 1967 and 1970, the software maker licensed more than 1,000 Autoflow systems.[17]

Informatics was another of the early software contractors that made the transition to marketing corporate software products. Walter Bauer, the former head of TRW's computer division, and his partners established Informatics in 1962. In the mid-1960s Informatics acquired the AIS division of Hughes Dynamics, which housed a group of talented programmers under the direction of John Postley, a 20-year veteran of computer programming. Together with the AIS division, Informatics acquired Mark III, a file-management system invented by Postley.

Mark IV, a new and improved version of the system that Postley had created, became *the* corporate software product of the late 1960s, the 1970s, and the early 1980s. Developed originally for IBM's System/360, Mark IV was marketed by an IBM-style national sales force with a hefty price of $30,000. Although this generated "sticker shock" among customers accustomed to free software, the product sold well from the beginning. By the spring of 1969, Informatics had secured 121 Mark IV installations in the United States and an additional 16 in Europe, well in excess of the company's most optimistic expectations.[18] From the time of its introduction in 1967 until its peak in the early 1980s, Mark IV was the best-selling corporate software product from an independent software vendor.

SERVICE BUREAUS

Service bureaus continued to account for a large majority of all services revenues in the second half of the 1960s. As data-communications technology improved, the traditional messenger- or mail-based batch model morphed into an "online batch" approach in which transactional data and outputs were transmitted between customers and service bureaus using leased telephone lines.

ADP, one of the leading companies in the service-bureau business, expanded in the second half of the 1960s by acquiring smaller operations in regions outside its original geographic base of the Greater New York City area. It also diversified from the payroll-processing business into an adjacent market, the brokerage accounting business. By 1970, ADP had annual revenues of about $39 million.[19]

Similarly, EDS grew rapidly in the 1960s by tailoring its data-processing abilities to specific industries and markets. In 1963, the same year in which it signed its first long-term facilities management contract with Frito Lay, EDS entered into its first insurance company contract with Mercantile Security Life. The company started setting up Medicare and Medicaid claims-processing systems in many states in 1965, and three years later signed its first data-processing contract with a financial institution, a Dallas-based bank. By 1973, EDS was generating $100 million in annual revenues.[20] Eventually, it became one of the top players in health care claims processing, financial and banking information, and insurance claims processing.

COMPUTER TIME-SHARING COMPANIES

Time-sharing, which started developing as an industry in the mid-1960s, shared one key feature with online-batch services: both enabled customers to access a central mainframe computer remotely. By definition, however, the time-sharing model offered interactivity, which the batch model lacked. When customers accessed a time-sharing computer from their place of business, they used a simple terminal to "converse" with a powerful mainframe, which for all practical purposes functioned as their own computer for the duration of the session.

Time-sharing was primarily a problem-solving facility. Once logged on to the mainframe, customers could undertake problems such as estimating the parameters of a statistical or econometric model, analyzing the performance of an investment portfolio, or solving a linear-programming problem. The time-sharing company supplied library programs for such problems, and users could also develop their own programs.

Two main types of companies offered time-sharing services early on—large and established computer companies such as GE, and small independents such as Tymshare and Comshare. GE came to time-sharing through its connection with Dartmouth College professors John Kemeny and Thomas Kurtz, who pioneered time-sharing in an academic setting (for which they also invented the BASIC programming language). Using computers supplied by GE, Kemeny and Kurtz developed a time-sharing system at the college to encourage computer use and computer-assisted learning by science and liberal arts students. GE quickly transferred to the commercial world the experience it gained from the development of the Dartmouth College time-sharing system. By the end of the 1960s, GE Information Services (GEIS) had established a national time-sharing network organized around a computer supercenter based in Cleveland, Ohio, and claimed 40 percent of all time-sharing revenues in the United States. As of 1975, GEIS had annual revenues of $100 million.[21]

Tymshare was a leading independent provider of time-sharing services. Founders Thomas O'Rourke and David Schmidt had worked for GE in California and kept abreast of the development of the time-sharing model in academic settings. Tymshare Associates was established in 1965 to sell timesharing services to the academic and scientific community in the San Francisco Bay Area. After Tymshare Associates became Tymshare Inc. in 1966, the company grew at a steady pace and expanded geographically, with its annual revenues rising by a factor of 100 between 1966 and 1970, to more than $10 million. In the early 1970s, Tymshare set up a proprietary network, Tymnet, which consolidated its position in the American and international time-sharing market. Tymshare's annual revenues reached about $64 million by 1975.

CHAPTER FIVE

IBM's System/370 in the American Market

As explained in Chapter 4, the introduction of System/360 changed the competitive landscape of the computer industry, both in the United States and abroad. From 1965 on IBM's competitors faced the Shakespearean dilemma of "to be or not to be" compatible with IBM.

FROM THE 1960S INTO THE 1970S

Some of IBM's competitors decided to confront IBM not only in the marketplace but also in the courtroom. In 1968, CDC opened fire: it sued IBM for allegedly attempting to monopolize the industry. The lawsuit claimed unfair practices on IBM's part, stemming from the company's announcement that it would add powerful models at the top of the System/360 range to compete with the CDC 6600. The 6600 had been selling well prior to this announcement, but soon after it, orders started to decline. CDC's president, William Norris, accused IBM of announcing "phantom machines" or "paper tigers"—computer models that existed only in the planning documents of IBM staff and that IBM made public to weaken the demand for CDC's supercomputers. The CDC lawsuit ended in a settlement through which IBM ceded its Service Bureau Corporation to CDC and paid the plaintiff $100 million in compensation.

In January 1969, the U.S. Department of Justice filed suit against IBM with several claims including unfair competition by bundling, premature product announcements, and predatory pricing. Four months later, the software company ADR followed suit. One of ADR's claims was that IBM had exaggerated the capabilities of its Flowcharter product, which competed with ADR's Autoflow. More fundamentally, ADR alleged that, by bundling hardware and software, IBM had stifled the development of an independent software industry. Between 1969 and 1974, a variety of computer companies—including Greyhound, Hudson, and Transamerica among the leasing firms, and Memorex, Calcomp, and Telex among the makers of plug-compatible equipment—filed antitrust suits against IBM.

ADR's bundling claim referred to a practice that was not exclusive to IBM.[1] In the early years of the computer industry IBM and many other computer vendors supplied customers with not just hardware but rather a "total solution" to their data-processing needs. In practice, this meant that customers received software, education, and maintenance and support services "bundled" with the hardware—that is, at no separate charge. Bundling benefited customers in that it made their data-processing costs more predictable, and it also gave them assurances that unexpected problems arising from the use of computing technology would be addressed by the vendor. Although bundling was a common practice among computer makers, IBM laid particular emphasis on customer education and support, which likely contributed to its becoming the leading company in the industry.

Just as IBM's customers benefited from bundling, some of IBM's competitors were harmed by it, particularly those companies competing in software and services. IBM considered unbundling software and services from hardware as early as 1964, but did not take any practical steps in that direction until a few years later. At the end of 1968, and with the hope of preempting an antitrust suit, it made the unbundling announcement. Even though the government went ahead and filed suit against IBM, the company went ahead as well and fulfilled its unbundling commitment. In 1969 it began to charge separately for 17 system and application programs, although it kept operating systems bundled until the late 1970s. It also began to charge separately for programming and educational services.

Of all the lawsuits launched against IBM, the one filed by the Justice Department had the greatest impact on the firm—not because it imposed a structural remedy, which it did not, but because it forced the company to devote massive resources to defend itself from the government's allegations. The suit dragged on for 13 years. The trial did not begin until May 1975 and lasted for six years. As of October 1980, 81 live witnesses had provided testimony, 928 depositions and 11,644 documents had been introduced in evidence, and the transcript of the case had grown to more than 100,000 pages in length.[2] In 1982, the second year of the Reagan administration, the Justice Department determined that the suit was "without merit" and dropped it.

THE INTRODUCTION OF IBM'S SYSTEM/370

Transistors were invented in 1947 but replaced vacuum tubes in computers' central processing units only in 1959, which was also the year in which integrated circuits were invented. Integrated circuits combined many transistors into a single semiconductor device.[3]

When IBM introduced System/360, there was already some debate about the weaknesses and virtues of Solid Logic Technology (SLT) versus monolithic integrated circuits. SLT, which was at the core of System/360, used several silicon chips to make one integrated circuit, whereas monolithic technology used a single silicon chip. IBM's decision to build System/360 on the basis of SLT was criticized both by government agencies that were funding the development of monolithic technology and by component vendors that were negatively affected by IBM's decision to make its own circuits.

By early 1968, when System/360 Model 85 was introduced, semiconductor technology groups at IBM had developed true integrated circuits. This progress in semiconductor technology laid the foundation for the first two models in the new IBM family of computers, System/370's models 155 and 165, announced in June 1970.[4] Although System/370, which was compatible with System/360, was evolutionary rather than revolutionary, two technological features of the System/370 computers made them considerably better in price-performance than the System/360 machines they replaced. First, the 370 computers used monolithic integrated circuits as opposed to SLT technology. Second, they also included a "cache" memory that enhanced the performance of the computer's main memory.

Two additional features of System/370 only became available when IBM introduced later models in the family: one was the industry's first all-semiconductor main memory, and the other was the concept of "virtual memory." Semiconductor-based main memory, which IBM introduced with System/370 Model 145 in September 1970, was as radical a technology change in memory as ferrite-core memory had been in the mid-1950s. Virtual memory, on the other hand, was not IBM's creation: it had been first implemented on the Atlas computer, built in Britain by Ferranti and Manchester University. The key contribution of virtual-memory technology was that it made it feasible for the system to move ("page") information between secondary storage and main memory—that is, it enhanced the size of main memory by transferring information between it and a slower storage technology without this having to be explicitly programmed.

At the same time that IBM was introducing the first System/370 models in 1970, the computer industry experienced a deep recession. This led to concerns at IBM, and in the industry as a whole, that computer purchases would remain weak for a long time. Adding to these fears was also the projection that computer storage costs would decline steadily at a fast pace, and that IBM would not be able to compensate for the sinking price of storage with increased sales and rentals of its other goods and services. In this context, the company established a task force very much like the one formed to develop plans for System/360. This task force, which began meeting in mid-1971, was charged with defining what was called the Future System (FS).

Two of the key goals of FS were to develop a new approach for organizing computer memory and storage and to reduce the cost of creating software.[5] The background for the FS project was the growing realization that about two-thirds of the costs associated with operating a computer were for software and services. IBM viewed FS as a completely new design that would displace System/370 as radically as System/360 had eliminated all of its predecessors. Although IBM devoted increasing resources to ensure the success of FS, the introduction of the new family kept on being postponed, to the point that by the spring of 1974 it was still 45 months away, just as it had been in 1971.

IBM realized that FS would not be ready soon enough to fend off the attacks that competing vendors were launching on System/370 and thus decided to terminate the FS project and extend the System 360/370 architecture. Although there were many reasons why FS never became a reality, the fact that a radically new system would have forced IBM and its customers to rewrite a massive stock of software programs was clearly the most significant. System/360 and its successor, System/370, had become a standard, and breaking with such a standard had become an extremely costly undertaking. After killing the FS project, the company continued to introduce new computers within the System/370 family throughout the 1970s. It launched System/370 Model 158 and Model 168 in 1975, considerably improving upon the price-performance of the early 370 computers.

In 1977, IBM introduced the 303X processors (the 3031, 3032, and 3033), all of them compatible members of the System/370 family. The 3033 model, introduced in response to competition from the Amdahl Corporation, represented almost a 100 percent improvement in performance over the previous model, at only a 12 percent increase in price. The 3031 and 3032 computers also offered impressive gains in price-performance relative to earlier models of the System/370 family.[6]

In January 1979, IBM announced two additional System/370 compatible computers, the 4331 and 4341. These models offered remarkable price-performance improvements, even in comparison with those IBM had made in the recent past. The machines represented such a radical price cut for a given performance level that they changed the competitive landscape of the industry in the next decade both in the United States and abroad.[7]

REACTIONS TO SYSTEM/370 IN AMERICA

When System/360 was announced in the mid-1960s, observers described market conditions in the computer industry as "IBM and the seven dwarfs."[8] IBM was, of course, Snow White to Burroughs, CDC, GE, Honeywell, NCR, RCA, and Sperry Rand's seven dwarfs. GE and RCA left the industry in the early 1970s. The GE customer base was acquired by Honeywell, and the RCA base by Sperry Rand; in both cases, about 60 percent of existing customers stayed with the acquiring firm.[9] Although GE exited mainframe production, it remained active in the time-sharing business. The five companies that remained were renamed the BUNCH—Burroughs, the UNIVAC division of Sperry Rand, NCR, CDC, and Honeywell.

American competitors reacted to IBM's strategic moves in the 1970s the way they had in the second half of the 1960s. Aside from the fact that GE and RCA exited the industry, the ones that stayed—and those that entered for the first time—confronted IBM in one of three ways: with a range of machines incompatible with System/370, with one or more machines compatible (and competing directly) with System/370, or with a niche approach.

Most of the big players—including Burroughs, Honeywell, NCR, and Sperry Rand—responded to each new wave of IBM computers with a new, IBM-incompatible wave of their own. The Amdahl Corporation pioneered a new approach to competing with IBM: the plug-compatible mainframe (PCM). Whereas plug-compatible peripherals substituted for IBM's peripherals, a PCM replaced the processor at the heart of an IBM installation. While working for IBM between the early 1950s and 1970, Gene Amdahl participated in the design of some of the company's early computers, including System/360. When he quit his job in 1970, he explicitly announced he was leaving to compete with his former employer by creating mainframe computers that would run on IBM's software. He founded the Amdahl Corporation in 1970, and within two years managed to raise considerable funding from Japan's Fujitsu and a Chicago venture-capital firm.[10]

Rather than confronting IBM across the performance range, Amdahl initially targeted the 370 Model 168, a powerful system first installed in the mid-1970s. The IBM-compatible Amdahl 470 V/6 machine performed about 50 percent better than the 370 Model 168 and rented for somewhat less.[11] A user could substitute an Amdahl processor for IBM's while continuing to use IBM's peripherals, software, and services. By the end of 1977, Amdahl had installed enough of its V/6 computers for IBM to take notice.

After killing the FS project, IBM took a couple of years to respond to the Amdahl threat. The 3033 computer, specifically designed to compete with the Amdahl 470 V/6, had some success at fending off the Amdahl attack at the top of the performance spectrum. Unfazed, Amdahl announced the 470 V/7 machine, about 1.5 times faster than the 3033 but only 3 percent more expensive. It also announced a smaller machine, the V/5, in an attempt to cover a broader portion of the performance range with IBM-compatible mainframes.

Amdahl's revenues soared between the time it shipped its first mainframe in 1975 and the late 1970s, attracting additional players into the plug-compatible mainframe business. IBM responded not only by introducing computer models such as the 3033, which embedded impressive gains in price-performance, but also by increasingly shifting its sources of revenues from mainframes to software; in the late 1970s, for example, it started charging separately for operating-system programs. Although the shift away from hardware and toward software had started taking place earlier, the growing threat from Amdahl and its peers accelerated the transition.[12]

SMALL COMPUTERS AND SUPERCOMPUTERS

Throughout the 1960s, four major barriers to entry had prevented the emergence of new vendors in the mainframe business: first, the R&D costs of producing a full range of computer processors and peripherals; second, the cost of developing operating-system and applications software; third, the need to ship large volumes to secure economies of scale; and fourth, the need to deploy a sophisticated and effective sales force. In the late 1960s and early 1970s, the first three of these barriers were lowered by the development of low-cost integrated circuits and the advent of the independent peripherals and software industries. This led to new entrants in the field, mainly of two types: the plug-compatible mainframe makers, discussed above, and the manufacturers of small computers (minicomputers and small business computers).[13]

The market-leading minicomputer manufacturer DEC was joined by dozens of new entrants into minicomputers in America.[14] These included Wang (beginning in 1964), Interdata (1966), Data General (1968), and Prime (1971). Among the minicomputer start-ups, few generated as much excitement in the 1970s as Data General. Its founder, Edson de Castro, had played a key role in designing DEC's early minicomputers. He established Data General in the late 1960s and achieved remarkable success in the 1970s with its NOVA minicomputer.[15] Several mainframe manufacturers, including Burroughs, Honeywell, NCR, and Sperry Rand, entered the minicomputer business as well.

A few companies that up to this point had been operating in markets other than computers entered computer production via minicomputers. Hewlett-Packard (HP)—a maker of measuring instruments founded by the Stanford electrical engineering graduates Bill Hewlett and Dave Packard in the late 1930s—acquired a small computer group from Union Carbide and launched a computer division in Cupertino, California. The HP computer group designed what in the early 1970s would have become the world's first 32-bit minicomputer (at a time when 16-bit machines were the rule). Fearing that a 32-bit machine would lead the company to a direct confrontation with IBM and its mainframe business, however, HP transformed the 32-bit computer into a sophisticated 16-bit machine and marketed it successfully as the HP3000 starting in 1972.[16]

Small business systems, which took off in the 1970s, also attracted customers on a budget. They were a complementary market to minicomputers, however. Minicomputers were designed primarily for scientific and engineering applications (process control, lab automation, and typesetting, for example), and had little manufacturer-supplied software. Manufacturers assumed that users would build their own, one-of-a-kind applications. Small business computers, on the other hand, were designed for business applications, and thus required both high-quality data-processing software and reliable after-sales support.

Since small business systems tended to operate in a more demanding market than minicomputers, they attracted two types of companies: first, a select group of minicomputer manufacturers, including DEC, Wang, and HP, which had achieved success in minis and were seeking to penetrate new markets; and second, established business-equipment manufacturers trying to diversify into computers by acquisition. Among the latter, Singer Business Machines, for example, entered the small business computer segment by acquiring Friden in 1963.

IBM introduced *the* archetypical small business system, System/3, in 1970. Based on a product originally developed in Germany, System/3 used a new 96-column punched card—the last spasm of this aged technology. System/3 was popular in two market segments not well exploited up to that point— small- and medium-sized businesses that were still using traditional accounting machines, and large decentralized companies where multiple small computers were preferred to one centralized mainframe. IBM subsequently marketed a sequence of equally popular small business systems, culminating in System/38 in 1980, with which it captured an important portion of the small business segment.[17]

There were 275,000 minicomputer installations in the United States by 1978. DEC had 38 percent of the minicomputer market, Data General had 15 percent, and HP had 8 percent. There were also about 73,000 small business computer installations in the States, and IBM's share as of 1978 was 31 percent.[18]

Two companies, CDC and Cray Research, implemented niche strategies at the high end of the performance spectrum. From the late 1960s, important philosophical differences started developing between CDC and its star computer designer Seymour Cray. CDC wanted to produce machines for both scientific and commercial users, whereas Cray wanted freedom and resources to focus on achieving top speeds in mathematical calculations for scientific and technical users. In the 1970s, CDC's management decided to broaden its portfolio into computer services and peripherals; this did not involve discontinuing supercomputer development, but rather slowing its pace. Cray, who was bent on pushing the performance frontier, left CDC and founded Cray Research in 1972. After his departure, CDC dropped out of the supercomputer business for a while but later returned, lured in part by the success of Cray Research.[19]

In 1976, Cray Research introduced the CRAY-1, a machine too powerful for IBM to even try to match. From then on, the company implemented a business model that relied on selling a few dozen supercomputers to highly sophisticated technical and scientific customers at prices roughly equivalent to three times manufacturing costs. Supercomputers sold for between $8 million and $10 million apiece, and the early customers included the nuclear weapons laboratories at Livermore and Los Alamos.[20] Over time, the Cray machines developed a following in the aerospace sector and in the oil, automotive, and chemical industries.

SERVICES AND SOFTWARE IN THE 1970S

The 1970 recession put some of the independent vendors of software, services, and peripherals out of business and forced others to undergo a few unprofitable years. As a whole, however, this segment of the industry kept on growing in the 1970s.

Total revenues from software (contracting and products) and services grew from $1.76 billion in 1970 to $7.69 billion in 1978. Table 5.1 presents the long-term (1955–1978) evolution of the main segments within the software and services business: traditional batch, online (or remote) batch, interactive (that is, time-sharing), software, and other (mainly, facilities management).

Although traditional batch services (the mail or messenger service bureau model) continued to account for a large portion of total revenues throughout the 1970s, other segments, including interactive and remote batch, expanded at a considerably faster pace. As of 1978, the online processing services segment (remote batch and time-sharing) had revenues of $2.8 billion, considerably more than the traditional batch segment. Revenues from software increased from $375 million in 1970 to over $2 billion in 1978.

Table 5.1.   Total Revenues (in USD Billion) from Services and Software in the
United States, 1956–1978

Year	Traditional batch	Remote batch	Interactive	Software	Other	Total
1956	0.020					0.020
1957	0.025					0.025
1958	0.040					0.040
1959	0.090					0.090
1960	0.125					0.125
1961	0.180					0.180
1962	0.220					0.220
1963	0.260		0.005	0.005		0.270
1964	0.285		0.010	0.020	0.002	0.317
1965	0.340		0.015	0.050	0.005	0.410
1966	0.410		0.020	0.100	0.010	0.540
1967	0.480		0.050	0.175	0.030	0.735
1968	0.600	0.010	0.110	0.270	0.050	1.040
1969	0.740	0.050	0.160	0.340	0.080	1.370
1970	0.945	0.087	0.243	0.375	0.110	1.760
1971	1.075	0.115	0.335	0.415	0.145	2.085
1972	1.235	0.145	0.440	0.470	0.190	2.480
1973	1.405	0.205	0.630	0.605	0.255	3.100
1974	1.580	0.280	0.825	0.830	0.335	3.850
1975	1.740	0.350	1.025	1.090	0.415	4.620
1976	1.860	0.565	1.160	1.375	0.495	5.455
1977	1.935	0.840	1.410	1.730	0.575	6.490
1978	2.100	1.077	1.738	2.110	0.660	7.685

Source: M. Phister, *Data Processing Technology and Economics* (Bedford, MA: Digital Press, 1979), 277 and 610.

Moreover, by the late 1970s, software and services as a whole had become considerably more important in the overall scheme of the industry than they were at the beginning of the decade. Whereas in 1970 software and services accounted for about 28 percent of total computer industry revenues, within eight years they represented about 43 percent of the total. Toward the end of the 1970s, some companies that had come to life as hardware producers, such as CDC, were already deriving more revenues from services than from mainframes and viewed mainframes as supporting those services.[21]

During the 1970s many companies supplying software made the transition from delivering programming services to developing software products.[22] Taxonomies of software products in the 1970s usually distinguished between systems software, industry-specific applications, and cross-industry applications. Systems software encompassed operating systems, database management systems, programming aids, utilities, and teleprocessing monitors (a complex piece of software "plumbing" that connected a user's application program to an operating system and a database). Hardware manufacturers dominated the operating-system segment and split the database-management segment with independent vendors. The programming-aid and utility-software segments were considerably more fragmented. IBM led (and continues to lead) the teleprocessing-monitor segment with its highly lucrative CICS program. This software product—little known outside the industry— is a complex software component that is indispensable for thousands of on-line services around the world. Each day, it is used in billions of electronic transactions, and—since its commercialization following unbundling in 1970—it has earned IBM billions of dollars in profits.

Industry-specific applications made up the largest portion of the incipient software-products industry in the 1970s; within this segment, applications for the financial services industry tended to outnumber those for any other sector of the economy. The supply side was highly fragmented, with many small players serving a small number of clients in a restricted geographic area. Cross-industry applications encompassed accounting and finance, human resources (including payroll), planning and analysis, engineering and science, and office automation. Table 5.2 presents a summary of the various software-product segments in the 1970s with some representative vendors and products in each.

Among computer services firms, ADP, CSC, and EDS, the sector leaders, grew steadily in the 1970s. EDS continued to develop its Medicare and Medicaid claims processing business. It expanded its data-processing services to banks and savings and loans associations, and began servicing credit unions around 1974. It also started signing computer-services contracts with foreign governments, including Saudi Arabia and Iran (1976), and diversified from facilities management contracts into "systems integration" for large customers and "turnkey systems" for small businesses. (Systems integration involved the development of large-scale applications and included the selection

Table 5.2.   Taxonomy of Software Products in the 1970s and the Early 1980s

I. Systems software

Subcategory	Examples of products and vendors
Operating systems	OS/360 family (IBM, 1965)
Database management systems	IMS, DL/1 (IBM, 1969, 1973); TOTAL (Cincom, 1968)
Teleprocessing monitors	CICS (IBM, c. 1970)
Programming aids	Autoflow (ADR, 1965); Mark IV (Informatics, 1967)
Utilities	SyncSort (SyncSort Inc., 1968); CA-SORT (Computer Associates, 1976)

II. Industry-specific applications

Subcategory	Examples of products and vendors
Manufacturing	Manufacturing Systems (MSA, c. 1972)
Banking	BankVision (Hogan Systems, c. 1980); CIS (Anacomp, c. 1980)

III. Cross-industry applications

Subcategory	Examples of products and vendors
Accounting	General Ledger (MSA, c. 1972)
Payroll	Pay (CSC, 1967)

Source: M. Campbell-Kelly, *From Airline Reservations to Sonic the Hedgehog: A History of the Software Industry* (Cambridge, MA: MIT Press, 2003), chap. 5.

of computer equipment. Turnkey systems were smaller solutions supplied to customers as complete hardware-software products dedicated to specific tasks, such as typesetting.) In the late 1970s EDS started providing data-processing services to government organizations.

CSC grew on two fronts: time-sharing and systems integration. First, it entered the computer time-sharing business with a proprietary system, Infonet, which provided both remote batch and interactive data processing. In 1972, Infonet was selected to provide time-sharing services to the U.S. government; within three years, it had become a 100,000-mile network reaching 125 cities and almost every government agency. Toward the late 1970s, CSC expanded the Infonet service to cover some European countries.[23] Second, the company solidified its preeminence as a systems integrator. In 1970, for example, it won a contract for the U. S. Navy's Aegis program, a sophisticated naval weapons system. Later in the decade, it helped modernize the U.S. Federal Aviation Administration systems used by air traffic controllers.

In 1972, ADP expanded into a new adjacent market—computerized inventory and accounting services for auto dealers. It also continued acquiring small service-bureau operations in almost every major city in the country and ventured into some foreign countries with its payroll-processing business—the Netherlands in 1974, Britain in 1977, and Canada in 1979. In the late 1970s, the company diversified into two new markets: payroll tax filing services, closely associated with the payroll business, and automated claims estimating services for insurance companies such as State Farm and Allstate.

COMPUTER LEASING AND PERIPHERALS IN THE 1970S

Contrary to what many industry observers believed would happen, the computer leasing business did not fade in the 1970s; instead, it became considerably more sophisticated as the decade went by. Some of the major computer leasing agreements of the late 1970s, orchestrated by companies such as Itel, turned out to be complex financial transactions in which the leasing company functioned as a sophisticated intermediary between several parties. However, strategic moves that IBM made at the end of the 1970s and early 1980s, including the introduction of the 4300 mainframes, brought renewed pressures upon the leasing companies, and Itel ended up filing for bankruptcy in 1981.

The significance of the peripherals business as a revenue generator grew considerably throughout the 1970s. By 1979, peripherals and terminals represented the largest revenue source for the companies that populated the "Datamation100" index: they accounted for about 36 percent of total revenues, topping software and services (30 percent), computer processors (30 percent), and media (4 percent).[24]

By the late 1970s, the independents had between a quarter and a third of the IBM plug-compatible peripheral business. Three companies remained in this market: CDC, which at this stage of its evolution derived more revenues from peripherals than from any other portion of its business; Memorex, which was in a precarious financial condition but not ready to exit yet; and a newcomer called STC (Storage Technology Corporation). STC had been founded in 1969 by four former IBM engineers with a focus on tape drives, and considerable success in this area led to a later expansion into disk drives.[25]

THE U.S. COMPUTER MARKET, 1965–1980: TAKING STOCK

IBM did not rest on its laurels after launching System/360. The first System/370 models, introduced in 1970, embedded impressive price-performance gains. If System/370 was evolutionary relative to System/360, the Future System was conceived to be revolutionary. And even though the

Table 5.3.   Stock of Computer Installations in the United States, 1959–1978: Mainframes (GP), Minicomputers, and Small Business Computers (SBC) (Units in Thousands and Values in USD Billion)

Year	GP (units)	GP (value)	Minis (units)	Minis (value)	SBC (units)	SBC (value)
1959	3.110	1.340				
1960	4.400	1.865				
1961	6.150	2.605				
1962	8.100	3.485				
1963	11.700	4.550				
1964	16.700	6.000				
1965	21.600	7.800	0.200	0.015		
1966	27.100	9.400	1.200	0.045		
1967	31.000	12.400	3.000	0.095		
1968	37.000	15.700	5.200	0.158		
1969	40.000	19.100	11.500	0.309		
1970	41.900	21.400	20.000	0.481	0.080	0.003
1971	45.000	23.300	28.500	0.654	0.260	0.011
1972	50.200	24.700	45.000	0.970	0.730	0.035
1973	58.300	27.300	65.100	1.325	1.500	0.080
1974	61.500	30.200	96.100	1.900	4.500	0.230
1975	62.100	33.800	126.300	2.535	12.400	0.530
1976	59.600	37.900	162.300	3.410	27.200	1.110
1977	58.200	42.900	214.500	4.770	48.800	1.950
1978	58.000	48.700	275.300	6.515	72.800	2.990

Source: M. Phister, *Data Processing Technology and Economics* (Bedford, MA: Digital Press, 1979), 600–601.

Future System never became a reality, IBM kept on shaking the industry at regular intervals with new and improved models within the 370 family. The introduction of the IBM 4331 and 4341 models in 1979 was so disruptive that many of the companies that were in the plug-compatible business— peripherals and mainframes—attempted to join forces to confront IBM. In a search for diversification Amdahl, Memorex, and STC engaged in merger negotiations in 1979, all of which eventually failed.

By the end of the 1970s, the computer industry had undergone a radical transformation. In the domestic market, two trends are worth highlighting: first, minicomputers and small business systems increased their share of all installations; and second, software and services increased their share of all computer-related revenues.

Mainframes still generated the most revenues of all computer types at this time, but they were no longer dominant in installed volume. Table 5.3 tracks changes in the composition of the computer stock (mainframes, minicomputers, and small business computers): by the late 1970s many more minis and small business machines than mainframes were installed in the United States.

Software and services had come to represent a much larger portion of total industry revenues than they did in 1965. The growth of software and services came from two sources. First, independent companies continued entering the business despite the 1970 recession. Second, computer makers increasingly looked on software as a source of revenues and profits. In the late 1970s, for example, IBM completed the process it had started a decade before by unbundling operating-system software.

However, the key development in the computer industry of the 1970s was neither the growth of small computers nor the rise of software and services as revenue generators—it was rather the consolidation of the IBM System/360 standard for mainframes through the System/370 computers, compatible with System/360. That IBM was forced to abandon plans for a completely new standard—the Future System—only a few years after introducing System/360 speaks strongly of the inertia created by successful standards.

CHAPTER SIX

International Reactions to System/360 and System/370

The impact of the IBM System/360 standard was not limited to the American market: in the mid-1960s, non-U.S. computer companies and governments reacted to what they perceived as the impending U.S. domination of the international computer industry, driven to a large extent by the unstoppable rise of System/360. Non-American computer companies faced the well-known strategic choices—compatibility, incompatibility, and niche. Foreign governments also faced a choice: to pick a winner—a national champion in computers—or not. While governments in Britain, France, and West Germany promoted national champions in the computer industry, the Japanese government took a different path.[1]

BRITAIN IN THE SECOND HALF OF THE 1960S

After the mergers of the early 1960s, there were three domestic computer companies in Britain: two major players—ICT and English Electric Leo Marconi (EELM)—and the smaller Elliott-Automation. EELM was the result of the acquisitions of Leo Computers and the Marconi computer group by English Electric in 1963–1964, and ICT had been formed following the merger of BTM and Powers-Samas, the punched-card machine vendors. The key competitor for all of them was IBM, which had disrupted the British computer market with the introduction of the 1401 model in 1961.

Prime Minister Harold Wilson's Labour government, elected in late 1964 and reelected in early 1966, made a consistent effort to bolster the development of British industry, including the computer industry. For this purpose, it established the Ministry of Technology (Mintech), and the newly appointed minister repeatedly encouraged ICT and EELM to merge to fend off American domination.

At first, the British computer manufacturers opted for a go-it-alone strategy. EELM, which had a technology-licensing agreement with RCA for some time, began planning for a third-generation computer range in early 1963. However, following IBM's announcement of System/360, it decided to manufacture the RCA Spectra 70 family (under the Series 4 name) as an RCA licensee. ICT, on the other hand, chose to develop an IBM-incompatible range of computers, the 1900 Series, based on an existing design. It announced the series in late 1964 and delivered the first model in early 1965, well before IBM delivered its first System/360 computer. The ability to get computers into the market ahead of IBM gave ICT a temporary, though significant, advantage.

After facilitating the absorption of Elliott-Automation by EELM in 1967, Mintech launched a new round of talks with the two British computer leaders with an eye toward a merger. In order to expedite the process, Mintech offered a nonrepayable £25 million grant (about $70 million in early 1967) to subsidize the creation of a new computer company and the development of a new family of computers, the New Range.[2] While the potential merger partners assessed the pros and cons of the operation, British economic conditions worsened considerably. The merger that gave rise to International Computers Limited (ICL), the British national champion, finally took place in the summer of 1968.

By that time, the government had cut its subsidy offer by half, and ICL ended up receiving £13.5 million (about $32.13 million). ICL accounted for almost half of the British computer market (in value) by 1969, and all U.S. companies combined for about 47 percent.[3] With the New Range underfunded from the beginning, ICL went through tumultuous times in the early 1970s and did not complete the development of the new computer family until the mid-1970s.

FRANCE IN THE SECOND HALF OF THE 1960S

Starting in the early 1960s, the introduction of the IBM 1401 created as much disruption in France as it had in Britain. CMB, the traditional data-processing equipment company, resorted to licensing computer technology from the American RCA, but this approach was not effective in counteracting IBM's penetration of the French market. The French government's attempts to encourage CSF and CGE to merge their computer operations with CMB's were unsuccessful, and the American conglomerate GE acquired a controlling stake in a new company created under the Bull-GE name; Bull-GE owned the former CMB's network of commercial interests in France and abroad. (At the same time, CMB became a holding company, a minority partner of GE in the American conglomerate's computer operations in France.) The creation of Bull-GE gave rise to a situation in which over 90 percent of the French computer market belonged to American companies, with two French-owned companies sharing the rest: SEA, which produced mainly scientific computers, and CAE, which marketed machines licensed from an American company.[4]

Like Britain, France created a computer national champion, the Compagnie Internationale pour l'Informatique (CII), in the second half of the 1960s.[5] The British and French governments thus reacted similarly to the American threat in that both chose to use public funds to subsidize the development of a national computer company. There was a key difference, however: ICL, the British national champion, subsumed in itself the data-processing and electronics expertise of every major player in the British computer industry, but CII, the French national champion, excluded Bull-GE, the quintessentially French (and pan-European) data-processing company. This implied foregoing immediate access to Bull's 5,000 customers in France and abroad.[6]

The confluence of a number of factors gave rise to the so-called Plan Calcul, the French industrial policy for computers. First, starting in the early 1960s, French policymakers became increasingly aware of the technological gap that separated their country from the United States. Second, Bull came under GE's control in 1964 with the formation of Bull-GE. Third, that same year, IBM announced System/360. Finally, in 1966, the Pentagon prevented CDC from selling one of its supercomputers to a French governmental agency in charge of military applications of nuclear energy; although the incident had few, if any, practical implications for the development of France as a nuclear power, it had important repercussions in the French press and served as a rationale for General Charles de Gaulle's Plan Calcul.

The First Plan (1967–1971), which cost the government about FFr 567.1 million (roughly $109.5 million), involved the creation of a number of institutions and companies, with CII at the core.[7] CII came to life by absorbing the two French-owned computer companies—SEA and CAE—and was charged with the task of developing a family of computers to confront IBM. Although the French government made a strong commitment to provide consistent financial support to CII, the company itself was private, not state-owned, and its main shareholders were Thomson and CGE, the two largest French-owned electronics manufacturers. Early on CII concentrated on government sales, which represented only 20 percent of the French market.

The CII computer range, the IRIS family, comprised the mid-sized IRIS 50 (with its derivatives) and the large IRIS 80. The IRIS 50 was based mainly on technology that CAE had licensed from SDS, whereas the IRIS 80 was a domestically designed system and thus achieved the goal that was at the heart of Plan Calcul—to build a wholly French mainframe able to compete with IBM's System/360. With the IRIS range, first delivered in 1969, CII adopted a peculiar strategic approach to compete with IBM: the computers were incompatible with IBM's System/360 but also only partially compatible with one another. CII also chose to confront IBM at the level of System/360 Models 40 and 50, where IBM enjoyed phenomenal profit margins and could easily lower prices if necessary. Although from a technical standpoint the IRIS machines performed reasonably well, CII sold them at a loss; and even though the French government subsidized CII's R&D heavily from 1967 to 1971, the French national champion lost money over the same period.[8] By the end of the First Plan in 1971, CII had a 7.5-percent share of the French computer market, a trivial improvement relative to the combined share held by SEA and CAE immediately before the creation of CII.[9]

WEST GERMANY IN THE SECOND HALF OF THE 1960S

From 1967, two domestic companies remained in the German computer market—Siemens and AEG-Telefunken. That year AEG took over Telefunken, while Siemens, which had earlier absorbed SEL's computer operations, acquired a controlling stake in Zuse KG from Brown, Boveri.[10] Their main competitor was IBM, which had transformed the German market with its 1401 model as much as it had transformed the British and French markets.

In 1964, Siemens entered into an agreement with RCA whereby the German conglomerate acquired the right to manufacture RCA's Spectra 70 in West Germany under the Siemens 4004 name.[11] Three years later, the German government launched the First Data Processing Program, an industrial policy to prop up the domestic computer industry. The government invested almost $90 million in supporting R&D programs for the development of computer hardware.[12] Siemens—in practice the German national champion during the first program—received most of the funding, and AEG-Telefunken got a considerably smaller portion of it. As in Britain and France at about the same time, the government also attempted to bring about a consolidation of the domestic computer industry: it encouraged merger talks between Siemens and AEG-Telefunken, but nothing came out of them. In the latter half of the 1960s, Siemens's share of the domestic market improved from about 5 percent to roughly 13 percent.[13]

Around the same time, West Germany witnessed the rise of a start-up—Nixdorf Computer AG—that became an important international player. Heinz Nixdorf, the founder, was a physics student who had worked for the Remington Rand electronics department in Frankfurt in the early 1950s.[14] In 1952, he set up his own company, Labor für Impulsetechnik (LFI), to develop and market electronic calculating machines. Early on, the company survived thanks to its contacts with Exacta, later known as Wanderer Werke, a maker of office machines. Nixdorf's breakthrough came in 1964, when it developed the Logatronic, a small computer for billing purposes. Four years later, Nixdorf bought Wanderer and renamed the firm Nixdorf Computer AG. The company expanded quickly, marketing small business computers that were well received in the banking and retail sectors. By 1970, Nixdorf had even started to make inroads into the American market through a subsidiary.

JAPAN IN THE SECOND HALF OF THE 1960S

A number of Japanese companies—NEC, Fujitsu, Hitachi, OKI, Toshiba, and Mitsubishi Electric—had entered the computer industry by the mid-1960s. All of them, apart from Fujitsu, signed technology agreements with American computer companies, and three of them—Fujitsu, NEC, and

OKI—participated in the FONTAC project, a cooperative research venture aimed at creating a domestic computer system competitive with the IBM 1401. The Japanese government implemented various policies to prop up the domestic computer industry, including the creation of the JECC—a computer rental company subsidized by the state and established with the goal of stimulating the demand for Japanese computers.

Like the computer industry in the rest of the world, Japanese manufacturers had to reshuffle their product offerings after the announcement of System/360. Hitachi, NEC, and Toshiba quickly introduced IBM-compatible computers. Fujitsu, which had taken advantage of its leadership in the MITI-funded FONTAC project to develop the architecture for its 230 Series of computers, manufactured the FACOM 230-60 model, influenced by System/360 but incompatible with it. The success of the 230-60 model in Japan boosted Fujitsu's position in the domestic market: among Japanese companies, Fujitsu went from third in 1965 to first in 1968, overtaking NEC and Hitachi.[15]

The Japanese government also reacted to System/360. In 1966, MITI produced the Electronics Industry Deliberation Council Report, which identified computers as key to the country's long-term growth and set three goals: (1) strengthening the domestic computer capabilities, (2) raising the share of domestic producers in the local computer market, and (3) increasing their profitability. Within this framework, MITI launched its second cooperative research venture, the "Very High Speed Computer System Project" (VHSCS), involving Hitachi (as the leader), Fujitsu, NEC, Toshiba, and OKI. The project (1966–1972) aimed at producing a computer powerful enough to compete with System/360, plus peripherals, specialized memory devices, and logic circuits.

In addition to loans to the computer industry totaling $410.3 million, government subsidies and tax benefits to the industry amounted to about $131.7 million during the 1960s.[16] Thanks to the combination of public intervention in the industry and marked improvements in the quality of Japanese computers, the share of domestic producers in the Japanese market went up from about 38 percent of all installations in 1960 to about 71 percent in 1970.[17]

OTHER EUROPEAN DEVELOPMENTS

Apart from the national champions, which attempted to compete with IBM with computer families that covered most of the performance range, there were dozens of smaller computer vendors in Europe that focused on niche markets. The German Nixdorf, discussed earlier, was the most successful of these niche vendors, but there were many others.

Datasaab, for example, was originally the computer division of the Swedish aircraft manufacturing Saab. After creating a prototype transistorized computer in 1960, the group continued its computer activities in two directions—the creation of a navigational computer to be installed on a Saab jet fighter, completed in 1971, and the development of a line of minicomputers and mainframe computers for the commercial market. One of the computers Datasaab designed for civilian purposes was used to set up a large terminal system for the Scandinavian banks.

Olivetti—the Italian, family-owned office-equipment vendor—introduced in 1965 what some have identified as the world's first desktop computer, the Programma 101. (Although it was not a personal computer in the modern sense, the Programma 101 was widely sold for calculating and small-scale accounting operations.) After that, it marketed the Audiotronic range of office computers, as well as bank terminals, word processing systems, and various other dedicated systems.[18]

In the Netherlands in the late 1950s, N. V. Electrologica started developing a commercial computer line, and the electrical equipment firm Philips built several experimental computers. After acquiring Electrologica in 1965, Philips entered the office-computer market in which companies such as Nixdorf and Olivetti were also active.[19]

In West Germany, a key player in the small computer market (other than Nixdorf) was Kienzle Computer, the computer group of the namesake precision instruments manufacturer. It became an important supplier of office computers and by the mid-1970s was fourth in the European market after Nixdorf, Philips, and Olivetti.

THE FIRST HALF OF THE 1970S IN EUROPE: UNIDATA

Foreign companies and governments spent the latter half of the 1960s reacting to System/360. They did not have too much time to catch up, however, since in the early 1970s they were forced to deal with System/370.

CII, Siemens, and Philips formed the Unidata joint venture in the early 1970s to compete with IBM.[20] The idea of a pan-European joint venture of some sort had been advocated in the late 1960s in two influential books,

Jean-Jacques Servan-Schreiber's *Le défi américain* (1967) and Christopher Layton's *European Advanced Technology: A Programme for Integration* (1969).

The time for a joint venture between the key European computer companies—or at least some of them—appeared to have arrived. Siemens, the German champion, had grown its computer business in the late 1960s on the basis of technology licensed from the American RCA. But, after RCA exited the computer industry in 1971, Siemens was left with a solid international network of commercial outlets for computer products but with no computer technology. It was anticipated that a link with CII would benefit both companies: Siemens would obtain the technology it was now lacking, and CII, which was weak in computer sales outside the French public sector, would obtain the marketing channels it had never had.[21]

The Unidata venture, formalized in the summer of 1973, called for the development of a family of machines, the Series X. Siemens and CII would produce two computer models each, and Philips would develop a processor at the bottom of the range, the market segment in which the Dutch conglomerate had expertise. Despite the fact that CII was supposed to provide technological leadership in the context of the venture, it was agreed that the operating system would be based on Siemens's and the series would offer upward compatibility with the Siemens Series 4004 (the German version of RCA's Spectra 70).

The partners did start developing the X Series, but an array of technical and political factors weakened the venture from the beginning. One of the key issues preventing Unidata from moving forward was that one of CII's main shareholders, CGE, was a strong competitor of Siemens in markets other than computers, and thus was not disposed to facilitate the collaboration of CII with Siemens in a joint computer project.[22] Although some commentators have linked the demise of Unidata to the arrival of Valéry Giscard d'Estaing to the French presidency in 1974, others have pointed out that the venture was essentially destined to fail from its inception because of the conflicting interests of the bargaining parties.

WEST GERMANY AFTER UNIDATA

The negotiations between Siemens and its potential partners in connection with the failed Unidata consortium took place against the background of the German government's second Data Processing Program (1970–1975). The government invested almost 10 times as much in the second program as it had in the first—the enormous sum of $765.5 million—and expanded the scope of its subsidies to cover software, applications, electronic components, and peripherals.[23]

Important realignments in the German computer industry occurred in the mid-1970s. Siemens acquired AEG-Telefunken in 1974. Soon after, it became obvious that Unidata would never gain traction, which in practice meant that Siemens would be left with only a portion of an IBM-compatible computer family. By 1975, however, Siemens had already accumulated advanced computer know-how and developed the smaller members of what would have become the Unidata X family, so it was well positioned to develop the larger members of the family by itself. This meant that Siemens remained strongly committed to being an important player in the European computer scene, even though its computer operations had never turned a profit. The company also agreed to continue offering IBM-compatibility. In order to strengthen its position in large mainframes, Siemens signed a technology licensing agreement with Fujitsu in 1978.[24]

Around 1975, the German government launched its third Data Processing Program, again with a massive budget—this time of $625 million.[25] The German marketplace had changed considerably relative to the late 1960s, with minicomputers and small business computers now taking center stage. Consequently, the third German program anointed not just one national champion but two—Siemens in large mainframe computers, and Nixdorf in minicomputers and small business systems. Like the second program, the third included peripherals, terminals, software, and university research and training.

FRANCE AFTER UNIDATA

In the first half of the 1970s, while involved in the Unidata negotiations, CII received government support within the context of the second Plan Calcul (1971–1975), which cost the government about twice as much as the first plan—FFr 1.0 billion versus FFr 567 million ($219.7 million versus $109.6 million).[26] That the French government made CII the main beneficiary of Plan Calcul I and II did not mean that Bull-GE disappeared from the national computer scene. Although the first few years after the GE takeover were unprofitable for Bull-GE, from 1968 on the company incorporated fresh blood in its management ranks and started a turnaround that lasted well into the 1970s: after operating at a loss every year between 1963 and 1968, Bull-GE (Honeywell Bull after 1970) turned a profit each year between 1969 and 1980.

Bull-GE became Honeywell Bull (HB) in 1970, after Honeywell took over GE's computer operations. In 1974, HB announced an IBM-incompatible range of mainframes and small business systems, the Series 60, designed for a face-off with the American computer giant across the performance range. The so-called Level 61 and Level 62 computers competed with IBM's small machines (System/3 and later on System/32), the various Level-64 models covered the middle of the performance range, and the Level-66 models confronted the IBM System/370 computers at the top of the range.

Around 1973, the political winds started changing in France. The French government began a process of negotiations with HB that led, in 1975, to the abortion of the Unidata consortium and the establishment of a new French national champion, CII-HB. Born from the fusion of CII and HB, the new company—in which the French CMB had a 53-percent stake and the American Honeywell the remaining 47 percent—was linked to Honeywell by contracts that had both commercial and technical implications. For example, CII-HB and Honeywell granted one another free licenses to the products designed by the other. The new French national champion would receive financial support from the French government for a period of four years, after which it was expected to be profitable without public aid.

In 1977, with the goal of unifying its various computer lines, CII-HB announced the DPS 7, a more powerful successor to the Level-64 mainframes. The company did reasonably well in the late 1970s and had about 25–30 percent of the installed value of general-purpose computers in France in 1980.[27]

BRITAIN IN THE 1970S

Prime Minister Edward Heath's Conservative government took over power in 1970 and quickly adopted a noninterventionist stance toward the domestic computer industry. It narrowed the scope of Mintech and refused to provide the funds that ICL requested to deal with the downturn of the early 1970s. Eventually, however, the Heath government agreed to a £40 million ($95.73 million) loan to ICL, which the national champion used to continue developing the New Range.[28] While working on the new computer family, ICL participated in a number of merger discussions (with both American and European companies) that ultimately failed.

Harold Wilson's Labour government was reelected in 1974, and ICL's "golden age" began. The company launched the New Range—marketed as the 2900 Series—late that year, introducing the computer family with a top-down approach by announcing first the most powerful models in the series, the 2970 and the 2980. By following this strategy, the company attempted to protect the 1900 installed base. In order to serve the small- and medium-sized business segment, ICL introduced the 2903 model, which became its best-selling computer, and in 1976 it acquired the international operations of Singer Business Machines. (Singer had diversified into the business-equipment market in the early 1960s, especially through its acquisition of Friden Inc., and had introduced a range of innovative and successful computer products in the late 1960s and early 1970s.)

While ICL enjoyed its golden age, the British industrial policy toward the computer industry changed yet again. In 1975, the government formed the National Enterprise Board (NEB), through which it made direct investments in an array of companies. The NEB took a 25 percent stake in ICL, invested in several computer start-ups, and financed the launch of two major enterprises, Inmos (semiconductors) and Nexos (office automation), both of which ultimately failed.[29] The Thatcher government, elected in 1979, was radically noninterventionist and reversed the policies of the previous government.

JAPAN IN THE 1970S

In the early 1970s, a constellation of factors brought about a "perfect storm" for the Japanese computer industry. First, at a time when Japanese computer makers were still trying to catch up with System/360, IBM introduced System/370. Second, a radical revaluation of the yen made Japanese exports considerably less attractive in several foreign markets (and foreign imports considerably more attractive in the Japanese domestic market). Third, foreign governments intensified pressures on the Japanese government to lessen its import barriers. Fourth, some Japanese firms were licensees of U.S. computer manufacturers that were realigning, changing ownership, or exiting the business altogether.

In the United States, GE exited mainframe production in 1970, and Honeywell, which acquired GE's computer operations, decided to adopt GE's architecture. This raised issues for both Toshiba (it had a long-standing technology licensing agreement with GE) and NEC (it had a similar contract with Honeywell). RCA also exited the industry in 1971, which forced the strategic realignment of Hitachi, an RCA partner since 1961.

In the first half of the 1970s, the Japanese government removed quantitative restrictions on imports of mainframes and peripherals and lowered tariffs on both. At the same time, however, MITI launched a number of initiatives with the goal of closing the technology gap that separated Japanese producers from their Western counterparts. During these years, MITI's goal was to help the domestic industry produce computers able to compete with System/370 while restraining the competition among domestic producers.

In order to achieve these goals, MITI launched the New Series Project in the early 1970s. The idea behind the project was that the Japanese computer makers, which could not compete with IBM's System/370 individually, would be able to do so successfully by cooperating and segmenting the market. MITI encouraged the Japanese computer manufacturers to form three joint research ventures: Fujitsu partnered with Hitachi to produce the M series of IBM-compatible computers; NEC partnered with Toshiba to develop the ACOS-77 family, based on the GE-Honeywell architecture (and especially Honeywell's 60 series); and Mitsubishi partnered with OKI to develop the COSMO line.

Computer models in the M family, the ACOS-77 range, and the COSMO line—all of which jointly made up the New Series—started becoming available in the Japanese market in 1975, and kept on being introduced through the late 1970s. The New Series Project achieved the general objective of helping domestic producers catch up with IBM technologically, albeit with foreign help (Fujitsu benefited from technology transfers from Amdahl Corporation, and NEC-Toshiba from Honeywell). The Fujitsu-Hitachi M series was particularly successful; it competed effectively with the large System/370 machines and displaced them consistently in Japan in the late 1970s. By 1979, Fujitsu had surpassed even IBM and held the largest share in the Japanese computer market. Toshiba's mainframes did not sell well, however, and the company ended up withdrawing from mainframe production in the 1980s, as did Mitsubishi and OKI.

In order to solidify the progress achieved with the New Series Project, the Japanese government launched another initiative, the Very Large Scale Integration (VLSI) Project. There were actually two VLSI projects, one sponsored by NTT (1975–1977) and another one by MITI (1976–1980). NTT funded R&D work by Fujitsu, Hitachi, and NEC related to the production of semiconductor memory chips (a market which Japan later dominated). MITI's VLSI Project supported the development of the production equipment that would be used in large-scale integration (that is, very dense packing of integrated circuits). The VLSI Project included five participating firms—Fujitsu, Hitachi, Mitsubishi, NEC, and Toshiba—which between them tried a wide variety of approaches. Progress made under these projects turned out to be crucial for Japan's entry into the production of supercomputers in the 1980s.

Leaving aside loans, the Japanese government supported the domestic computer industry with subsidies and tax benefits amounting to $632.4 million in the first half of the 1970s and $1.025 billion in the second half.[30] The share of Japanese producers in the domestic market increased consistently during the 1970s, from about 60 percent of annual computer value shipped in 1970 to about 72.5 percent in 1980.[31]

WORLD COMPUTER MARKETS, 1965–1980: TAKING STOCK

The extent to which IBM's System/360 became an international standard is reflected in the fact that foreign governments and computer companies felt compelled to respond to it in one way or another. The competitive responses followed the familiar patterns we have already observed in the American market.

There was, first, the IBM-compatible route, which a number of companies followed in the late 1960s, including EELM in Britain, Siemens in Germany, and Hitachi, NEC, and Toshiba in Japan. The IBM-incompatible alternative was chosen by ICT (and later ICL) in Britain, CII in France, and several of the Japanese computer manufacturers. Finally the niche strategy was chosen by Nixdorf and several other companies in Europe. These three competitive responses continued in the 1970s, with Siemens in Germany and Fujitsu and Hitachi in Japan on the IBM-compatibility path, CII-HB in France and ICL in Britain opting for incompatibility, and Nixdorf thriving in small computers.

Governments in several Western European countries reacted to System/360 not by creating state-owned computer companies but rather by subsidizing private firms that thus became computer national champions. The Japanese government did not choose a national champion but instead created a protected domestic market within which it fostered competition and cooperation among domestic manufacturers.

The period 1965–1980 was also the time when the global nature of the computer industry manifested itself clearly in a variety of ways. First, by 1980,

many of the top American computer companies generated a significant portion of their revenues outside the United States. Second, by 1975, countries
other than the United States accounted for about 46 percent of the value of
the world computer installed base, and the trend pointed toward an increasing
role of foreign markets in the international computer scene. Table 6.1 tracks

Table 6.1. Worldwide Computer Installations, 1960, 1970, and 1983: Number of Systems
and Value (in USD Billion) of Computers and Equipment

	United States		Japan		Western Europe		Rest of the World	
Year	Number	Value	Number	Value	Number	Value	Number	Value
1960	5,500	8.80	400	0.50	1,500	2.60	1,600	0.80
1970	65,000	92.60	6,000	7.50	21,000	40.50	18,000	9.60
1983	400,000	300.00	70,000	50.00	225,000	220.00	205,000	130.00

Source: U.S. Congress, Office of Technology Assessment, *International Competitiveness in Electronics*
(Washington, DC: U.S. Congress, Office of Technology Assessment, November 1983), 151.

Table 6.2. Top Computer and Office-Equipment Import Markets in 1978
(Values in USD Million)

Country	Imports	Exports	Export/import ratio
World Total	14,983.20		
United States	1,961.50	4,682.80	2.39
West Germany	1,875.40	2,001.90	1.07
United Kingdom	1,533.10	1,478.90	0.96
France	1,531.30	1,238.90	0.81
Canada	787.40	483.70	0.61
Italy	782.10	756.10	0.97
Netherlands	640.10	469.60	0.73
Japan	544.10	1,654.30	3.04
Belgium	436.30	198.50	0.45
Switzerland	366.90	204.50	0.56

Sources: B. Szuprowicz, "The World's Top 50 Computer Import Markets," *Datamation,*
March 1978 and January 1981.

computer installations (in volume and value) in the United States, Japan, Western Europe, and the rest of the world between 1960 and the early 1980s; the table clearly shows the rising importance of the non-U.S. installed base.

Third, during the 1970s several non-U.S. firms became forces to be reckoned with in their own domestic markets. By 1979, CII-HB had roughly 25–30 percent of the French market and about 10–12 percent of the European market, Siemens had about 21 percent of the German market and 9 percent of the European market, and English computer companies— ICL principally—had managed to secure more than 50 percent of their own domestic market.[32] As of 1975, Japanese producers had a larger share of the Japanese market than American computer manufacturers—54 percent for Fujitsu, Hitachi, NEC, Toshiba, and OKI (combined) versus 42 percent for IBM, Univac, Burroughs, and NCR combined.[33] And by 1979, Fujitsu had surpassed IBM and ranked first among all vendors in the Japanese market.

Fourth, the increasingly global nature of the industry was reflected in the international flows of computers, which grew rapidly as the 1970s went by. Table 6.2 presents the major computer importers and exporters toward the end of the 1970s.

Worldwide computer imports grew by nearly a factor of three between 1972 and 1978, and the United States became both the top computer importer and exporter in the world in 1978. In addition, a typology of countries emerged in the way they related to the world computer market, with two countries—Japan and the United States—becoming the archetypical net exporters, and several smaller ones, including Switzerland and Belgium, the typical net importers.

Even though an increasingly aggressive confrontation between American and Japanese companies seemingly dictated market trends in the international computer industry of the late 1970s, under the surface a revolution was in the offing. Three relatively unknown companies—Tandy, Apple, and Commodore—appeared on the 1980 "Datamation 100" index. They heralded the microcomputer revolution that, starting in the early 1980s, would change the face of the industry.

PART III

THE RISE OF THE
PERSONAL COMPUTER
1980–1995

CHAPTER SEVEN

Microcomputers and Personal Computers in the American Market

C hapters 7, 8, and 9 cover the period from 1980 to 1995, the era of the IBM-compatible PC standard. The advent of the microcomputer started around 1975 but went mostly unnoticed until 1981. IBM was again a major part of it, not because it lit the fire, which it did not, but because it introduced a personal computer (PC) in 1981 that became the standard of the new era of computing. IBM's competitors faced strategic choices similar to those of the 1960s and 1970s—either to produce computers compatible with the standard and beat IBM in price-performance, or to create a successful alternative to the standard. The standard of the 1980s was like System/360 in that IBM played the key role in introducing and consolidating it, but also unlike System/360 because IBM did not own the core components of the standard.

There are two common misconceptions associated with this period of the computer industry. The first is that the rise of personal computers caused the overnight demise of more traditional computing machines. We show that much was happening in the world of mainframes and minicomputers during the 15 years from 1980 to 1995. The other misconception is that microcomputers and personal computers were the exclusive domain of American companies (such as Intel, Microsoft, Compaq, and Dell). In Chapter 9, we describe computer developments outside the United States: we examine the way in which the traditional players in Europe and Japan reacted to the advent of microcomputers and personal computers, and also highlight the entry of a new set of countries that had played no role at all in the mainframe era of computing.

MICROCOMPUTER HARDWARE BETWEEN 1975 AND 1981

Although the rise of microcomputers and personal computers is often associated with IBM, and especially with the introduction of the IBM PC in 1981, there was an emergent microcomputer industry in the United States before then—several small firms started manufacturing microcomputers in the second half of the 1970s. Apple, Commodore, and Tandy Radio Shack entered the industry in 1977; HP, Texas Instruments, and Zenith entered in 1979–1980.[1]

Integrated circuits (or microchips) were independently invented in the late 1950s by Robert Noyce (Fairchild Semiconductor) and Jack Kilby (Texas Instruments). Noyce had worked at Shockley Laboratories—the firm that William Shockley, the coinventor of the transistor, set up after leaving Bell Labs—but left in 1957, disenchanted with the research direction that the company was pursuing. With a group of Shockley defectors that included Gordon Moore and with funding from Fairchild Camera and Instrument, Noyce founded Fairchild Semiconductor. In 1968, Noyce and Moore left Fairchild and launched Intel, a company that would later play a key role in shaping the evolution of microcomputers and personal computers. At this time, the semiconductor industry was growing rapidly: integrated circuits were being used in the logic boards of mainframe computers and other electronic goods, and semiconductor memory was on its way to replacing traditional core memory.[2]

At Intel in 1971, Ted Hoff, an engineer, invented the microprocessor, a complete computer processing unit on a single chip. Initially, the primary uses for microprocessors were in industrial automation (such as gasoline pumps) and consumer goods (such as sophisticated microwave cookers). However, the power of microprocessors increased year on year in accordance with Moore's Law, formulated by Intel's cofounder. Moore's Law, originally formulated in 1965, predicted that the number of transistors on a chip would double approximately annually due to manufacturing process improvements into the indefinite future (in fact, the doubling time averaged about 18 months). The 4004 microprocessor that Hoff invented had 2,300 transistors. In 1972, the 8008 came out with 3,500 transistors, and in April 1974 Intel unveiled the 8080, which packed 6,000 transistors and would soon become the brain of the Altair microcomputer.[3]

In 1968, the hobby-electronics entrepreneur Ed Roberts founded Micro Instrumentation Telemetry Systems (MITS) in Albuquerque, New Mexico, to sell radio transmitters for model airplanes. The company quickly diversified and developed a successful electronic calculator business. Soon, however, intense price competition drove down calculator prices and forced MITS to search for a new business. Roberts committed to build a computer kit based on the Intel 8080 microprocessor and to publish an article about it in *Popular Electronics*. Roberts's Altair kit, described in the January 1975 issue of the magazine, sold for just under $400 and is often credited with having unleashed the microcomputer era.[4]

The Altair appealed mainly to hobbyists: programs for the machine had to be written in 8080 machine code and entered by flipping switches. The microcomputer became considerably easier to program after William (Bill) Gates and Paul Allen—the young founders of Micro-Soft (later Microsoft)—developed a version of the BASIC programming language for the machine. The BASIC translator that Gates and Allen created for the Intel 8080, and which they then modified to run on a wide variety of microprocessors, became the lingua franca of computer programming in the early years of the microcomputer.[5]

A key feature of the Altair computer was its so-called S100 bus structure, which became a short-lived industry standard. The S100 bus enabled users to plug in other circuit boards to expand the machine's capabilities. Early on, MITS designed its own 4k memory boards to extend the Altair's storage capacity, but the boards did not work well. Third-party vendors, including Processor Technology and Cromemco, entered the market supplying memory boards that did work, and thus an industry of Altair complements was born.

Many of the companies founded to produce memory boards for the Altair moved later on to the production of computer kits. Most competitors of MITS—Polymorphic Systems and IMSAI, among them—copied the Altair's S100 bus and thus became known as the S100 companies. By late 1976, the IMSAI 8080, manufactured by MITS's key competitor, had become a serious threat for the Altair machine.

Nineteen seventy-seven marked a turning point in the business history of the budding microcomputer industry: the three firms that would briefly dominate the industry—Apple Computer, Commodore Business Machines, and Tandy Radio Shack—introduced key products.

Steve Jobs and Steve Wozniak founded Apple Computer in Cupertino, California, in April 1976.[6] Jobs had worked for HP and the videogame manufacturer Atari, and Wozniak still worked at HP when they launched their start-up. The first Apple computer was designed by Wozniak and introduced at a meeting of a hobbyist computer club in California. A prototype of the Apple II, another Wozniak creation, was ready in August 1976. The Apple II was perhaps the first personal computer that appealed to an audience broader than the hobbyists. Capable of showing color graphics on the screen and endowed with a robust version of BASIC, it had a formal debut at the West Coast Computer Faire in 1977 and quickly became the product that supported Apple Computer's early growth. By the end of the year, the company was making a profit and doubling production of the Apple II every three months.

The Apple II benefited from the popularity of two complementary developments: the floppy disk and the spreadsheet. In mid-1978, the company began shipping a floppy disk drive that made it feasible for the Apple II to readily run software applications created by third-party developers and to store transactional data. This made the Apple II potentially useful for organizational and business users in addition to its existing hobbyist, educational, and domestic customers. VisiCalc, the original spreadsheet that the entrepreneurs Dan Bricklin and Bob Frankston created in 1979, boosted the demand for the Apple II in corporations.

Commodore Business Machines and Tandy Radio Shack were not computer start-ups but rather electronics companies that diversified into computers. Commodore, a Canadian company that moved from Toronto to Silicon Valley, developed a profitable business in the 1970s selling electronic calculators built on a Texas Instruments chip.[7] It made a name for itself in the microcomputer market with the Commodore PET, introduced at the West Coast Computer Faire in 1977. The PET competed with the Apple II in the late 1970s but failed to become as important in the American market, mainly because Commodore delayed the introduction of a disk drive and concentrated its marketing efforts on Europe.

By the mid-1970s, Tandy Radio Shack was the leading consumer electronics retailer in the United States. The founding company, Tandy, had started in 1927 as a wholesale leather business but in the early 1960s transformed itself by acquiring Radio Shack, an ailing chain of electronics stores that Tandy quickly turned around. Its first microcomputer, the TRS-80, introduced in August 1977, sold much better than the company expected, and helped Tandy Radio Shack become the top microcomputer company in America until the success of the Apple II gave Apple Computer the lead.

Three large electronics instruments companies—Texas Instruments, Hewlett Packard, and Zenith—tested the microcomputer waters in 1979–1980. Texas Instruments, a leading semiconductor manufacturer, entered the industry with a machine for the mass market, the TI 99/4. HP, the maker of scientific instruments that had become an important player in the minicomputer industry of the 1970s, took a radically different approach: it introduced a relatively expensive microcomputer, the HP-85, designed with professional and scientific users in mind. Zenith, a large American manufacturer of television sets and electronic components, entered the industry in late 1979 by acquiring the Heath Company, a maker of electronic kits for the hobbyist market. Zenith established Zenith Data Systems (ZDS) with the goal of selling microcomputers in the small business market. None of them became a serious challenger for Apple Computer and Tandy Radio Shack.

MICROCOMPUTER SOFTWARE BETWEEN 1975 AND 1981

Without software to make them useful for ordinary users and organizations, personal computers would have remained nothing other than sophisticated gadgets for hobbyists and technical experts. By making it easier for people to write applications software, Microsoft's BASIC played a key role in helping to make microcomputers popular. From this point on, the desktop "personal computer" became the most visible form of microcomputer.

Microsoft was formed in the wake of the *Popular Electronics* article that publicized the Altair computer in early 1975. Gates and Allen, who had started tinkering with computers at an early age in Seattle, contacted MITS's Ed Roberts and agreed to write a BASIC translator for the Altair. The software was delivered on time and worked as promised. The royalties accrued from MITS and other personal computer companies supported the early growth of Microsoft, the company Gates and Allen founded in Albuquerque, New Mexico, and later relocated to the Seattle suburbs. Although Microsoft developed other programming languages for microcomputers, BASIC remained its core product in the early years. By 1982, the Microsoft BASIC translator was running on about one million personal computers and had become the most widely used piece of systems software ever written.[8]

Digital Research's CP/M operating system was the other piece of systems software that played a central role in the early development of the industry. Digital Research was founded by Gary Kildall, who in the early 1970s had worked as a computer science instructor at the Naval Postgraduate School in Monterey, California. Kildall consulted on a part-time basis for Intel, advising and writing software for its microprocessors. Intel introduced the 8080 around the time floppy disk storage appeared for the first time on the microcomputer scene. Kildall wrote code to control the operation of the floppy disks and developed a number of related programs. By 1975, he had created a complete set of utilities—the core of what would soon become CP/M.

Kildall founded Digital Research in 1976 and started selling CP/M to hobbyists. The next year, he wrote the CP/M BIOS, an operating-system interface that could be customized to enable CP/M to work with a broad swath of computer hardware. This design made it possible for many early personal computer manufacturers to run CP/M on their own machines. By 1982, about half a million microcomputers made by hundreds of manufacturers used CP/M.

The BASIC programming language and the CP/M operating system were the most important early systems software products for microcomputers. Users, of course, were much more interested in applications software that performed useful business or other tasks. Three main genres of software applications for business users came to dominate the personal computer market: spreadsheets, words processors, and simple databases. Network effects were very powerful, and a single firm came to dominate each of these sectors. Among the early application software products, the most prominent was a spreadsheet named VisiCalc.

As mentioned earlier, Dan Bricklin and Bob Frankston first developed VisiCalc for the Apple II. Bricklin had worked as a software engineer for DEC and was a Harvard MBA student, intending to reorient his career toward management, when he conceived the idea that led to VisiCalc. Frankston, who had complementary talents, was a technically oriented math graduate who had been tinkering with computers since he was a teenager. In 1979, they incorporated a software start-up company, Software Arts, designed and wrote VisiCalc, and contracted with a software distribution start-up, Personal Software, to serve as the publisher. Sales of VisiCalc took off meteorically in the second half of 1980.

VisiCalc was later adapted for the microcomputers of various other manufacturers, including Tandy Radio Shack, Atari, HP, and Commodore Business Machines. By 1982, about 300,000 copies of VisiCalc had been sold, making it by far the most popular application software product for microcomputers.[9] VisiCalc represented a new paradigm in financial planning software because, unlike mainframe-based financial-modeling packages, it was interactive and provided instant results.

The leading word processor in the early years was MicroPro's WordStar. MicroPro was founded in 1978 by Seymour Rubinstein, a veteran of the mainframe computer industry who had migrated to microcomputers. By September 1978, MicroPro had two products for microcomputers, a data-sorting program (SuperSort) and a text editor (WordMaster), both of which sold well from the start. Revenues from sales funded further development, and Word-Master evolved into a full-blown word processor, WordStar, which quickly started outselling Electric Pencil, the leading word processor for microcomputers at the time. Unlike Electric Pencil, WordStar offered users a what-you-see-is-what-you-get feature: the text on the screen looked the way it would when printed.

The dominant database product for personal computers was Ashton-Tate's dBase II. Software Plus, the software publisher later renamed Ashton-Tate, was established in 1980 by George Tate, a former electronics industry salesman. The first version of the dBase II software was small enough to fit within the storage capacity of the early microcomputers and useful enough to generate a strong demand from the beginning. It quickly gave rise to a small industry of consultants who learned how to code in the programming scheme that came with the package. By 1981, dBase II had become the top-selling database program for personal computers.

MICROCOMPUTER AND PERSONAL COMPUTER HARDWARE BETWEEN 1981 AND 1995

IBM's entry in 1981 radically changed the competitive dynamics of the micro-computer industry. Its presence legitimized personal computers as a viable option for corporate computing. IBM also originated the acronym "PC," which became a common if not loosely used shorthand for any "personal computer," whether it was compatible with the IBM machine or not. (In this book, we use "PC" for an IBM-compatible personal computer, and "personal

Table 7.1.   Main Intel Microprocessors, 1979–1993

Product	Number of transistors	MIPS	Start of design work	Public unveiling	Volume shipments
286	134,000	1	1979	1982	1983
386	275,000	5	1982	1985	1986
486	1,200,000	20	1985	1989	1990
Pentium	3,100,000	100	1989	1993	1993

Source: Steffens, *Newgames—Strategic Competition in the PC Revolution* (Oxford: Pergamon Press, 1994), 214, and Intel, "Microprocessor Quick Reference Guide," http://www.intel.com/press room/kits/quickreffam.htm, accessed July 8, 2013.

Note: MIPS=millions of instructions per second.

computer" more generally for both IBM-compatible and non-IBM-compatible machines.) Many of the early start-ups did not survive IBM's entry into this market and those that did were forced to rethink their competitive strategies.

Just as in the decades prior to the advent of microcomputers, the evolution of technology played a key role in shaping the dynamics of the computer industry after 1981. By introducing a new microprocessor generation roughly every three years, Intel underpinned the development of new systems and applications software, which in turn attracted new users. In 1979, Intel introduced the 16-bit 8088, which had 29,000 transistors and was used in the IBM PC. Intel unveiled the 80286 (134,000 transistors) in 1982, the 386 (275,000 transistors) in 1985, the 486 (1.2 million transistors) in 1989, and the Pentium microprocessor (3.1 million transistors) in 1993, improving performance by a factor of four to five with each new introduction.[10] Table 7.1 summarizes the characteristics of these microprocessors, along with the dates when they were introduced and first shipped in large quantities.

By the early 1980s, several microcomputer market segments had taken shape, including consumers, professionals, hobbyists, small businesses, educators, and industrial users. Table 7.2 presents a summary. After IBM's entry, these segments tended to collapse into two: the $1,000–$3,000 segment and the $3,000–$6,000 segment (which quickly came to be dominated by IBM).

By the time IBM entered the microcomputer industry in August 1981, it had been forced by the pace of industry developments to outsource many of its components: the 8088 microprocessor came from Intel, the DOS oper-

Table 7.2. Personal Computer Market Segments in 1980–1981

User group	Main applications	Retail hardware price range
Consumers	Education, entertainment, personal management	$300–$1,100
Professionals (engineers, scientists, analysts, managers)	Solutions to profession-related applications problems	$1,000–$4,000
Hobbyists	Experimentation	$1,000–$4,000
Small businesses (retailers, service organizations, small manufacturers)	Business management operations	$4,000–$15,000
Educators (elementary, high school, college, commercial education)	Computer instruction and programming, computer-aided instruction	$600–$1,500
Industrial users (process/plant engineers, electronic equipment suppliers)	Process monitoring/control, quality control, resale activities	$600–$2,000

Source: Steffens, *Newgames,* 125.

ating system and the BASIC programming language from Microsoft, and the VisiCalc spreadsheet program from Software Arts. In addition, IBM included a series of business programs from Peachtree Software, a company that focused on the low end of the personal computer software market, and a word processor, EasyWriter, from a software start-up called Information Unlimited Software. IBM also broke with tradition in choosing to sell its PC through ComputerLand, an IMSAI spin-off that had quickly become the most popular chain of computer retail outlets in America.

Xerox entered the personal computer market in 1981 as well. In the late 1970s, the company had developed a highly innovative personal computer, the Star workstation, which pioneered many of the user-friendly features later found in the Apple Macintosh. Priced at around $15,000, however, the Star was too expensive to develop a large following.[11] In 1981, Xerox tried again with the Xerox 820, but the CP/M-80-based machine failed to take off despite the reputation of its maker.

Two other large players entered shortly after IBM: Wang Laboratories and DEC. Wang, which had formerly specialized in minicomputers and word processing systems, launched its personal computer in 1982 with hardware and software designed in-house. Focusing almost exclusively on

Fortune 1000 companies, Wang's personal computer never managed to expand its sales beyond its established office-products customer base and achieved a paltry 2 percent share in the $3,000–$6,000 segment. DEC introduced three different personal computers, all of them priced at a premium and with limited initial software support. Although it did somewhat better than Wang in the $3,000–$6,000 segment, it failed to become a major challenger for IBM.[12]

During the first half of the 1980s, the IBM PC standard became entrenched in the American—and international—personal computer market. Because IBM did not own the key components of the standard, both Microsoft and Intel were contractually free to sell (or license) their products—the operating system and the microprocessor—to any company willing to pay for them. Thus, while Apple Computer and a few other manufacturers remained IBM-incompatible, many companies—the "IBM clone-makers"— entered the market in the post-1981 period to sell personal computers that adhered to the IBM (or rather Microsoft-Intel) standard, but offered better price-performance than the IBM PC. Over the years, two of the IBM clone-makers—Compaq and Dell—became major players in the world personal computer marketplace.

Compaq was founded in 1982 by three Texas Instruments alumni with many years of experience in computers—Rod Canion, William Murto, and Jim Harris—with additional support from Ben Rosen, a Silicon Valley venture capitalist. Compaq quickly became the fastest-growing company among the IBM clone-makers and, more generally, the fastest-growing firm in the computer industry. The company's strategy was simple: on the one hand, it competed with IBM by offering clones that beat the IBM machines in price-performance; on the other, it actively cooperated with all the other players—computer dealers, component makers, and software houses—that made up the ecosystem built around the IBM PC standard. The fact that Compaq managed to design a new computer in six to nine months, much faster than almost all of its competitors, coupled with the smooth relationships it maintained with Intel, enabled the clone-maker to bring to market a family of microcomputers in 1988 based on the new Intel 80386 microprocessor even before IBM itself. By 1990, Compaq ranked third among American personal computer manufacturers, behind IBM and Apple Computer.[13]

Michael Dell, the founder of Dell Computer, started selling IBM-compatible machines from his University of Texas dorm room in 1984. Dell's core innovation was more in marketing than in technology: the company pioneered an approach for selling personal computers directly to customers via mail-order. By eliminating the middle-man, Dell—and a swath of similar companies that followed Dell's lead, including Northgate, Compuadd, and Gateway—managed to undercut competitors such as IBM and Compaq.[14] By 1990, Dell ranked tenth among American personal computer manufacturers and continued to climb steadily thereafter.

Throughout the 1980s and beyond, Apple Computer was the archetypical IBM-incompatible player in the personal computer market. The Macintosh, introduced in 1984, borrowed and adapted a number of concepts developed at Xerox's Palo Alto Research Center (PARC), including the windowing system and the idea of launching programs by using a "mouse" to "point and click." (Xerox had deployed these features in its own personal computing forays, which had failed due to their high cost.) Although the Macintosh had unique features, its sales did not meet expectations; the company's financial health was sustained by the consistently good performance of the Apple II, which sold very well into the mid-1980s. Apple Computer introduced a new generation of Macintosh computers in the late 1980s, but its business model—based on premium prices and high profit margins—did not change. Through the early 1990s, the company retained a share of the world personal computer market in the 6–8 percent range by volume and in the 9–11 percent range by value.[15]

Figures 7.1a and 7.1b track the evolution of unit shipments and the installed base of personal computers in the United States from the early 1980s through the early 1990s, distinguishing between Intel-based IBM PCs and compatibles, and the others.

Between 1981 and 1992, annual shipments rose from 780,000 to more than 10 million, and the installed base from 1.7 million to about 63 million. As Figure 7.1a shows, there was a shakeout in the industry around 1984, when sales of personal computers stalled (in part due to a flagging interest in computer gaming). The IBM PC standard was not established overnight: it took about five years for IBM-compatible personal computers to account for 50 percent of all shipments, and about seven years for them to account for half of the total installed base.

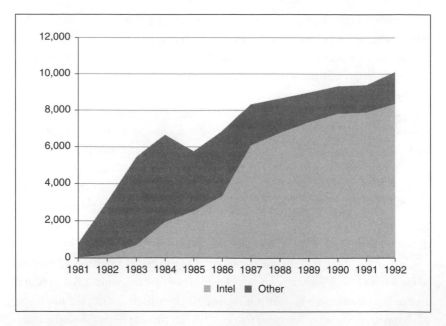

Figure 7.1a. Personal computer shipments in the United States, 1981–1992. Intel-based and other, units in thousands.
Source: J. Steffens, *Newgames—Strategic Competition in the PC Revolution* (Oxford: Pergamon Press, 1994), 210–211.

Table 7.3 tracks worldwide revenues for the top American personal computer manufacturers between 1981 and 1991.

Total personal computer revenues in the international market grew nearly twentyfold between 1981 and 1991. IBM went from zero to almost half of the American industry's total revenues in about four years. Although the revenues of the first movers—namely, Apple Computer, Tandy Radio Shack, and Commodore Business Machines—increased over the decade, their market shares declined steadily after 1981; Apple, however, remained the most successful throughout the 1980s. Compaq was the rising star in the second half of the 1980s, growing its share from about 1.6 percent in 1983 to about 12 percent in 1991. Finally, although IBM led the industry throughout the 1980s, it never reached the kind of dominance it achieved in mainframes—IBM's share of personal computer revenues peaked at about 46 percent in 1985 and declined consistently thereafter.

In the early 1990s, a second shakeout, driven largely by fierce price competition, reshuffled the personal computer industry. Compaq began cutting

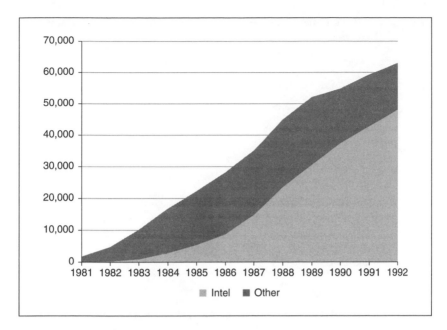

Figure 7.1b. Installed base of personal computers in the United States, 1981–1992. Intel-based and other, units in thousands.

Source: J. Steffens, *Newgames—Strategic Competition in the PC Revolution* (Oxford: Pergamon Press, 1994), 210–211.

prices in 1991, partly in response to a series of Dell ads that made Compaq's machines look overpriced. In mid-1992, Compaq introduced a new family of machines that sold for a third less than its predecessors, and from then on it continued cutting prices at a rate of about 30 percent a year through 1994.[16]

Competing vendors tried to keep pace with Compaq, and profit margins collapsed. Some of the large clone-makers, including Dell and AST Research, operated at a loss despite seeing their revenues rise; some of the smaller clone-makers exited the business altogether. Apple was seriously affected as well: with IBM-clone prices plunging, the Macintosh machines looked increasingly overpriced, and Apple's profits fell hard in 1993. By 1995, the trade press was announcing that the good times were over for the American personal computer industry. Overall, the industry carried on as a commodity business but never recaptured its early growth and profit margins.

Table 7.3.   Worldwide Microcomputer Revenues (in USD Million) for Top American
                 Manufacturers, 1981–1991

	1981	1983	1985	1987	1989	1991
Apple	401	1,085	1,603	2,269	3,574	4,900
IBM		2,600	5,500	7,008	8,343	8,505
Tandy	293	598	797	1,132	1,330	750
Commodore	162	927	600	514	866	1,039
Compaq		111	504	1,224	2,876	3,271
Other	551	1,648	2,863	4,158	4,668	8,308
Total	1,406	6,969	11,866	16,306	21,657	26,773

Source: "The Datamation 100," *Datamation,* June 1, 1982; June 1, 1984; June 15, 1986;
June 15, 1988; June 15, 1990; and June 15, 1992.

PERSONAL COMPUTER SOFTWARE BETWEEN 1981 AND 1995: OPERATING SYSTEMS

By the time IBM introduced its PC in 1981, Microsoft's BASIC had become
the standard programming language for microcomputers. In light of Microsoft's solid reputation, IBM charged the company with the task of developing a version of BASIC for the IBM PC. IBM tried to obtain a license for
the CP/M operating system from Kildall's Digital Research. When negotiations with Kildall failed, Microsoft proposed to design not only a BASIC
translator for the PC but an operating system as well. After IBM gave them
the go ahead, and under extreme time pressure, Gates and Allen decided
to acquire an operating system—QDOS (Quick and Dirty Operating
System)—from Seattle Computer Products rather than developing a new one
from scratch. With some modifications introduced by Microsoft, QDOS
turned into MS-DOS, one of the key components of the IBM PC standard.

The original version of MS-DOS (version 1.0) contained about 4,000 lines
of code and was a relatively simple software product. Even a small software
company had the resources to design a competitive product, and many did.
Two of the most important ones—Digital Research's CP/M-86 and SofTech's
USCD p-System—were offered by IBM on the PC as alternatives to
MS-DOS. Digital Research could have built upon CP/M's reputation to try
to make CP/M-86 into the standard operating system for the IBM PC (and

the clones that followed), but it did not play its cards well. First, because CP/M-86 was not ready for the IBM PC launch in 1981, IBM's PC came with MS-DOS only, which gave Microsoft a lead of several months to build a user base. Second, Digital Research priced CP/M-86 at a considerable premium relative to Microsoft's MS-DOS; by the time Digital Research cut the price of its product, it was too late.

Throughout the 1980s, Microsoft built its fortune on the back of MS-DOS, which had a dominant share in the IBM-compatible operating-system market for most of the decade. MS-DOS, however, had two fundamental shortcomings: first, it was a "command line" operating system, and thus not particularly user friendly; and second, it did not allow for multitasking (the operation of more than one program at a time).

By 1982–1983, a consensus had arisen in the programming community that a windowing system offered the best approach for achieving multitasking, and several companies were attempting to develop such a system for IBM-compatible personal computers. In 1984–85, some of these companies, including VisiCorp (the successor to Software Arts), Digital Research, IBM, and Microsoft, introduced windowing systems—VisiOn, GEM, TopView, and Windows, respectively. None of them was successful because the software technology was too immature and most machines were not sufficiently powerful to run them.

Only Microsoft and IBM kept on trying. The companies started collaborating in 1985 on the development of a new operating system, OS/2, which they viewed as the long-term replacement for MS-DOS. Cooperating with IBM on OS/2 did not preclude Microsoft from continuing to work on Windows. In late 1987, Microsoft introduced Windows 2.0, which received better reviews than Windows 1.0. Some of the main applications software publishers then started converting their programs to run on Windows 2.0, which by early 1989 had sold 2 million copies. At this stage, however, Windows was far from rivaling the popularity of MS-DOS, which was selling roughly 5 million copies per year.[17]

OS/2, introduced shortly after Windows 2.0, never took off in the market, probably because it was expensive, offered only marginal improvements over Windows 2.0, and lacked compatibility with MS-DOS. As soon as it became obvious that OS/2 would fail to gain traction, Microsoft withdrew from the joint development with IBM and focused all of its resources on Windows. Microsoft's third attempt, Windows 3.0 (May 1990) was, finally, the game changer. In a virtuous circle, users started switching to Windows, which made the operating system attractive to third-party software developers, who in turn devoted more of their time and resources to design applications for the operating system, which in turn attracted more users. By the mid-1990s, Windows had become the dominant operating system in the personal computer market, both in the segment of IBM-compatibles and overall.

PERSONAL COMPUTER SOFTWARE BETWEEN 1981 AND 1995: PRODUCTIVITY APPLICATIONS

The term "productivity application" originated around 1982 and encompassed the most commonly used personal computer software applications: the spreadsheet, the word processor, and the personal database. By 1983, productivity applications accounted for about 70 percent of the business personal computer software market; small business software applications made up the remaining 30 percent.[18]

The productivity applications segment also witnessed the decline of companies and products that once seemed invincible. In 1982, the entrepreneur Mitch Kapor founded Lotus Development Corporation to compete with the VisiCalc spreadsheet. A Yale University graduate, Kapor had developed an add-on program for VisiCalc called VisiPlot, which presented spreadsheet data graphically. Kapor sold the rights to VisiPlot and used these funds, together with additional venture capital, to establish Lotus. In January 1983, the company introduced the 1–2–3 spreadsheet, which surpassed VisiCalc in usability and speed. By the end of 1984, 1–2–3 had almost completely displaced VisiCalc.

Version 2 of Lotus 1–2–3 was launched in late 1985 and quickly came to dominate the personal computer software charts. Release 3 of Lotus 1–2–3, however, was a misstep: the company decided to rewrite the whole product from the beginning, which delayed the software's introduction until 1989. In addition, it bet that OS/2—the operating system that IBM was designing in collaboration with Microsoft—would soon replace MS-DOS, and invested resources accordingly. Like many other companies, it failed to foresee the rise of Microsoft's Windows.

In the meantime, Microsoft had been improving its own spreadsheet product on the Apple platform. MultiPlan, Microsoft's first spreadsheet, was launched in 1982 for the Apple II and the IBM PC. Although the product was greeted with enthusiastic reviews, it did not become a serious threat to Lotus 1–2–3. Microsoft thus made the strategic decision to focus on the Macintosh platform: it created a new spreadsheet software product, Excel, which quickly captured 90 percent of Macintosh spreadsheet sales. The company introduced Excel for Windows together with Windows 2.0 in late 1987, at a time when Lotus, and many other companies, were betting on IBM's OS/2.

When sales of Windows 3.0 started taking off in 1990, Lotus did not have a spreadsheet product for the new operating system, but Microsoft did. With a lead of several months over Lotus 1–2–3, Excel built a user base on the operating system that was becoming dominant. By 1995, Excel had more than 70 percent of the world's spreadsheet revenues and Lotus less than 20 percent.

The displacement of WordStar by WordPerfect was as sudden and unexpected in word processing software as that of VisiCalc by Lotus 1–2–3 had been in spreadsheets. WordPerfect was founded in Utah in 1979 by two academic computer scientists, Bruce Bastian and Alan Ashton, who originally wrote their word processor for the Data General minicomputer and later adapted it for personal computers.

In 1984, WordPerfect had less than 1 percent of the market for PC word processing software, and WordStar had 23 percent. Within two years, the picture changed dramatically: WordStar's share dropped to 15 percent, whereas WordPerfect's share rose to 30 percent. The turning point came in late 1984, when MicroPro introduced a new product, WordStar 2000, to replace WordStar. WordStar 2000 had a completely new interface and thus forced users to relearn how to use the software; many of them shifted to Word-Perfect 4.0, the best alternative to WordStar available at the time. By 1990, WordPerfect had 80 percent of word processing software revenues. WordPerfect shared a strategic mistake with Lotus, however: it bet on OS/2, rather than Windows, as the successor to MS-DOS. When Windows 3.0 was introduced in 1990, WordPerfect had no Windows version of its software ready.

Microsoft, in the meantime, had been perfecting its own word processing product, Microsoft Word. Microsoft had launched Word in 1983 and introduced a Macintosh version two years later. From then on, it used Apple's platform to improve its own word processing technology far away from the industry's attention, which was focused on the IBM PC and WordPerfect. After introducing Word for Windows in 1989, Microsoft was able to launch a new version (Word 2.0) that took advantage of the rising sales of Windows 3.0. By 1995, Word had 90 percent of the market.

In 1990, Microsoft bundled its productivity applications for Windows into a suite of programs called "Office," which included Excel, Word, and the new PowerPoint presentation graphics program, and sold for not much more than the cost of one of the stand-alone programs. Although competitors, including Lotus, introduced rival bundles, they were unable to compete effectively. By 1994, Microsoft dominated the market for office suites with a 90 percent share.

CONSUMER ONLINE SERVICES, 1980–1995

The diffusion of personal computers in the 1980s created a mass demand for consumer online services. The key types of enterprise in this market were bulletin board systems (BBSs) and consumer networks. Both gained traction in the early 1980s.

The first BBS went online in early 1978 and was the creation of two Chicago-based computer hobbyists. Since only one user at a time could access the system, the operating software emulated a cork-and-thumbtack bulletin board where users left messages for one another. The more capable systems allowed simultaneous users and provided online conferences for them to interact with one another. There were commercial BBSs as well—vendors of computer hardware and software used them to distribute product information and software upgrades; others operated as online stores, and still others facilitated multiuser online game playing. By 1993, there were reportedly 57,000 BBSs in the United States and perhaps as many as 100,000 worldwide with 10 million users.[19]

BBSs operated rather like the websites of today, providing a specialized service or a sliver of knowledge. By contrast, commercially run consumer online networks attempted to cater to all of a user's online needs.[20] The most successful consumer network of the 1980s was, by far, CompuServe. Born in 1969 as Compu-Serv in Columbus, Ohio, it operated in the 1970s as a time-sharing service for insurance companies. By the end of the decade it was searching for new ways of generating revenues from its computer plant, which remained unused outside office hours. Working in collaboration with the Midwest Association of Computer Clubs, Compu-Serv established a bulletin-board-style system called MicroNET. The service (later renamed

CompuServe) expanded quickly, to the point that by mid-1984 it claimed to have 130,000 subscribers nationwide, 600 employees, and 26 mainframe computers in its Columbus headquarters.[21]

The basic CompuServe services included email to other users, conferences, and forums; online chat rooms; a National Bulletin Board for posting classified ads and notices; and computer games. Other services supplied by third parties and repackaged by CompuServe included weather forecasts, AP wire services, newspapers and magazines, stock quotes, banking, and online shopping. CompuServe faced some competition, although rivals were few because of the high entry costs associated with building a national network. They included The Source (a joint venture between the Reader's Digest Association and CDC), GEnie (a spin-off from GE Information Services), and Prodigy (a joint venture between IBM and Sears). During the 1980s, none of these services posed a serious threat to CompuServe, which benefited both from its superior content and from network effects—CompuServe's larger user base funded better services, which in turn attracted more users.

America Online (AOL), a relative latecomer to consumer networks, provided much more effective competition for CompuServe. AOL developed an exceptionally user-friendly and accessible interface. Although its network and content may not have been much differentiated from that of the competition, AOL excelled in getting consumers online with the least effort and disappointment. In the early 1990s, AOL expanded rapidly, to the point that by late 1995 it had overtaken CompuServe's two-million-plus subscribers.

CHAPTER EIGHT

Beyond Personal Computers in the American Market

Although microcomputers and personal computers became the most dynamic sector of the industry in the 1980s, this did not mean that mainframe and minicomputer developments ceased. The rise of microcomputers and personal computers brought about a *relative* decline of mainframes and minicomputers, which up to the late 1970s had dominated the computer industry. Customers continued to buy mainframes and minicomputers, but at a much slower pace than before.

MAINFRAMES AND MIDRANGE COMPUTERS

Throughout the 1980s, the mainframe industry was fundamentally stable: the names of the key manufacturers changed little, and the market shares of individual players moved up and down only slowly. As it did in the personal computer industry after 1981, IBM set the pace and direction of change in the mainframe industry. None of IBM's competitors challenged its dominance: IBM had a 67 percent share of all mainframes manufactured and installed in the United States (in units) both in 1978 and in 1988.[1] IBM's competitors continued to face the compatibility-versus-incompatibility dilemma—the plug-compatible manufacturers (PCMs) remained IBM-compatible, whereas the members of the BUNCH (Burroughs, Sperry UNIVAC, NCR, CDC, and Honeywell) remained incompatible.

Amdahl Corporation and National Advanced Systems (NAS) were the leading American plug-compatible mainframe manufacturers. Fujitsu and Hitachi, the key foreign players, also had a presence, albeit small, in the American market through their investments in Amdahl and NAS. Amdahl Corporation increased its share of all U.S. mainframe installations from 2.6 percent in 1978 to 6.7 percent in 1988. The evidence suggests that IBM took the PCMs into account in designing its competitive strategy (product introduction and pricing), even though their share of the U.S. mainframe market remained relatively small.

The members of the BUNCH held market shares in the low single digits throughout the 1980s. In 1986, Burroughs launched a hostile tender bid for Sperry UNIVAC that valued the target at about $4.1 billion. The company created by the acquisition was named Unisys and became, with annual computer-related revenues of about $10 billion, the second largest firm in the computer industry. Although the combined company achieved a market share that none of the members of the BUNCH would have been able to acquire on its own, Unisys was not much better equipped to confront IBM than either Burroughs or Sperry UNIVAC alone. The companies complemented one another in that Burroughs was strong in the financial and distribution industries and Sperry UNIVAC had a history of sales to the federal government. However, they decided to keep their computer families separate and incompatible with one another, which limited the impact of network effects and economies of scale. By 1988, Unisys accounted for 9.7 percent of all mainframes installed in the United States (in units), a smaller proportion than the sum of the partners' premerger shares—an indication that the transaction had not produced the results the companies expected.[2]

IBM remained heavily invested in mainframe R&D and manufacturing throughout the 1980s and early 1990s. In 1985, it announced a new range of machines, the 3090, that embedded a 20–25 percent improvement in price-performance. The 3090 computers, which still responded to the System/370 architecture introduced in the early 1970s, consolidated IBM's dominance in the second half of the 1980s. By early 1989, four of the five top-selling mainframe computers in the United States (by value) were IBM 3090 models.[3]

Table 8.1. Worldwide Mainframe Revenues (in USD Million) for Top American
Manufacturers, 1981–1991

	1981	1983	1985	1987	1989	1991
IBM	12,000	11,444	14,010	11,193	12,509	9,100
BUNCH	5,209	5,006	4,755	2,508	1,848	1,350
PCMs	510	771	734	1,280	1,471	987
Cray Research	92	170	333	588	634	863
Total	17,811	17,390	19,831	15,569	16,462	12,300

Source: "The Datamation 100," *Datamation,* June 1, 1982; June 1, 1984; June 15, 1986;
June 15, 1988; June 15, 1990; and June 15, 1992.

In 1990, IBM started replacing System/370 with a new family of mainframes, the System/390 Series, upwardly compatible with System/370. It described the introduction of the 390 computers as the firm's most significant
product announcement in decades and promised that the most powerful of
the 390 machines would have twice as much computing power as the equivalent model in the 370 series.

Table 8.1 presents worldwide mainframe revenues for the main American
manufacturers between 1981 and 1991.

The mainframe market started shrinking in the mid-1980s—except for
Cray Research, which thrived in its profitable niche as a manufacturer of super-
computers. Not even the creation of Unisys prevented the members of the
BUNCH from losing market share throughout the 1980s. The PCMs—and
Amdahl especially—increased their share in the second half of the 1980s, al-
though IBM remained by far the top player overall in the industry.

IBM was also the top player in midrange systems in the 1980s and the
early 1990s, but in this segment it confronted stronger opposition: DEC
threatened IBM's dominance in midrange computers more seriously than
any competing vendor did in mainframes. Throughout the 1980s, IBM's share
of midrange system revenues generated by U.S. manufacturers was, on average, around 33 percent, and DEC's was about 21 percent. There was, in
addition, a plethora of other companies producing minicomputers and small
business systems in the United States, including HP, Prime, and Data
General—in combination they accounted for about 46 percent of midrange
revenues in the 1980s.[4]

One of the main problems IBM faced in the midrange segment throughout the 1980s was that it offered several mutually incompatible hardware-software platforms. In small business systems, for example, IBM introduced S/38, which was incompatible with the highly popular S/3 series. DEC offered a range of models compatible with one another within the remarkable VAX family, which covered the whole middle sector of the performance spectrum from the equivalent of a high-end personal computer to that of a low-end mainframe. By 1989, DEC had nine different models among the top 20 mini-computers in the American market, and most of them belonged to the VAX range.[5]

Even though IBM's S/38 was not compatible with S/3, it sold well for about 10 years, from 1978 to 1988. When sales of S/38 started to slow down, the company introduced the AS/400, a small business computer that was upwardly compatible with S/38. The AS/400 became a hit for IBM in the 1990s, selling strongly throughout the decade.[6]

SCIENTIFIC WORKSTATIONS AND THE CLIENT-SERVER COMPUTER MODEL

By the early 1990s, the mainframe and minicomputer businesses of companies such as IBM and DEC were feeling the effects of a rise in alternative computing modes: the client-server paradigm and powerful scientific workstations. From the mid-1960s to the mid-1980s, typical computer networks were organized such that a central mainframe did all the computing and several "dumb" terminals facilitated input-output. Beginning in the early 1980s, the development of microcomputers and powerful workstations enabled the diffusion of more complex topologies. Among these was the client-server model, featuring personal computers or workstations ("clients") that were attached to one or more powerful "server" computers within a local area network. The servers provided services—file storage, database access, and running enterprise applications, among others—for the clients.

Although the first client-server networks relied on the UNIX operating system and on high-performance servers, less expensive PC-based client-server schemes proliferated in the late 1980s. These were clusters of IBM-compatible personal computers connected to one or more low-cost Intel-based servers. At the software level, the clients typically used MS-DOS or Windows and the server a Novell Netware network operating system. Over time, the client-server model replaced the traditional mainframe-based computing scheme in many American corporations. In a 1994 *Datamation* survey, for example, 58 percent of corporations that had traditionally used mainframes were implementing client-server computing. A year later, the share had grown to 67 percent.[7]

Just as client-server networks competed with traditional mainframes, scientific workstations began to displace minicomputers. Workstations relied on a high-performance microprocessor to make the power of a scientific mainframe available within a desktop form factor. The first workstation company was Apollo, founded in Chelmsford, Massachusetts, by Bill Poduska, one of the cofounders of the Prime minicomputer company. In 1981, Apollo Computer delivered its first product, a machine that sold for $40,000 and up and used a proprietary operating system.[8] Apollo soon faced competition from Sun Microsystems, a company established in Silicon Valley in 1982 by Stanford University graduate students Andy Bechtolsheim, Vinod Khosla, and Scott McNealy. Sun benefited from technology transfer from the academic world: the hardware was derived from the Stanford University Network workstation project, and the operating system was the University of California at Berkeley's variant of UNIX, usually known as BSD UNIX. (Bill Joy, who had played a key role in the development of BSD UNIX, joined the company soon after its founding and is considered a cofounder.) Sun advocated open standards, a strategy that worked well against Apollo and HP, both of which remained committed to their proprietary operating systems. By the end of the 1980s, Sun Microsystems dominated the workstation market, and HP, which had acquired Apollo, remained far behind.

COMPUTER MANUFACTURERS AS SOFTWARE VENDORS

In the realm of computer hardware, sales of mainframes and minicomputers were negatively affected by personal computers and scientific workstations during the 1980s; at the same time, software and services grew. In the case of IBM, for example, the share of software in total revenues went up from about 3.8 percent in 1980 to about 17.6 percent in 1995.[9]

IBM took two steps that laid the foundation for this transformation. First, in 1979, it completed the process it had started in the late 1960s by unbundling mainframe operating systems. Second, in 1983, it closed the software's source code. In that year, it replaced full access to the source code with a policy known as "object code only" (OCO): from then on developers would be able to interact with IBM's software only via "application programming interfaces" (APIs). Just like many others in the computer industry, IBM had come to view software as valuable intellectual property that needed to be protected.

IBM remained the top seller of software products throughout the 1980s and a good portion of the 1990s, even in the presence of personal computer software companies such as Lotus and Microsoft that rose from obscurity to membership in the software elite in a matter of years. Lotus and Microsoft sold far more units of their software products than IBM, because personal computers sold by the million whereas mainframes sold only in the hundreds. Software products for large computer systems, however, were vastly more expensive than personal computer software products, and thus IBM remained the top software vendor (by value) well into the 1990s.

In 1986, for example, IBM sold about $5.5 billion worth of software, roughly 6.4 times as much as Unisys, which ranked second in the *Datamation* "Top 15 in Software," and around 20 times as much as either Lotus or Microsoft. Even as late as 1992, IBM's software revenues were four times as high as those of Microsoft and about 14 times as high as those of Lotus. But IBM was not the only American computer manufacturer that invested resources to develop software products: Unisys, DEC, and HP were among the top 15 software vendors in the world in 1986, and DEC and Unisys remained in that elite group in 1992.[10]

During the 1980s, IBM had a dominant position in the market for systems software for its own mainframes. It had a monopoly in operating systems, roughly 50 percent of the market for databases, and a 90-percent share in teleprocessing monitors.[11] IBM's systems software prices formed a price umbrella under which independent software vendors mushroomed and thrived.

INDEPENDENT SOFTWARE VENDORS

It was almost impossible to compete with IBM in operating systems or teleprocessing monitors for IBM-compatible mainframes. It was possible, however, to find areas of the mainframe software-products market in which IBM was either absent or not competitive: Computer Associates, Oracle, and SAP are examples of companies that found those highly profitable niches.

Computer Associates (CA) was founded in 1976 by Charles Wang, a Chinese immigrant who had studied mathematics and physics and worked as a programmer and salesperson for a software house based in New York. CA started with one sorting utility and by 1980 had grown its portfolio to 20 software products. It had its IPO in 1981, and the next year it started an almost uninterrupted chain of acquisitions that turned it into one of the top independent software companies in the world.

CA acquired four different types of companies and products: firms such as Sorcim (1984) that designed PC applications; firms such as Software International (1986) that marketed utilities and applications for VAX mini-computers; companies such as ADR (1988) and Cullinet (1989) that commercialized database products for mainframes; and firms that created mainframe systems software and applications, among them Uccel (1987) and Legent (1995). The database-related acquisitions turned CA into an important player in this market, second only to IBM by the early 1990s. The strategy catapulted the company to the upper echelons of the software rankings: by 1995 it was third among independent software providers in the United States, behind Microsoft and Oracle.[12]

Oracle became a major player in the software world by commercializing a relational database product. By the early 1980s, the database market was reasonably mature and was dominated by companies such as ADR, Cincom, Cullinet, and IBM. At the time, the predominant database software followed the hierarchical model, which organized information into an inverted tree structure, with each branch dividing data into smaller categories. The model worked well as long as the user followed the preexisting hierarchy while searching, but it was less useful when somebody was interested in answering a data query that went across the hierarchy.

In the early 1970s, Ted Codd, an IBM researcher, invented the relational database, which organized data into a collection of tables. These tables were indexed in such a way that they could be connected or "joined" to access information in different ways using a simple query language known as SQL. Relational database technology moved from IBM's San Jose laboratory to academia and then to the commercial world. Although relational databases needed more computer power, they gained in simplicity of use—and computer speeds caught up with the technology within a few years.

Larry Ellison, Oracle's founder, had been a programmer, first at the Ampex Corporation and then at Precision Instruments, where he had worked on information storage software. In 1977, he launched System Development Laboratories, a custom programming firm, with help from two colleagues. For their first project, Ellison and his partners developed a relational-type database called Oracle for a customer. The next year, they renamed their company Relational Systems Inc., and shortly thereafter started shipping Oracle for DEC minicomputers. By 1982, when the company was renamed Oracle Systems, relational technology had reached a certain degree of maturity and was beginning to compete with traditional databases.

IBM, one of the key incumbents in the database market, decided to hedge its bets by implementing a dual database strategy: it continued to support users of its traditional database product, IMS, while at the same time introducing a relational product, DB2. Cincom, another leading incumbent in traditional database software, made a large R&D investment that enabled it to pursue a similar, dual strategy. ADR and Cullinet, the other two major players, did not adjust well and ended up being acquired by CA.

Oracle's first-mover advantage enabled it to grow rapidly as the market switched to the new database technology. It ranked fourth among software vendors overall and second among database vendors (behind IBM) as of 1988. While IBM and CA remained strong in sales of databases for mainframe computers, Oracle made most of its revenues from products for the client-server paradigm that was emerging in the late 1980s. By 1995, Oracle had become the second-largest independent software vendor in the United States, behind Microsoft and ahead of CA.[13]

Computer users were frequently confronted with the difficulty of integrating software products from different vendors. CA addressed this problem by acquiring a broad portfolio of products, ensuring they integrated smoothly, and offering a "one-stop" solution for all of a customer's software needs. SAP addressed the same problem by offering a monolithic product that catered to all of a customer's application software requirements in a single program. SAP invented the so-called Enterprise Resource Planning (ERP) software segment and did not face serious contenders in that category until the 1990s.

SAP was founded in 1972 in the town of Walldorf, south of Munich, by five programmers who had worked for IBM Germany—Hasso Plattner, Dietmar Hopp, Klaus Tschira, Claus Wellenreuther, and Hans-Werner Hector. For a few years, it operated as a software contractor, developing a financial accounting program, System R, for Imperial Chemical Industries and then enhancing the software each time it obtained a new contract. Thus, instead of writing bespoke software to meet each customer's requirements in the traditional way, SAP continually enhanced its core software asset to meet the needs of an increasingly diverse user base. In 1978, it made the transition to a software products firm: its first product, named R/2 and introduced in 1981, was quickly adopted by German corporations.[14]

SAP's R/2 starting selling outside Germany because of a Trojan horse effect: multinational corporations that used the software in their German offices started installing it in their non-German operations as well. R/2 grew in complexity both because new functions were added to it over time and because, in the process of becoming multinational, it was enhanced to deal with multiple currencies and tax regimes. The scarcity of individuals able to help corporations install the SAP software slowed down SAP's expansion, and the company responded by introducing training courses for consultants in the early 1980s and an international training center in 1987. The next year, SAP opened its first American office in Philadelphia and later on set up branch offices in most major U.S. cities. It established a user group, held an annual conference for installers, and entered into partnerships with some of the major computer-services firms, such as CSC and EDS, and computer manufacturers, such as IBM, DEC, and HP.

As of 1990, SAP was one of the world's largest suppliers of business applications software for mainframes but had barely penetrated the American market. It started conquering the U.S. market only with R/3, released in Germany in 1992 and in the United States the following year. Unlike R/2, which was mainframe centered, R/3 was designed for client-server computing. Starting in 1993, SAP's revenues skyrocketed as U.S. sales took off and the company introduced per-workstation pricing, which resulted in some corporate installations costing in the millions of dollars.

SAP's growth established the market for ERP software. By 1995, other players had entered this market to capitalize on its growing potential. SAP's most significant competitor was Oracle, which supplied database software for about 80 percent of R/3 installations and introduced Oracle Applications to compete with R/3. Other established U.S. software companies, such as J. D. Edwards, PeopleSoft, and System Software Associates, developed an ERP product as well. By 1996, SAP had about 33 percent of the ERP market, Oracle had about 10 percent, and several smaller vendors had single-digit shares.[15]

COMPUTER SERVICES: ADP, CSC, AND EDS

In the early 1980s, the rise of personal computers spelled doom for certain forms of computer services that had thrived in the 1970s, particularly the time-sharing industry. Priced roughly between $1,500 and

$6,000, the personal computer was a cheaper and more effective alternative to the $10-an-hour time-sharing terminal. As corporations migrated to personal computers after the introduction of the IBM PC, the demand for time-sharing collapsed; by the mid-1980s, the industry had practically disappeared.

Companies such as ADP, EDS, and CSC, all of which in the early 1980s dominated the American market for data-processing services, were relatively unaffected by the rise of the personal computer. The top eight American computer-services companies in 1985 and 1995 are shown in Table 8.2.

Table 8.2. Top 8 U.S. Companies in Computer Services, 1985 and 1995 (Revenues in USD Million)

	Ranking	Service revenues	Total IT revenues	Services as a percent of total IT
1985				
ADP	1	1,102	1,102	100%
CDC	2	1,059	3,680	29%
GM/EDS	3	978	978	100%
GE	4	950	1,130	84%
CSC	5	801	801	100%
McDonnell Douglas	6	650	1,105	59%
Martin Marietta	7	430	430	100%
Sperry	8	303	4,755	6%
1995				
IBM	1	20,143	71,940	28%
EDS	2	12,422	12,422	100%
DEC	3	6,498	14,440	45%
HP	4	6,258	26,073	24%
CSC	5	3,895	4,100	95%
Andersen Consulting	6	3,798	4,220	90%
Unisys	7	3,535	6,202	57%
ADP	8	3,157	3,157	100%

Source: "The Datamation 100," *Datamation,* June 15, 1986, and June 1, 1996.

The extraordinary revenue growth of individual firms such as CSC and ADP hints at the increasing importance of computer services within the industry. ADP, CSC, and EDS remained among the top eight through the mid-1990s, although by 1995 they were contending with the large computer manufacturers, some of which were deriving sizable portions of their total IT revenues from computer services by then.

The rise of personal computers posed a challenge for ADP's business model. Even as late as the early 1980s, the company's Payroll and Brokerage divisions were still delivering services to clients using traditional batch processing—manual input was picked up by an ADP driver from the client's site, processed on ADP's computers, and then delivered back to the client as a collection of paychecks or reports. The Dealer Services and Claims Services divisions were slightly ahead: clients accessed data through terminals, but these terminals could not compete in power and functionality with the personal computers that were starting to come to market.

ADP's strategic planners suggested that increasingly powerful personal computers and application software would threaten the company's existence. ADP, however, found ways to work *with* the personal computer rather than *against* it: all of its business units developed ways to use it as a channel to deliver their products and services. A substantial portion of payroll- and HR-related services supplied by ADP, for example, became accessible via personal computers. By 1993, ADP had become a powerhouse with annual revenues of about $2 billion.[16]

During the 1980s, CSC profited heavily from its expertise in systems integration. The plethora of different computer technologies that coexisted in the marketplace—mainframes, minicomputers, personal computers, servers, and scientific workstations, with various degrees of compatibility or incompatibility—created an opportunity for computer-services companies to advise clients on what technologies to acquire and how to combine them. CSC became a leader in this field: it secured contracts all over the world, some of them as large as the nationwide computer system that connected about 75,000 items of hardware in Saudi Arabia.

In the early 1990s, CSC benefited from another trend that became commonplace in large corporations—IT outsourcing. In 1991, for example, CSC and General Dynamics (GD) entered into a $3 billion contract, the largest outsourcing agreement up to that date: CSC bought GD's IT assets, hired many of GD's former IT employees, and began providing IT services for

GD. Later in the 1990s, CSC entered into similar multibillion-dollar agreements with J. P. Morgan and DuPont.[17]

The other major computer-services firm, EDS, was acquired by General Motors (GM) in the 1980s. In what was GM's largest-ever diversification and one of the largest acquisitions at that time, GM paid $2.5 billion for EDS in 1984.[18] In theory, the transaction made sense for the automaker, which was searching for ways to better structure and rationalize internal communications and data-managing processes. While under the GM umbrella, EDS set up the largest private computer network in the world by interconnecting about 100 separate GM networks. As of 1990, this gigantic network had eight million kilometers of cable and linked 300 mainframe computers, 2,000 minicomputers, 300,000 computer terminals, and 250,000 telephones. The network started as a GM-only resource but later expanded to encompass most of EDS's customers, which in 1990 numbered about 7,000.[19]

Flush with revenues from services supplied to the car-making giant, EDS expanded into other, non-GM-related areas of work, and other geographies, especially Europe. The spectacular growth of EDS and the computer-services industry more generally encouraged traditional computer companies such as IBM and nontraditional ones such as Arthur Andersen to enter the market. As EDS continued to grow, GM came to account for a constantly declining portion of its revenues. A demerger finally came in the mid-1990s, at a time when EDS was one of the most admired companies in the world and, with offices in 36 countries, dominated the worldwide market for computer services.

CHAPTER NINE

International Developments

Computer companies all over the world adjusted their competitive strategies to take the rise of microcomputers and personal computers into account, while seeking to protect their traditional markets. This chapter explores the evolution of the computer industry in Europe and Asia between the early 1980s and the mid-1990s.[1]

A key development of the 1980s was the rise of "open standards," which were standards that were open to all and free from onerous licensing conditions. By adopting open standards, it was possible for manufacturers to source computer-system components from a variety of providers knowing that they would integrate without difficulty. The machine-independent UNIX operating system developed by AT&T and client-server computing, particularly, contributed to the rise of open systems. Although open standards were adopted by some of the U.S. manufacturers, they had a much stronger resonance in Europe, where they had the potential to create an ecosystem of co-operating suppliers. In this chapter, we focus first on the traditional computer markets and then on personal computers.

EUROPEAN DEVELOPMENTS: BRITAIN

Throughout the early 1980s, ICL remained Britain's national champion in computer manufacturing, but it did go through a rocky period. It had been created by a government-promoted merger in 1968, with the aim of designing a new range of computers to compete with IBM's mainframes. In the transition from the 1970s to the 1980s, ICL's situation did not look promising. First, as explained earlier, IBM introduced a new family of mainframes, the 4300 series, in 1979. This series embedded a fourfold improvement in price-performance and put considerable pressure on competitors, both in the United States and abroad. Second, the Thatcher administration's public stance against state intervention in industry created uncertainty as to whether ICL would receive any financial support at all from the British government. Third, a recessionary environment plus an appreciating domestic currency weakened ICL's sales volumes in Europe. By 1980–1981, the company was deeply unprofitable.

Although the Thatcher government had made public pronouncements against intervention in the computer industry, it did provide ICL with loan guarantees. It also facilitated discussions between ICL and Fujitsu, which led to the deal that underpinned ICL's subsequent prosperity. The ICL-Fujitsu agreement (October 1981) specified that ICL would obtain advanced microchip technology from Fujitsu and would market high-end IBM-compatible Fujitsu mainframes in Britain.[2] By 1982, ICL was profitable again.

ICL was taken over by the British telecom-equipment maker STC in 1984, and it did better than its European peers. Its relative success rested on strategies begun in 1981–1982. First, rather than competing with IBM across the full spectrum of applications and customer types, it chose to focus on specific niches of the European market, including local governments, retail, defense, and office automation. Second, the agreement with Fujitsu enabled ICL to concentrate more on computer design and less on component manufacture. Finally, ICL embraced open standards, including the UNIX operating system, earlier and more consistently than the other large European computer makers.

By the late 1980s, STC was searching for a new partner to share the burden of ICL's R&D budget. ICL participated in merger discussions with Siemens, Groupe Bull, Olivetti, Philips, and Nixdorf, but all of them failed. Subsequently Fujitsu, ICL's technology partner, announced it was ready to purchase an interest in the British computer company; in July 1990, it bought an 80 percent stake.[3] At this stage, ICL ranked fifth in revenues among European computer companies, had strong software assets, and was profitable despite the recession of the early 1990s. The Fujitsu acquisition of ICL generated strong reactions in Europe—ICL came to be viewed as a Trojan horse through which the Japanese would penetrate European markets, just as they had used Amdahl to make inroads into the American market. The British computer company was excluded from some of the research programs sponsored by the European Commission and expelled from the European computer-industry trade group.[4]

After taking over ICL, Fujitsu became the second-largest computer company in the world. The takeover benefited ICL as well—at a time when the computer operations of all the other big European players were operating at a loss, ICL continued growing and remained profitable, at least through the mid-1990s.

EUROPEAN DEVELOPMENTS: FRANCE

By the late 1970s, CII-HB was steadily consolidating its position in the French computer market. After taking power in the early 1980s, President François Mitterrand's Socialist government announced a comprehensive plan of state intervention in various branches of the domestic industry, which led to the nationalization of several major industrial groups in 1981. In April 1982, CII-HB, which had been formed by the merger of CII, the French national champion, and Honeywell Bull (HB) in 1976, was brought under state control. From then on, it became known as Groupe Bull.[5]

Between 1983 and 1992, Groupe Bull's operations were heavily subsidized by the French government. The company continued to sell its own mainframes in the domestic market and entered into an agreement with NEC in 1984 to sell its high-end ACOS mainframes in France under the DPS-90 name. It also made various attempts to introduce UNIX-based machines that reflected the trend toward open standards.

During the late 1980s and early 1990s, Groupe Bull embarked on a number of acquisitions. In 1987, it acquired a stake in Honeywell Information Systems, the Honeywell subsidiary that held all of its computer assets. The deal created a computer company, Honeywell-Bull Inc, headquartered in Minneapolis, Minnesota, with parents of three different nationalities— Groupe Bull owned 42.5 percent of the new company, Honeywell another 42.5 percent, and NEC the remaining 15 percent.[6] In 1989, it made another attempt to penetrate the U.S. market by acquiring Zenith's microcomputer operations—a deal that failed to deliver the expected results. Then, in 1993, Groupe Bull acquired a 20 percent stake in Packard Bell, a low-cost IBM clone-maker that had built a respectable share in the American PC market by undercutting the likes of Compaq.

Because Groupe Bull decided to support the software of each company it acquired, it found itself with a portfolio of nine different operating systems, which prevented it from realizing economies of scale. Moreover, in a world in which open systems were on the rise, it continued to give a strong preference to its own proprietary systems, even though it made attempts to explore UNIX-based computing in partnership with both European and American companies.

Groupe Bull experienced massive losses in the early 1990s, and several companies, including France Télécom, IBM, and NEC, were encouraged to take stakes in the ailing national champion. In 1994, the French government announced a two-stage privatization process that reduced the state's share in Groupe Bull from 77 to 40 percent, increased the NEC stake from 4 to 17 percent, and allowed the American electronics maker Motorola to own 10 percent of the company.[7]

EUROPEAN DEVELOPMENTS: GERMANY

During the 1980s, Siemens remained the key mainframe producer in the German market, and Nixdorf was the main small computer maker. Siemens continued to commercialize a range of IBM-compatible computers based on Fujitsu's technology. As in Britain and France, the German national champion had more success selling computers to the domestic public sector than to private corporate customers. Throughout the 1980s, Siemens's computer division accounted for a small portion of company revenues and was barely profitable.

At the same time, Nixdorf was *the* German success story in computers. Between 1982 and 1987, it almost doubled its annual sales and tripled its net profits. By 1988, however, there were signs of impending trouble, and observers had started envisioning the likely demise of the company. Like DEC and Data General in America, Nixdorf thrived in Europe in the 1970s and early 1980s by offering a cheap alternative—minicomputers and small business computers—to mainframe-based computing. However, like many other makers of small computers, Nixdorf remained heavily invested in its own, proprietary technology, and its business model was further threatened by the rise of client-server computing systems.

As Nixdorf began to experience financial difficulties, rumors spread of a possible acquisition by a foreign computer company. In order to prevent foreigners from developing a presence in the German market through Nixdorf, Siemens stepped in and acquired a controlling stake in the firm.[8] Siemens Nixdorf Informationssysteme (S.N.I.), the company created by the transaction, was heavily dependent on the German domestic market and encompassed a wide range of incompatible hardware-software systems, which prevented it from achieving significant economies of scale. Radically different corporate cultures made the transition to a single company even more difficult, and by the mid-1990s, S.N.I. was facing financial difficulties. The S.N.I. computer operations ended up becoming part of a joint venture with Fujitsu—Fujitsu Siemens Computers—established in the late 1990s.

PERSONAL COMPUTERS IN EUROPE

In the late 1970s, the same companies that had taken the lead in the American personal computer market—Apple, Tandy, and Commodore—captured the top spots in the Western European markets as well. Commodore, in particular, benefited from its preexisting network of office-equipment distribution outlets in Europe to become the most successful personal computer manufacturer on the continent for several years.[9]

IBM entered the European personal computer market in 1982 and, with the advantage of its brand name, became the leading vendor in most European countries. Beginning in the mid-1980s, two developments shaped the evolution of the European market. First, Apple implemented a systematic strategy for the continent centered on the Macintosh family of computers. Second, some of the PC clone-makers—Compaq and HP, most prominently—competed successfully with IBM in several national markets. Generally, American companies held leading positions in most European countries throughout the 1980s and into the early 1990s.

Two types of European companies started manufacturing microcomputers in the 1980s. First, the established computer companies—ICL, Nixdorf, Siemens (and later S.N.I.), and Groupe Bull—took a defensive approach to personal computers: they continued to focus most of their resources on mainframes and minicomputers, and marketed personal computers to their existing corporate customers in their home markets. Most of them failed to develop a Pan-European strategy. Second, microcomputer start-ups were founded in several European countries and some of them became important players in their home markets, with a few of them even managing to develop a Pan-European presence. Among the most successful were Acorn, ACT, Amstrad, and Sinclair in Britain, and Tulip in the Netherlands.[10]

By the early 1990s, some of the leading American manufacturers—IBM, Compaq, and Apple—were either at, or very close to, the top in each one of the key European markets. In addition, the traditional European computer companies were among the top six vendors in their local markets—ICL in Britain, S.N.I. in Germany, and Groupe Bull in France. Toshiba was the only Japanese company that managed to achieve some success in Europe, and Olivetti was the only European company that became an important vendor in several European personal computer markets.

Some lesser known brands were also among the top vendors. The early 1990s brought considerable turbulence to the European personal computer market. A number of local, low-cost manufacturers—including Vobis in Germany, Elonex and Viglen in Britain, and Kenitech in France—entered the industry and built respectable market shares. Prices dropped, margins collapsed, and the industry entered an adjustment phase not unlike the one that the United States experienced in the first half of the 1990s.

ASIAN DEVELOPMENTS: JAPAN

In Japan, unlike the rest of the world, no microcomputer standard dominated, and personal computers diffused only slowly until the early 1990s. Cross-country wage differentials made it possible for a new generation of countries, including South Korea, Taiwan, and Singapore, to become an increasingly important part of the computer industry once microcomputers and personal computers started gaining traction.[11]

Even though in the early 1980s the Japanese mainframe makers appeared ready to compete internationally, they did not live up to expectations. By the early 1990s, the three leaders—Fujitsu, NEC, and Hitachi—had about 75 percent of the Japanese market but only about 3 percent of computer markets in the rest of the world. At that time, sales outside of Japan accounted for only 12 percent of NEC's computer revenues, 18 percent of Hitachi's, and 29 percent of Fujitsu's.[12] The Japanese presence abroad took mostly the form of computer sales through, often combined with shareholdings in, local companies.

By the early 1980s, Japan appeared to be in a strong position to play a central role in the fledgling personal computer era: Japanese companies had world-class computer capabilities and had accumulated considerable expertise in developing electronic components. They ended up controlling world markets for components such as DRAM chips, flat-panel displays, and floppy-disk drives, but failed to become top players on the world personal computer scene.

MITI, the agency in charge of developing and coordinating industrial policy, failed to design and implement the kind of computer policies in the 1980s that underpinned the development of the Japanese mainframe computer industry in the 1960s and 1970s. Four major policy initiatives were launched in the 1980s: the Fifth Generation Computer Systems Project, the Supercomputer Project, the Sigma Project, and the TRON Project. The only one with implications for personal computers, the TRON Project, failed to take off. The lack of a policy focus on personal computers in Japan, however, was only part of the story.

NEC was the first Japanese company to develop a 16-bit PC on the basis of an Intel-compatible microprocessor and a nonstandard version of the DOS operating system: in 1982, it introduced the PC-9801 for the business market and encouraged developers to create software for the machine. Due to its first-mover advantage, NEC was able to attract a massive number of developers to its platform. Network effects worked their magic, and NEC held at least a 50 percent share of the Japanese personal computer market through the mid-1990s.[13]

In the United States, dozens of clone-makers entered the market to compete with IBM on the basis of what eventually became the Intel-Microsoft standard, but in Japan NEC prevented other firms from cloning the PC-9800. As a result, a number of rivals—including Fujitsu, Hitachi, IBM Japan, and Toshiba—entered the Japanese market with personal computer models that ran mutually incompatible versions of the DOS operating system. Japan thus ended up with an industry that was radically different from the one that existed in the United States. The U.S market quickly became populated with hundreds of companies that competed within the Intel-Microsoft standard; in Japan, however, there were as many operating systems as competitors, and no standard was established. With the exception of IBM, American personal computer companies did not attempt to enter the Japanese market, mainly because developing distribution channels and modifying systems to deal with Japanese characters represented significant hurdles. Prices remained high, and personal computers diffused relatively slowly.

This situation changed considerably in the early 1990s. In 1991, IBM introduced the DOS/V operating system, which could handle Japanese characters. DOS/V enabled IBM clone-makers (of any nationality) to market in Japan the same computers they were selling elsewhere, which facilitated the invasion of the Japanese market by companies from the United States (Dell, Gateway 2000), Asia (Acer), and Europe (Olivetti). Moreover, some of the top Japanese personal computer makers, including Fujitsu, converted their machines to DOS/V, and software developers started creating application packages for the operating system.

Apple gained market share in Japan during the 1990s with a Japanese version of the Macintosh computer. Between 1990 and 1994, Apple's share rose from 1 percent to over 15 percent. In 1993, Microsoft introduced a Japanese version of Windows 3.1 that could run on both NEC and DOS/V computers. Two years later, Windows 95 became as popular in Japan as it did in the United States. The shift from DOS to Windows meant that software applications that had been created for the NEC version of DOS, and that supported NEC's dominance in the Japanese market, no longer played the role they once did.

Compaq broke into the Japanese market in 1992: it introduced personal computers at half the price of equivalent NEC machines. Some of NEC's Japanese competitors started cutting prices as well, and NEC's share of the market fell from 52 to 43 percent between 1991 and 1994. In 1995, Fujitsu launched its own price war: it cut prices even more deeply than Compaq and grew its share from about 9 percent in 1994 to 22 percent in 1996. That same year, NEC announced that it would start selling DOS/V machines in Japan. The supremacy of the PC-9800 had finally come to an end.

The only Japanese company that became a key player in the international personal computer industry before the mid-1990s was Toshiba, which had played only a minor role during the mainframe era of the computer industry in Japan. A latecomer to the Japanese personal computer market, Toshiba failed to become a serious challenger for NEC in the domestic market but relied on its capabilities in precision engineering to turn into an international leader in a less-populated niche—the portable personal computer. By the early 1990s, Toshiba was among the top 10 personal computer manufacturers in the American market (in units shipped). It was also among the top 10 in several European national markets and on the European continent overall (both in units and value shipped).[14]

ASIAN DEVELOPMENTS: SOUTH KOREA

The newly industrializing countries of South Korea, Taiwan, Singapore, and Hong Kong became important players in the international computer industry in the 1980s. All of them had grown at a fast pace in the 1960s and 1970s on the basis of international wage differentials and export-oriented manufacturing; however, by the end of the 1970s, rising labor costs were starting to set limits to further expansion. In this context, the governments of three of these nations—South Korea, Taiwan, and Singapore—introduced policies to facilitate their countries' transition to more capital- and technology-intensive manufacturing. By fostering foreign direct investment and technology transfer, and by facilitating the development of domestic technical skills, governmental action laid the foundation for the growth of the computer industry in these nations.

South Korean companies successfully challenged the Japanese giants in the market for consumer electronics, such as TVs, VCRs, and microwave ovens, and caught up with American and Japanese producers in semiconductors. Their impact on the international computer industry, although important, was somewhat more limited.[15]

The domestic conglomerates (chaebol) that entered computer production in the 1980s—Samsung, Hyundai, LG, and Daewoo—had grown rapidly over the two previous decades by developing consumer electronic products for world markets with public subsidies and government-set export targets. Beginning in the late 1970s, the South Korean government also helped the conglomerates capture an important portion of the world market for memory chips (DRAMs), which the Japanese had come to dominate: the share of South Korean firms in the DRAM market rose from zero to 30 percent in a decade, and Samsung displaced NEC as the world's leading producer of memory chips in 1994.[16]

Unlike the Japanese, the South Koreans did not play any role in the world computer industry before the advent of the microcomputer. The computer pioneers were not the chaebol, but rather a small group of start-ups, such as Trigem and Qnix, which began manufacturing personal computers for domestic consumption. Trigem introduced the first microcomputer in the country in 1981 and the first IBM-compatible PC in 1984. From then on, it ranked among the top two vendors in the South Korean personal computer market every year until the mid-1990s.

The chaebol became involved in personal computer manufacturing only when the government banned computer imports in 1982. The domestic market, by far the largest of the newly industrializing economies, remained closed to imports of computers and peripherals for about six years, which created enough incentives for the conglomerates to enter computer production. After the ban was lifted, the dealer networks that the chaebol sponsored prevented foreign companies from capturing more than a small share of the domestic personal computer market. In practice, the leading vendor in South Korea was always either a local start-up (such as Trigem) or a local conglomerate (such as Samsung).

Although South Korean computer companies targeted mainly the domestic market, some of them—including Daewoo and Hyundai—ventured overseas. Daewoo turned out to be the most successful in the United States by far: in the late 1980s and early 1990s, it made inroads in the States by taking over Leading Edge, one of the early IBM PC clone-makers. Daewoo manufactured personal computers for Leading Edge, which in turn marketed them in America at a steep discount relative to IBM's prices.

As discussed in Chapter 7, the competitive dynamics of the personal computer industry changed in the early 1990s. The crisis that engulfed the world personal computer industry at that time, and particularly the U.S. market, hit South Korean manufacturers especially hard. Accelerated product cycles and price wars depressed profit margins, particularly for IBM clone-makers. Hyundai pulled out of the United States in order to concentrate on its home market and Europe. Daewoo sold its American Leading Edge subsidiary and retreated to focus on the domestic market. Some of the conglomerates acquired stakes in American computer companies to retain a presence, albeit small, in the U.S. market: Samsung, for example, purchased a 40-percent interest in AST Research, an IBM PC clone-maker, and Hyundai bought a similar stake in drive-maker Maxtor.

ASIAN DEVELOPMENTS: TAIWAN

The Taiwanese personal computer industry, developed mainly by local entrepreneurs, became *the* Asian success story in the international market.[17]

The Taiwanese electronics industry took off in the 1960s, when American multinationals such as Texas Instruments and their Japanese counterparts—Sanyo and Matsushita, among others—outsourced the production of consumer electronic products and parts to Taiwan. The 1970s witnessed a new wave of foreign direct investment involving companies such as RCA, Philips, and IBM. As suppliers and subcontractors to foreign multinationals, Taiwanese companies gained experience and skills that were readily transferable to personal computer production.

By the late 1970s, some local firms were already creating unauthorized clones of the Apple II, and after 1981, some of them started manufacturing IBM-compatible PCs. Drawn by Taiwan's low-cost but skilled labor force, foreign computer manufacturers set up production facilities in the country in the 1980s. Local entrepreneurs, in turn, started manufacturing small components for personal computers as subcontractors, and then slowly transitioned to the design and manufacturing of more advanced computer components, including motherboards, monitors, and graphics cards. (A computer's motherboard is the main circuit board, containing the microprocessor and memory, whereas graphics cards, also known as video cards, control the computer's display monitor.) During the 1980s, it became common for major U.S. firms such as Apple, IBM, Compaq, and Dell to outsource the production of computers to a wide network of Taiwanese small- and medium-sized enterprises. By the mid-1990s, Taiwan was the world's leading producer of notebook computers, monitors, and motherboards.

Some Taiwanese companies made attempts to develop their own brand, but few were successful; among them, Acer stands out.[18] Acer was founded under the Multitech name in 1976 by the entrepreneur Stan Shih and five others. (Shih was also the creator of Taiwan's first pocket calculator.) Although in its early days the company distributed electronic imports, it soon started designing and manufacturing its own computers. In 1981, for example, it introduced the Micro-Professor I, a basic system conceived as a training tool in microprocessor technology; the next year, it marketed the Micro-Professor II, an early clone of the Apple II. After 1981, Multitech started designing and promoting IBM-compatible PCs in Taiwan. Within five years, it became the second company (after Compaq) to introduce a personal computer based on the new 386 Intel microprocessor. After changing its name to Acer in 1987, it expanded rapidly in the late 1980s and early 1990s, so much so that by 1995 it ranked twelfth in sales in the world personal computer market.[19]

Although Acer did not receive direct financial support from the Taiwanese government, it was allowed to use technology developed in a public research institute in its first IBM-compatible PC. This technical contribution, combined with the assistance it received from the government in arranging bank loans, underpinned Acer's rise on the world computer scene.

ASIAN DEVELOPMENTS: SINGAPORE

Large multinational corporations—including National Semiconductor, Texas Instruments, and Fairchild—started manufacturing low-density chips in Singapore in the 1960s, lured by international wage differentials and the incentives provided by the Economic Development Board (EDB).[20] In the 1970s, another wave of multinationals—GE, Philips, and Matsushita, among them—set up facilities in the country, this time with a focus on consumer electronics products. In order to ensure that the country's workforce had the skills required to create world-class products, the Singaporean government started training workers in precision engineering in cooperation with the multinationals.

In the late 1970s and early 1980s, the EDB began targeting computer production, just as the American computer multinationals ramped up a global outsourcing process. Tandon was the first U.S. computer company to outsource production to Singapore in the 1970s for the manufacture of floppy disk drives. In 1982, Seagate, another U.S. disk-drive manufacturer, set up production facilities on the island, and many component and subcomponent manufacturers—including Miniscribe, Maxtor, Conner, Control Data, and Western Digital—soon followed Seagate's example. As the multinationals increased production over time, Singaporean workers acquired skills that, combined with the government-provided training, made them a valuable asset for manufacturers of a wide range of computer products, both foreign and domestic.

Apple set up production facilities in Singapore in 1981 for the manufacture of basic components. Over time, the company increased the complexity of the tasks that it assigned to Singaporean workers, to the point that it ended up building a design center on the island in 1993, the very first it set up outside the United States. Other microcomputer manufacturers, including Compaq and HP, followed Apple's example and made direct investments in Singapore.

Although the growth of the Singaporean computer industry was fundamentally driven by the foreign multinationals, a local company managed to establish an international standard for a specific personal computer component—sound cards. Creative Technologies was founded in 1981 to make add-on cards for the Apple II.[21] It subsequently manufactured a clone of the Apple II and, later, an IBM-compatible multimedia computer. After switching its focus to media technologies, it created an add-on sound card branded Creative Music System. Although this first product was not successful, Creative later developed the Sound Blaster sound card. Because Sound Blaster was marketed on personal computers that were based on the Intel 386 microprocessor and Windows 3.1, the popularity of the card grew with that of the operating system, making it by far the most popular sound card for PCs.

THE INTERNATIONAL COMPUTER INDUSTRY, 1980–1995: TAKING STOCK

In the late 1970s, it looked as though the international computer industry would be shaped by the confrontation between IBM and its Japanese rivals (Fujitsu and Hitachi); it also seemed that the industry of the 1980s would be dominated either by mainframe computing or by increasingly powerful minicomputers. The 1980s, however, brought a number of surprises.

The rise of personal computers was the most significant event. Personal computers started appearing in the American market in the mid-1970s but gained legitimacy in corporate environments in the early 1980s with the entry of IBM. During the 1980s, the PC segment, which quickly became the fastest-growing part of the industry, saw the establishment of a standard: the IBM PC. This standard prompted familiar responses among competitors, with dozens of clone-makers choosing to compete by adhering to the standard but beating IBM in price-performance; meanwhile, Apple Computer and a few others chose the incompatibility route. Because the owners of the core components of the new standard were Intel and Microsoft, the rise of the new standard did not benefit IBM as much as System/360.

Although the computer industry had become truly global before the 1980s, the dawn of the personal computer era added an extra dimension to the internationalization of the industry. The modularity of the personal computer, combined with the prevailing patterns of cross-country wage differentials

Table 9.1.   IT Production, by Region, 1985–1995 (Revenues in USD Million and Percentage of Total)

	1985	1987	1989	1991	1993	1995
I. Total revenues (in USD million)						
Europe	22,350	36,186	39,954	44,595	39,332	54,857
United States	47,122	47,635	49,296	47,965	52,176	76,284
Japan	17,519	38,248	51,790	56,489	55,162	70,882
Other Asia-Pacific	2,988	6,382	18,495	25,112	38,858	66,503
Total	89,979	128,451	159,535	174,161	185,528	268,526
II. Revenue shares (%)						
Europe	25	28	25	26	21	20
United States	52	37	31	28	28	28
Japan	19	30	32	32	30	26
Other Asia-Pacific	3	5	12	14	21	25
Total	100	100	100	100	100	100

Source: Reed Electronics Research, *Yearbook of World Electronics Data*, 1985–1995.

and with industrial policies implemented by national governments, facilitated the rise of a new cohort of countries—South Korea, Taiwan, and Singapore, among others—that had played no role in the mainframe era of computing. Table 9.1 shows that, by the mid-1990s, the Asia-Pacific region (excluding Japan) had become as important a player in worldwide IT production as Europe, the United States, and Japan.

The decline of mainframes and minicomputers cannot be tied directly to the growth of the personal computer. Minicomputers were largely displaced by scientific workstations, and mainframe-centered computing schemes gave way to the client-server model. However, it took at least a decade for this process to unfold, and mainframes remained central to many legacy computer operations and still do to this day. IBM remained king of the mainframe world, in both hardware and software, but many companies—CA, Oracle and SAP, among others—thrived in highly profitable niches of the mainframe software market.

The rise of open systems was another disruption to the established industry. The growth of Sun Microsystems and its UNIX-based workstations was one of the best examples of this trend. This led to the decline of companies (such as Nixdorf in the minicomputer segment) that were once the darlings of the computer industry but did not adjust quickly enough to the new world of open standards, a world in which the generous margins resulting from proprietary standards were a thing of the past.

By far the biggest surprise in the IT industry, however, was that the early 1990s witnessed the greatest fall from grace in corporate history: in early 1993 IBM, which had thrived through the mid-1980s, reported the largest single-year loss ever recorded by a corporation. Although IBM's decline has often been attributed to the rise of personal computers, the facts do not support this thesis. To a great extent, the roots of IBM's malaise date back to the mid-1970s and were unrelated to the rise of microcomputers. They stem, rather, from the commoditization of the mainframe: by the mid-1970s, the mainframe—the core and foundation of IBM's domination of the industry—had become an article that other competent manufacturers could produce. Moreover, IBM's expertise in systems integration was being taken over by software. As a result, computer users began switching to other, less expensive computer manufacturers, and IBM's traditionally fat profit margins evaporated.[22]

In the midst of the crisis, IBM brought in a new CEO, Louis Gerstner, Jr., who had previously served as chair and CEO of RJR Nabisco. Under Gerstner's direction, IBM implemented a short-term and a long-term strategy. In the short term, the company slashed the price of its mainframe products, both hardware and software, to regain market share. In the long term, IBM implemented more aggressively a transformation that was already in progress—it increasingly became a software and services company, while at the same time embracing open standards. This radical reorientation allowed the company to survive and thrive again after several difficult years in the mid-1990s.[23]

The first half of the 1990s, finally, was a turbulent time not only for IBM but also for the international computer industry more generally, and especially for the personal computer segment. Table 9.2 presents an international ranking of companies in mainframes and personal computers in 1989 and 1995.

The contrast between mainframes, a stable but slowly shrinking segment, and personal computers, a rapidly growing and volatile sector, is dramatic. Total mainframe revenues declined somewhat, whereas total personal computer revenues skyrocketed. With one exception, the same mainframe

Table 9.2. Top 10 Companies in Mainframes and Personal Computers, 1989 and
1995 (Revenues in USD Million)

	Mainframes, 1989			Mainframes, 1995	
Rank	Company	Revenues	Rank	Company	Revenues
1	IBM	12,509	1	IBM	6,475
2	Fujitsu	3,262	2	Fujitsu	4,824
3	Hitachi	3,117	3	Hitachi	4,376
4	NEC	2,392	4	NEC	3,870
5	Amdahl	1,471	5	Unisys	1,116
6	Unisys	1,200	6	Groupe Bull	795
7	Groupe Bull	841	7	S.N.I.	770
8	Cray Research	634	8	Amdahl	758
9	Siemens	612	9	Cray Research	412
10	STC/ICL	466	10	Mitsubishi	290

	Personal computers, 1989			Personal computers, 1995	
Rank	Company	Revenues	Rank	Company	Revenues
1	IBM	8,343	1	IBM	12,949
2	Apple	3,574	2	Compaq	9,176
3	NEC	3,117	3	Apple	8,534
4	Compaq	2,876	4	Fujitsu	6,432
5	Groupe Bull	1,681	5	Toshiba	5,690
6	Olivetti	1,523	6	HP	5,475
7	Toshiba	1,341	7	NEC	5,225
8	Tandy	1,330	8	Dell	4,558
9	Unisys	1,300	9	Packard Bell	4,300
10	Fujitsu	870	10	Sun	3,965

Source: "The Datamation 100," *Datamation,* June 15, 1990, and June 1, 1996.

companies appeared among the top 10 in 1989 and 1995, and their rankings changed little. By contrast, four companies dropped out of the top 10 in personal computers and four new ones took their spots.

The table reveals a striking growth in personal computer revenues but fails to show an equally important fact: by 1995, personal computer hardware had become a commodity, and margins had collapsed. Combined with falling mainframe revenues, the traditional computer hardware companies were actively searching for new sources of revenues and profits in software and services. IBM, which was already on the road to recovery by 1995, generated almost as much revenues from the combination of software and services (including maintenance)—almost 46 percent of the total—as it did from hardware—about 49 percent of the total.[24]

But a new era of computing was about to start: the Internet, which had been growing for years as an academic and scientific network of networks, was about to come to the forefront and transform the international computer industry one more time.

PART IV

THE INTERNET ERA
1995–2010

CHAPTER TEN

Software and Services

Chapters 10, 11, and 12 cover the period from 1995 to 2010, an "era of multiple standards," or more vividly, "a jungle of standards." During this time, numerous standards coexisted across and within different segments of the computer industry. In the mainframe sector, the System/360 standard remained dominant; the IBM PC standard defined most of the personal computer market. Within different segments of the industry, multiple standards competed, sometimes like David and Goliath, as in the case of the IBM PC versus the Apple Macintosh computers, and sometimes more equally, as between Apple's iOS and Google's Android in smartphones. Just below the surface was the commercial Internet, which irrupted in the mid-1990s and brought another plethora of standards, such as those for e-mail and the World Wide Web.

The Internet remains a work in progress and, to judge by its history so far, its future is impossible to forecast. We are conscious that the history presented here is necessarily transitional. We are aware that future historians will see things differently.

Before the mid-1990s, the Internet was a government-owned network of networks primarily for academic and scientific institutions.[1] In the first half of the decade, two developments led to the transformation of the Internet into a network with formidable commercial implications: first, it became a private entity, and second, the World Wide Web became the most popular means of navigating it. From then on, the expanding Internet transformed a variety of industries, including computer software and services and computing hardware.

The Internet and the web are often conflated, and the distinction needs to be made clear. The Internet is a network infrastructure that can support numerous applications—among them e-mail, file transfer, internet telephony, and of course the World Wide Web. The web, which was invented in 1993 by Tim Berners-Lee at the CERN European Particle Physics Laboratory in Geneva, Switzerland, transformed the Internet experience by providing a simple interface accessible to ordinary users.[2] Making this experience possible required significant advances in software, services, and hardware, which are the focus of the final part of this book. The majority of new Internet enterprises, such as Amazon, eBay, Yahoo, and Google, were made possible by the web, while older enterprises were transformed by it. Consumers accessed services through "web browsers" on personal computers, and those services were supplied by conventional computer hardware running "web server" software and more traditional software infrastructure such as databases. As we write, the hegemony of the web is being challenged by "apps" on smartphones and tablet computers, but the user experience and the supporting infrastructure are not radically different.

Although during this period the core of the industry continued to shift from hardware to software and services, computer hardware still played an important role. The period from 1995 to 2010 witnessed the remarkable persistence of computer mainframes as well as the expansion of the personal computer market and its subsequent decline as personal computers gave way to smartphones and tablets.

Over this 15-year span, the globalization of the computer industry accelerated and deepened. The period saw the continuing shift of computer production toward new regions, driven at least in part by cross-country wage differentials, and the rise of new global players in computer software and services.

Furthermore, the rise of the commercial Internet had a multifaceted impact on the computer software and service industries. First, it undermined the business model of the consumer online networks. Second, it gave rise to new personal computer software products, including web browsers, web publishing tools, and browser plug-ins. Third, it laid the foundation for a host of new web-based companies, including search engines, directories, portals, and social networks. Fourth, it facilitated the growth of open-source software, and enhanced the role of server operating systems and security software. Fifth, it paved the way for the development of software as a service (SaaS). Finally, it created incentives for mass-market software vendors to forward-integrate into enterprise software products, and for both mass-market and enterprise software vendors to forward-integrate into computer services.[3]

DISRUPTION OF CONSUMER ONLINE NETWORKS

The arrival of the Internet was not particularly disruptive for computer services firms in general, such as ADP and EDS. Although a degree of change came about during the transition from private networks to the public Internet, it was largely a case of adapting to a new infrastructure rather than a transition to a new business model. This was not the case for the consumer networks.

Consumer online networks were the first commercial operations to be threatened by the rise of the web. The web made the Internet much more attractive to consumers, since it offered features and experiences not unlike those they could find on a traditional consumer network—chat rooms, news groups, and some emerging entertainment. This opportunity led to the rise of hundreds of Internet Service Providers (ISPs) in 1993. An ISP offered a raw conduit into the Internet, and provided little or no mediation between users and the global network.[4]

The first of the incumbent consumer networks to adapt to the new world of the Internet was Delphi, a second-tier player that had recently been acquired by the News Corporation. In 1993, Delphi offered 20 hours per month of full Internet access for $23. In November 1994, a much more potent threat to the consumer networks emerged when MCI, the telecom giant, launched the InternetMCI service with 20 hours of monthly access at $19.95, about one third of the cost of a similar level of service from AOL or Prodigy.[5] These low rates were possible because, as a raw ISP, MCI provided negligible content and had few fixed investments. AT&T and WorldCom launched ISPs in 1996.

Of the major consumer networks, only AOL made a completely successful transition to the Internet. (Prodigy and GEnie had not been core activities for their owners and faded away in the second half of the 1990s.) During 1994–1995, AOL created an Internet Division, acquired two small web

software makers, and bought GNN, an Internet access provider. These acquisitions enabled the company to modify its user interface to include a
window onto the web. AOL created what proved to be the gentlest possible
introduction to the Internet—the web was offered as another "channel" sitting alongside its other content channels. AOL ended up acquiring CompuServe in 1998.[6]

In 1993, Microsoft, having failed to acquire AOL, CompuServe, or any
other of the major online service providers, started investing considerable
resources into the creation of its own service. The Microsoft Network (MSN)
was developed as an old-style consumer network—a closed network using
proprietary protocols, with content acquired from media suppliers. By December 1995, however, the company had decided to embrace the Internet,
even if that involved sacrificing MSN. Thereafter, MSN effectively became
an up-market ISP and was no real threat to AOL.

WEB BROWSERS, SERVERS, AND COMPLEMENTS

The rise of the web led to the emergence of three new software categories:
web browsers for personal computers, web servers for enterprises, and web
complements.

The two leading suppliers of web browsers were Netscape and Microsoft.
Although the attention of the press in the mid-1990s focused almost exclusively on the rivalry between these two firms, in 1994–1995 there were about
two dozen entrants producing browsers to run on personal computers.[7] What
distinguished Netscape and Microsoft from other browser suppliers was that
they also created servers and browser complements that offered a more comprehensive technological system.

Jim Clark, the founder of the workstation manufacturer SGI, and Marc
Andreesen, who had led the development of the most successful and user-
friendly early web browser at the University of Illinois at Urbana-Champaign,
established Netscape Communications Corporation in April 1994. Netscape's
Navigator browser was released as a "beta" program for early adopters
and made available as a free download in October. In two months, about 10
million copies were downloaded. In December 1994, Netscape released a
commercial-grade browser Navigator 1.0, together with complementary
server software; other related applications followed in the next few months.

The browser was free for noncommercial users and modestly priced for others.

Microsoft woke up to the Internet in early 1994, but it took the company another year or so to change direction. Both the Internet Explorer browser and the Windows 95 desktop operating system were released in August 1995. Microsoft recognized the need to supply not only a browser but also infrastructure complements; in February 1996, it introduced the Internet Information Server (IIS), its web server, bundled with the Windows NT server operating system.

Microsoft's early browsers were lackluster, achieving barely a 10 percent market share throughout 1996. The company gradually caught up with Netscape in successive releases. By release 4.0 (September 1997), the Microsoft browser had achieved technical parity with its competitor; by mid-1998, each company controlled about half of the browser market.

Microsoft's web software was either given away free or bundled with its operating system at no additional cost to the user, which reduced the opportunity for Netscape to derive revenues from software sales. Instead, Netscape had to generate income through advertising. Most Navigator users visited the company's home page, or "portal," when their browsers were opened, which generated about 100 million hits per day. As of 1997, the company derived annual revenues of $108 million in fees from advertising and search-engine referrals. In November 1998, Netscape was acquired by AOL for $4.2 billion, mainly for its portal operation, and the browser market was in practice ceded to Microsoft.

Just as IBM's practice of bundling software and services with hardware had created legal problems for the company in the 1960s, Microsoft's practice of "tying" and "bundling" the Internet browser with the operating system became one of the central issues in the lawsuit that the U.S. Department of Justice filed against the company in May 1998. Although one of the remedies the government proposed was the breakup of Microsoft into separate (operating-system and applications) companies, this idea was later abandoned and the legal process ended with settlements between Microsoft and the plaintiffs, which included several state governments as well.[8] Microsoft also unsuccessfully defended lawsuits in the European Union, which alleged tying and failure to disclose protocols to enable interoperation with its operating system.

There were two primary markets for web software complements: publishing tools for the efficient creation of websites, and auxiliary programs or "plug-ins" that provided additional browser functionality.

The broad space of web publishing tools extended from simple consumer products priced at about $50 to enterprise systems that cost up to $1,000 per user. By the fall of 1996, more than 50 products were reportedly on the market.[9] A key company in this space was Charles Ferguson's Vermeer Technologies, founded in April 1994. While Vermeer's publishing product, FrontPage, was under development, Ferguson negotiated with Netscape and Microsoft, both of which needed a powerful web publishing tool as a complement to their browsers and servers. Microsoft ended up acquiring FrontPage for $130 million in early 1996.[10] Armed with FrontPage, the NT operating system, the IIS web server, and its own database software, Microsoft was able to offer a complete system for establishing an e-commerce operation or a corporate website. Only Netscape had the technology to compete with Microsoft in offering a one-stop solution.

The early web browser was a rudimentary system intended primarily for the display of text and images. A rash of companies began to supply auxiliary helper programs that enabled a standard web browser to support a richer consumer experience. Hundreds of browser complements were developed, and in the more popular categories such as media players, there were many competing products.

One of the most successful web complements was Adobe's nearly ubiquitous Portable Document Format (PDF) document management system. Adobe's PDF technology, in fact, predated the web.[11] In 1991, John Warnock, cofounder of Adobe, conceived the idea of a portable document format that would enable electronic documents to be accessed on any computer platform. The product was launched under the Carousel name in November 1992. Although Carousel was not particularly successful, it was improved and relaunched as Acrobat in June 1993. The product did not become popular until Adobe made the reader free in September 1994, while deriving revenues from its document creation tools. Adobe encouraged personal computer assemblers to bundle the reader with new computers, and the product was also distributed through cover disks on personal computer magazines. Network effects worked their usual magic, and PDF became a popular document dissemination format long before the web took off. Adobe adopted a similar strategy for the web, enabling users to download the reader for free, while deriving revenues from its document creation and publishing tools. Adobe's PDF, today a mainstay of the publishing industry, is one of the few software products that has seamlessly bridged the divide between the old world of print on paper and the new world of electronic publishing.

DIRECTORIES AND SEARCH ENGINES

The expansion of the Internet created a platform on which a variety of new computer-services companies developed. Among them were directories, search engines, portals, and social networks.

In 1993, many people saw the need for services to help navigate the rapidly growing web. There were two main approaches: directories and search engines. In a directory, the universe of websites was organized into a hierarchy, very much like the yellow pages or a library catalogue. The first individuals to successfully organize a directory on a commercial basis were Stanford University computer science graduate students Jerry Yang and David Filo. In the spring of 1993, Yang and Filo created Yahoo!, a hobby website that listed the hundred or so websites of which they were then aware. The list grew with the web, and it soon became necessary to arrange the listings in a directory-like hierarchy. By the following January, Yahoo! had catalogued 10,000 sites and was receiving a million hits a day.[12] Two months later, the founders secured $1 million in venture funding, which enabled the company to employ additional indexers to seek out and list new websites on the ever-expanding web. Advertising was seen as a natural way to fund the enterprise: with increasing consumer interest in the Internet, major corporations were willing to spend a fraction of their advertising budgets experimenting with the web.

Search engines were a complementary and more economically sustainable approach. In this technology, an automated system—a web "spider" or "crawler"—systematically traversed the web, extracting keywords from web pages and documents. These keywords were then incorporated in a searchable index. Lycos, developed by Carnegie Mellon's Michael Mauldin, was the first commercial search engine. In July 1994, the system went live with a catalogue of 54,000 entries. By January 1995, it indexed 1.5 million items.[13] Because web crawling was easy to imitate and indexing consumed few human resources, barriers to entry were reasonably low; more than 30 firms entered the field—among them, entrepreneurial start-ups Lycos, Excite, and Info-Seek, as well as Alta Vista, a DEC subsidiary.

Few stories exemplify the power of feedback (or network) effects as clearly as the meteoric rise of Google, a search engine that Larry Page and Sergey Brin, two Stanford University computer science graduate students, set up in 1996. Google was named the search engine of choice in *PC Magazine*'s list of the top 100 websites of 1998 and was singled out for the outstanding "relevance" of its search results. After receiving $25 million in venture-capital funding in 1999, Google soon became Yahoo!'s default search engine provider and launched AdWords, its self-service ad program. By 2001, Google was indexing three billion web documents and 250 million images; as of 2004, those numbers had gone up to 4.28 billion documents and 880 million images. Users conducting searches flocked to Google in large numbers, which in turn attracted advertisers. By March 2006, Google accounted for roughly 43 percent of all online searches, Yahoo! for 28 percent, and MSN for about 13 percent.[14]

WEB PORTALS AND SOCIAL NETWORKS

In 1998, a new term, "portal," emerged. It was a website that offered a point of presence on the web with two main characteristics: it consolidated information and services from multiple sources and was sufficiently engaging to hold users' attention for significant periods of time. Directory and search services were fundamentally important as entry points into the web. In order to compete with their many imitators, the early market leaders—Yahoo!, Excite, Lycos, and InfoSeek—integrated other services into their portals. As of 1996, all of them had IPOs, collectively raising $162 million, which funded portal services such as e-mail, chat rooms, special interest groups, and instant messaging.[15] In the case of the traditional consumer networks that were migrating to the web (AOL and CompuServe, for example), portals were a means of differentiating their services from the no-frills ISPs that provided an Internet connection but no content.

Portal services were often created by firm acquisition in order to capture newly breaking technology. In 1996, for example, "webmail" promised to be the killer application for portals. Pioneered by Hotmail, webmail enabled users to access their e-mail from any web browser, from any computer, from anywhere in the world. In 1997–1998, MSN acquired Hotmail for $400 million, Yahoo! acquired Rocket Mail for $94 million, and Lycos acquired WhoWhere for $133 million. The late 1990s saw a frenzy of such acquisitions as portals integrated more and more services.[16]

Of all the new businesses that the rise of the commercial Internet made possible, few have changed people's lives more radically than social networking sites—websites that allow individuals to construct a more or less public profile and connect with other users. Websites for dating and reuniting friends were among the first social networking sites that started appearing around 1997.[17]

A second wave of social networking sites started around 2001, when the Ryze.com site was launched to help people leverage their business networks. The most successful among the second-wave sites was Friendster, founded in 2002. Friendster was set up to compete with Match.com, which by that time was already a profitable online dating site. Friendster was designed to facilitate encounters among friends-of-friends, under the assumption that romantic connections between friends-of-friends would have a better chance of success than those between strangers.

A group of Friendster members founded MySpace in 2003 to compete with Friendster and other social networking sites. Early on, MySpace benefited from the presence of Indie-rock bands, which created MySpace profiles and used the site to connect with fans. Teenagers started flocking to MySpace in 2004, and the site took off. In 2005, the News Corporation bought MySpace and its parent company, Intermix, for $580 million. At its peak, in December 2008, MySpace attracted almost 76 million unique monthly visitors in the United States.[18]

By the time News Corporation acquired MySpace, the service that would eventually change the social networking world—Facebook—had already been launched. In February 2004, Mark Zuckerberg set up the site under the name "Thefacebook.com" as a social networking site for Harvard University students. Later that year, the service expanded its reach to other colleges and universities around the United States. In a little over a year, Facebook was supporting more than 800 college networks, and later in 2005 it added high school networks. The next year it expanded its reach overseas and to cover workplace networks. In a classical network-effects story, users attracted more users, creating positive feedback effects that accelerated the site's growth. Software developers were attracted to create applications, such as multiplayer games, and advertisers allocated increasing portions of their budgets to the social networking site. By late 2011, Facebook had 845 million monthly active users. That year, it recorded revenues of $3.7 billion and net income of $1 billion, mostly from advertising.[19]

OPEN-SOURCE SOFTWARE, SERVER OPERATING SYSTEMS, AND SECURITY SOFTWARE

The Internet accelerated three major trends in infrastructure software. First, it increased competition in the industry by facilitating the development of open-source software. Second, it enhanced the role of server operating systems. Third, security software became one of the major software categories.

The term "open source" dates from 1998, but the concept of source-code-disclosed software is much older. (For the first 20 years of the industry, program source code was routinely disclosed to enable programmers to modify software packages. However, as software packages morphed into paid-for software products, suppliers sought to protect their intellectual property and no longer made the source code available. This remains the norm in the proprietary software industry.) The Internet fueled the ascent of open-source software, enabling programmers to collaborate on software projects even when they were thousands of miles apart.[20]

The Linux operating system, the centerpiece of the open-source software (OSS) movement, was originally developed by Linus Torvalds, a computer science undergraduate at the University of Helsinki. In September 1991, Torvalds released version 0.01, an experimental system consisting of 10,000 lines of code. From then on, Linux took on a life of its own as the number of collaborators grew into the hundreds.

A variety of complements—e-mail and web servers, security software, a database system, a web browser and an office suite, among others—were needed to make Linux a useful computing system. While Linux was evolving, many of these complements were being developed under the OSS model. Although they could be downloaded and integrated into a practical system, such integration was time-consuming and lacked stability.

In 1994, a number of "distributions" were offered on a commercial basis by firms such as Red Hat, Suse, Caldera, TurboLinux, and Mandrake. Commercial distributors packaged the Linux operating system plus all the complementary software, and offered telephone support and consultancy. Such packaging and support services were at the core of the early business model for OSS commercial companies. Because it entered early and adapted in a timely manner to the evolving OSS movement, Red Hat emerged as the leader in the Linux market: it accounted for 56 percent of all distributions by 1998.[21]

The advent of the Internet also enhanced the popularity of client-server operating systems in the second half of the 1990s, since it created a huge demand for dedicated servers for applications such as e-mail and web serving. At the same time, the rapid improvement of Intel microprocessors made Intel-based servers competitive with other, more expensive offerings in the computer server market.

The rising importance of client-server computing coincided with the maturing of Linux. The operating system received a massive boost in 2001, when IBM announced that it would adopt Linux and would donate the time of several hundred of its developers to OSS projects, including Linux. Several of the largest commercial websites, including Google and Amazon, adopted Linux for their "server farms." In 2006, Google was reportedly using Linux on all of its 450,000 servers installed worldwide.

The company that benefited the most from the rise of Intel-based servers was Microsoft. In 1993, Microsoft released Windows NT, a server operating system that was five years in the making. After the company recognized the importance of the Internet in 1994, it rushed to develop and incorporate facilities for web serving and other Internet technologies. Microsoft's server operating system continued to mature and incorporate new features as they arrived on the scene, becoming a phenomenal development effort for the company. Windows NT 1.0 (1993) had 4–5 million lines of code and was created by a team of about 200 people. Windows NT 5.2 (marketed as Windows Server 2003) was released in 2003, contained about 50 million lines of code, and was created by a team of 2,000 developers. NT became the dominant product in the server operating system market. In 2001, for example, about 4.26 million server operating systems were shipped worldwide— Windows NT accounted for almost 60 percent of the total, Linux for about 11 percent, Novell Netware for another 11 percent or so, and various UNIX flavors for the rest of the market.[22]

The rise of the Internet brought to the forefront the role of security software. The lack of built-in security has always been the most fundamental weakness of the Internet. Because the Internet was designed as a network for cooperating academics and research scientists, for whom security was not a major issue, security technology has had to be retrofitted onto the Internet, and security has become a major concern for corporations. In 2005, for instance, the annual economic losses due to security flaws were estimated to be in excess of $10 billion.[23]

Software Magazine's "Software 500" list for 2005 identified 29 software-product firms whose primary activity was computer security.[24] In that year, the leading security-software firm by far was Symantec, which had a one-third market share. Symantec was a modestly successful vendor of miscellaneous personal computer software packages with annual revenues of $438 million in 1995; a decade later, however, the company had become the fourth-largest independent software vendor with annual revenues of $2.5 billion.

Symantec's transformation started around 1996, when, after bringing in a new CEO, the company altered its strategy and set out to become a leading Internet security vendor. Symantec determined that, in order to become an industry leader, it would have to offer a complete security solution, and it made numerous acquisitions to fill out its security software portfolio. This set the company apart, since the norm throughout the 1990s was for security professionals to integrate products from multiple vendors, each specializing in a single product (intrusion detection, firewalls, antivirus software, identity management, encryption products, and so on). In 2000, Symantec moved decisively into computer-security outsourcing, assuming continuous responsibility for all of a client's computer security. To fulfill its security-management service, the company established two global-response centers, from which security experts remotely managed Symantec's client networks and monitored them for vulnerabilities or signs of an intrusion. With its portfolio of software and services, Symantec offered a one-stop security solution that took it to the top of the industry.

THE IMPACT OF THE INTERNET ON SOFTWARE AND SERVICES

Before the advent of the Internet, computer software and services consisted of three distinct segments. In the first, mass-market software products, vendors such as Microsoft supplied software products (word processors and spreadsheets, among others) for use on personal computers. In the second, enterprise software products, companies such as CA, Oracle, and SAP sold software packages for business administration and corporate computing infrastructure. In the third sector, computer services, firms such as ADP and EDS provided processing services remotely.

The Internet extended the boundaries of software products from the confines of an isolated computer system to a global network. This greater interconnectedness had two fundamental effects on the preexisting software industry. First, the boundaries between mass-market and enterprise software products became porous, creating the opportunity for mass-market software companies to forward-integrate into enterprise software. Second, both mass-market and enterprise software vendors extended the reach of their products into services delivered over the Internet.

Before the Internet, mass-market and enterprise software products evolved independently, selling in different markets. The most conspicuous differences were in product pricing and sales volume. Whereas a successful personal computer software package was usually priced at considerably less than $1,000 and might sell millions of copies, a typical enterprise software product started at $50,000 and sold a few thousand copies at most. When the personal computer became an Internet-connected machine, mass-market products for the client computer increasingly required server-side components, which blurred the sharp distinction between mass-market and enterprise software.

A few examples of how mass-market vendors forward-integrated into enterprise software have already been explored. Microsoft's main forays into enterprise software were into server operating systems (with Windows NT) and corporate databases. Adobe's most conspicuous transition in the Internet era was a shift from personal computer–based products for publishing on paper to products for electronic publishing and document management on the web, mainly through the exploitation of its PDF technology. Perhaps Symantec was the personal computer software vendor that most aggressively entered the enterprise software space. Whereas in 1995, Symantec was a relatively small vendor of software for personal computers, it became a software giant by 2005, with a product portfolio that covered both personal computing and network infrastructure.

Before the rise of the Internet, the service component of software products was relatively small, typically limited to revenues from telephone help lines or training and maintenance fees. In the Internet era, software vendors generated increasingly larger fractions of their revenues from services. Intuit, a company founded in 1983 to market a personal finance management program, provides a good example of a software-products firm integrating into services. Intuit's Quicken was an extremely successful product, to the point that, by the mid-1990s, it had reportedly become the best-selling consumer software product of all time. In 1992 and 1993, Intuit introduced

QuickBooks, an accounting package for small businesses, and Turbo-Tax, a program for personal tax filing. By the middle of the decade, as the Internet was gathering momentum, Intuit increasingly focused on supplying services to its existing customer base of consumers and small businesses. The company's most radical break with the past was the establishment of an online payroll service, which enabled it to compete head-on with ADP. By 2005, computer services accounted for 35 percent of Intuit's annual revenues.[25]

The Internet made it possible for new and existing firms to offer subscription-based software, also known as SaaS.[26] Among the new companies offering SaaS, Salesforce.com, a producer of software for customer relationship management (CRM), was the most successful. CRM was an established software genre whose major vendors included Siebel and BEA Systems. In the traditional CRM system, a mobile salesperson used a laptop computer loaded with CRM software, booked orders on the move, and periodically synchronized with the master database in the home office. Salesforce.com reconfigured this model so that the CRM software and the associated databases resided on its servers, and both mobile- and office-based users accessed the service through a web browser. The subscribing firm was thus relieved from maintaining an infrastructure to support the CRM application, and synchronization was automatic. By 2004, Salesforce.com was the leading company among half a dozen subscription-based CRM suppliers. That year, the company reported that it was serving 300,000 users in almost 17,000 organizations.[27]

CHAPTER ELEVEN

Computer Hardware

Perhaps the biggest surprise in computer hardware after 1995 was that—contrary to what many observers predicted—the market for computer mainframes did not vanish. And although personal computers remained a key component of the computer industry in the era of the commercial Internet, in recent years they have faced strong competition from smartphones and tablets.

MAINFRAMES AND CLIENT SERVER SYSTEMS

After 1995, the migration of "mission critical" software applications, particularly ERP applications, to client-server systems continued unabated, solidifying the trend discussed in Chapter 7. This process, however, did not kill the mainframe; it rather transformed the mainframe business into one largely based on maintenance and upgrades for existing users as opposed to revenue growth.[1]

The mainframe persisted as a computer platform partly because of "legacy" effects—banks, for example, that used very old, often bespoke, mainframe-based software applications to handle customer accounts found it too costly and risky to recreate them for new computer platforms. Moreover, the rise of the commercial Internet increased the demand for mainframes from legacy users. The explosion of e-commerce fueled the need for a computing platform with high levels of availability, fault tolerance, security, high throughput, scalability, and reliability—all of which were established attributes of the mainframe.

The battle between IBM and the plug-compatible manufacturers continued after 1995. By the late 1990s, worldwide mainframe revenues were declining steadily, but the mainframe market was too important for IBM, Hitachi, and Fujitsu to abandon. IBM continued dominating the industry, while Hitachi and Fujitsu competed by attracting customers with better price-performance than IBM. In the late 1980s, Hitachi and the Dallas-based EDS formed the Hitachi Data Systems joint venture and acquired National Advanced Systems (NAS), the computer division of National Semiconductor that produced IBM-compatible mainframes. In 1997, Fujitsu acquired Amdahl Corporation, the main American manufacturer of IBM compatibles.

IBM made a "green" transition in the 1990s from its proprietary "bipolar" electronics technology to conventional CMOS, which was slower but cooler running.[2] CMOS-based machines required considerably less energy and floor space than the older mainframes. While IBM was going through the transition and its CMOS technology was evolving, Hitachi Data Systems and Amdahl-Fujitsu gained market share. By the end of the decade, however, the technology had matured, and IBM's investments in CMOS started to pay off.

In the year 2000, IBM introduced a new mainframe family, the IBM zSeries, with which it consolidated its position in the market. Throughout the first decade of the twenty-first century, IBM became even more dominant in mainframes than it had been in the 1960s and 1970s. Although the zSeries embedded important gains in price-performance relative to its predecessors, it was still a descendant of the IBM System/360 introduced in the mid-1960s. Applications written 30 or 40 years earlier for System/360 and System/370 could still run, mostly unmodified, on IBM's new mainframes.

In the new millennium, IBM generated, on average, about $3.5 billion a year in mainframe-related revenues, selling computers priced at no less than $100,000 and often at several million dollars. Although mainframe sales reportedly accounted for only about 3.5 percent of the company's revenues, hardware expenditures were often accompanied by complementary and substantial expenditures in software and maintenance contracts. According to some estimates, as much as 40 percent of the company's profits in the 2000s were mainframe related.[3]

Other hardware manufacturers that had risen rapidly on the computer scene of the 1980s and early 1990s did not fare as well as IBM after the mid-1990s. DEC, for example, which in its glory days of the late 1980s had become the second-largest computer company (after IBM), saw its VAX line of midrange computers attacked on a number of fronts and ended up being acquired by Compaq in 1998; the deal was worth $9.6 billion, making it the largest transaction of its kind in the history of the computer industry up to that point.[4] For Compaq, the transaction made sense as a quick way to consolidate its position in enterprise computing—DEC was an attractive target for its strong computer server business.

Compaq, however, could not manage to remain independent for long; in 2002, it was acquired by Hewlett-Packard in a $25 billion operation.[5] The HP-Compaq merger was intended to create a company strong enough to compete both with Sun Microsystems and IBM in the server computer market and with major vendors in the personal computer market. The operation created a computer company almost as large as IBM.

The Compaq acquisition gave HP important computer assets in the server and personal computer markets but was less effective at enhancing HP's role in computer services. Whatever HP was lacking in this latter market it obtained through its $13.9 billion acquisition of EDS in 2008, a deal that more than doubled HP's revenues in the computer-services segment.[6]

The other superstar computer company of the 1980s and 1990s, Sun Microsystems, survived as an independent entity for a longer time by specializing, among other things, in workstations and servers that ran the company's flavor of the UNIX operating system. Its performance in the first decade of the twenty-first century was inconsistent, however, and it ended up being acquired by Oracle in 2010 in a $7.4 billion deal.[7]

The Oracle acquisition of Sun Microsystems was unusual in that it involved a company focused on software and services buying another firm that had strong computer hardware assets. One possible interpretation of the transaction is that, in the context of an industry operating under the shadow of a strongly diversified mammoth such as IBM, some companies decided to become diversified giants themselves in order to compete. After all, from its origins, the data-processing industry aimed at offering a "total solution" to clients involving hardware, software, and services.

PERSONAL COMPUTERS

The rise of the commercial Internet in the second half of the 1990s enhanced sales of personal computers. Some sort of "information appliance" was needed to gain access to the Internet, and the personal computer was, until recently, the king and queen of all such appliances.

In the years immediately after 1995, personal computer shipments grew at a steady rate, propelled by the rise of the Internet. The proportion of adults using the Internet in the United States, for example, grew very rapidly, from 14 percent to 50 percent, between 1995 and 2000. The proportion kept on rising thereafter, but at a slower rate—it had reached 74 percent at the end of 2009 and 87 percent by early 2014.[8] Worldwide, personal computer shipments grew from 80.6 million units in 1997 to 134.7 million units in 2000. Production stalled slightly during the dot-com bust of 2000–2001 but continued rising thereafter.

Competing personal computer vendors established different business models for PC assembly, distribution, and marketing. The "retail assemblers" were the small local suppliers that thrived on the basis of local-market knowledge, accessibility (typically being located in a retail park), customer service, and low production overhead. Until 2005 or so, they held a 25 percent share of the market in the United States and an even larger share in other countries.[9] They did not have the economies of scale of the larger producers, but their proximity to customers provided a profitable niche.

The "standard mass assemblers"—IBM, Compaq, HP, Siemens, Sony, NEC, Fujitsu, and Samsung, to name some of the largest—functioned on a quarterly plan: they forecast how many personal computers in different categories the market would be able to absorb, and then they built the PCs, or often subcontracted their assembly, in light of that forecast. In the late 1990s and early 2000s, much of this subcontracting involved Taiwanese firms. In fiscal year 2000, for example, Compaq had total sales of $35.6 billion and imported $9.5 billion worth of components from Taiwan alone. In the first decade of the 21st century, subcontracting and computer assembly moved toward China and other regions on the basis of cost differentials (discussed further in Chapter 12).

The "build-to-order" firms, such as Dell and Gateway, took customer orders first and then built personal computers on the basis of the orders received. This approach dealt effectively with some of the key problems the industry faced. One of them was that components lost value at an extremely fast pace, some as quickly as 1 percent per week. Since companies such as Dell and Gateway did not start building computers until the order was received, they minimized excess inventory issues. Furthermore, the build-to-order model eliminated much of the risk involved in projecting consumer demand. By contrast, for the standard mass assemblers such as Compaq and IBM, failed projections often led to oversupply and extreme discounting, or to undersupply and missed opportunities.

A Chinese company appeared for the first time among the top five when IBM sold its personal computer business to Lenovo in the mid-2000s. Acer, a Taiwanese company whose origins were briefly described in Chapter 9, appeared for the first time among the top five in 2004. In recent years, Dell, HP, Acer, Lenovo, and Toshiba have vied for the top spots, and the share of the rest has shrunk.

The ups and downs of the world's top personal computer makers convey the relative success of different competitive strategies. They also hide a more important fact: in recent years, new appliances—smartphones and tablets—have started eroding the role of the personal computer as the dominant computing device.

SMARTPHONES: THE FIRST ENTRANTS

The mobile phone (often termed a "cell phone" in the United States) emerged as a consumer item in the early 1990s, in effect riding on the technology and infrastructure for mobile telephony that had been developed earlier to satisfy the corporate communications market and elite customers.[10] The second half of the 1990s saw a wave of new single-function consumer devices, such as media players, digital cameras, and GPS systems, and infrastructure to support them. For a small increment to manufacturing cost, it became feasible to incorporate audio players and digital cameras into a mobile phone, which thus became a "feature phone"—an integrated bundle of special-purpose devices with capabilities that were frozen at the time of manufacture.

The term "smartphone" came into use in 1997 and represented a new way of thinking about mobile phones. Smartphones were no longer single-purpose or multipurpose devices, but rather universal handheld computers that incorporated a telephone. A key feature of smartphones was the ability to run software programs, later called "apps," that enabled them to perform tasks that had not been envisaged when the phone was manufactured. Smartphones are, at their core, classical universal computers.

Smartphones were built on the technology of handheld computers, often called personal digital assistants (PDAs), developed within the computer industry. All of the early smartphones had at their core software operating systems devised for PDAs. The main ones in the pre-2007 period were Palm OS, Windows CE (later called Windows Mobile), Symbian, and Black-Berry OS.

Palm Computing was founded in 1992 by Jeff Hawkins, the creator of one of the first handheld computers, the GRiDPad. In 1996, after being ac-quired by U.S. Robotics, Palm introduced the PalmPilot 1000, a PDA that incorporated handwriting recognition. Designed as an electronic Filofax-type organizer rather than a full-fledged computer, the PalmPilot 1000 sold more than a million units in the first 18 months after introduction.[11] The oper-ating system that controlled the PalmPilot PDA, the Palm OS, was first used in a smartphone in 2001.

The success of the PalmPilot 1000 generated a flurry of entry into the PDA market. Microsoft had started working on an operating system for mo-bile computing devices in late 1994.[12] By September 1996 it had entered into agreements with six hardware partners—Casio, Compaq, HP, LG Electronics (for Hitachi), NEC, and Philips—to bring to market PDA-like devices run-ning on the Windows CE operating system. These early Windows-based handheld computers were not particularly successful. By late 1997, Palm had about two-thirds of the market for handheld computing devices, and Win-dows came much further behind. Smartphones based on Windows CE were not introduced until 2002.

Symbian has its roots in an operating system named Epoc developed by Psion, a British computer company.[13] Psion was founded in 1980 by David Potter, an academic physicist, and in its early years became a leader in soft-ware for microcomputers. In 1994, Psion introduced a small handheld com-puter, the Series 3, which was a hit in the British market. After the Series 3 took off, Psion engineers started designing an operating system, called Epoc, to serve as the foundation for the long-term successor to the Series 3. While exploring the possibility of licensing its as-yet-unreleased operating system, Psion established a relationship with Nokia, the Finnish conglomerate, which was about to introduce the Communicator 9000, a combined mobile phone and PDA. Negotiations between the companies led to an agreement that would allow Nokia to use the Epoc operating system on its future line of Communicator devices.

Symbian, a spin-off of Psion, was founded in June 1998; it owned the Epoc operating system and was co-owned by some of the key players in the mobile phone industry (Nokia, Ericsson, and Motorola). The Symbian operating system was used on a mobile phone for the first time in 2001.

The story of the BlackBerry dates back to 1984, when two engineering students, Mike Lazaridis and Douglas Fregin, founded Research in Motion (RIM) as an IT consulting business in Waterloo, Ontario. From the beginning, the firm specialized in wireless data transmission.[14] In 1996, RIM introduced the first two-way messaging device, the so-called Inter@ctive Pager; three years later, it came out with the first product in a line that would bring the company international recognition: the BlackBerry, a device that allowed business executives to access their corporate e-mail wirelessly from anywhere at any time. RIM's first smartphone, the BlackBerry 5810, reached the market in 2002.

SMARTPHONES: APPLE'S IPHONE

The smartphone market changed radically with the arrival of Apple's iPhone in June 2007. Apple's management had started exploring the development of an Apple phone in 2002, soon after the introduction of the iPod.[15]

The iPod was a portable media player that Apple unveiled in October 2001. Early that year, Apple had also introduced iTunes, an application used to download, organize, and play digital audio. The iTunes Store opened for business in April 2003. One of the key problems consumers faced in the early 2000s, and especially after the introduction of the iPod, was mobile device proliferation—they were carrying around too many gadgets, including a PDA, a phone, a media player, and sometimes a digital camera. Around this time, some attractive "convergent" devices, such as the Palm Treo 600, started appearing on the market.

By 2004, the iPod business, which already accounted for 16 percent of Apple's revenues, looked promising but also vulnerable due to the increased sophistication of mobile phones. Furthermore, online music stores rivaling Apple's iTunes were proliferating. Apple responded with a "music phone," the ROKR, jointly developed with Motorola and introduced in 2005. The

ROKR—which had an unfriendly interface, could hold no more than 100 songs, and had to be synced with a personal computer to complete a purchase from the iTunes store—sold well below expectations despite an expensive marketing campaign.

As the ROKR episode was unfolding, Apple established a business relationship with Cingular, the wireless carrier. Apple and Cingular—which was acquired by AT&T in December 2006—held protracted negotiations that led to a deal centered on the introduction of an Apple phone. Apple's iPhone, developed in an atmosphere of complete secrecy during 2005–2006, was announced by Steve Jobs in January 2007.

Jobs presented the iPhone as a "revolutionary mobile phone" that combined the capabilities of a phone, an iPod, and an "Internet communicator."[16] The entire front surface of the iPhone was a touchscreen, and all of its functions were activated by touch. It ran the Mac OS X operating system (later rebranded iOS when used on the iPhone), offered a radically new and improved Internet access capability, and was able to wirelessly download music and movies from the iTunes store.

In the second quarter of 2007, when the iPhone became available commercially, Symbian was the undisputed leader in the world smartphone market with a share of almost 66 percent of all units sold. The iPhone market share grew quickly, from less than 1 percent when it was introduced to over 16 percent in late 2009. The rise of the iPhone was accompanied by a steep decline in the market shares of both Symbian and Windows CE; the share of the Blackberry OS kept on growing through late 2009 because the Blackberry phone was less of a consumer item and benefited from the inertia of being embedded in many organizations.

SMARTPHONES: GOOGLE'S ANDROID

By late 2008, the iPhone was the brightest star in the smartphone universe. Its ascent, however, did not remain uncontested for long. That September, T-Mobile released the first smartphone running on Android, a mobile operating system owned by Google.

The history of Google's Android goes back to Andy Rubin, a computer and electronics hobbyist who early in his career had worked for Apple.[17] In the late 1990s, Rubin and a group of engineer friends founded a start-up in Palo Alto, California, named Danger Inc., which in the early 2000s developed the Sidekick, one of the first smartphones to effectively combine web access, e-mail, instant messaging, and other applications. In 2002, Rubin met Page and Brin, the Google founders, who were pleasantly surprised to find that Google, which had a tiny share of the search market at the time, was the default search engine on the Sidekick.

The Sidekick developed a fan base among computer-savvy teenagers but never became a contender in the broader smartphone market. Rubin left Danger Inc. in 2004 and launched a new startup, Android, whose goal was to design an open-source mobile platform available to all developers and handset makers for free. The company would generate revenues by selling support services for the system.

In 2005 Rubin approached Page to obtain Google's endorsement for Android. Rather than just endorsing the start-up Google acquired it in July 2005 for an estimated $50 million. This unleashed speculation in the technology world about the potential implications of Google's turning into a smartphone vendor.

At the time it acquired Android, Google was reportedly concerned about two facts: first, web surfing had started to migrate from personal computers to mobile phones, and second, the Internet capabilities of existing feature phones were too primitive, because they were originally designed for low-bandwidth devices. Consumers' migration toward the mobile web could potentially undermine the foundations of Google's success because mobile phones were not particularly effective platforms for Google's services and ads.

Android's acquisition by Google did not turn it into a smartphone vendor per se. Unlike Apple, which sold the iPhone as an integrated and proprietary bundle of hardware and software, Google chose to follow a strategy not unlike that which Microsoft had employed in the 1980s in its relationships with PC makers—Google developed an operating system and licensed it to any and all handset makers. The key difference between Google's Android and Microsoft's operating systems was that Android was open-source and cost the handset manufacturers nothing. Rather than generating revenues from licensing, as Microsoft had done with its operating systems starting in the early 1980s, Google would make money from smartphone advertising.

In November 2007, shortly after the iPhone had reached the market, a group of technology companies that included Google, T-Mobile, HTC,

Qualcomm, and Motorola announced the formation of the Open Handset Alliance for the development of the Android operating system, somewhat in the model of the original Symbian consortium. The first successful Android smartphone was Motorola's DROID, which reached the market in October 2009.

The market share of Android in the world smartphone market grew quickly. By early 2011, Android had become the leading operating system in the market with a 36 percent share of all units sold, followed by Symbian (27 percent), Apple's iOS (17 percent), the BlackBerry OS (13 percent), and Windows Mobile (just under 4 percent).

SMARTPHONES: APP ECOSYSTEMS

The battle among smartphone vendors centered on attracting app developers to each platform. In March 2008, Apple unveiled a software development kit for the iPhone, and the venture-capital firm Kleiner Perkins Caufield & Byers set up the iFund, a $100 million fund to invest in applications for Apple's smartphone. Google responded with the $10 million Android Developer Challenge.[18] Although the Challenge could not rival the iFund in the magnitude of its monetary rewards, it attracted app developers in search of exposure.

In July 2008, Apple launched the App Store, which featured applications for both the iPhone and the iPod touch (a cut-down version of the iPhone, without communication facilities, sold as a media player).Two months after launch, over 3,000 apps were available on the App Store and users the world over had already made more than 100 million app downloads.

Google's own app store, Android Market, was announced in August 2008. By the following year, it had become clear that third-party applications would drive the growth of the smartphone business, and all the major smartphone players—including BlackBerry and Microsoft—were either seriously considering or already involved in the launch of an app store to compete with Apple's.

By September 2012, about 700,000 apps were available on Apple's App Store and users had made roughly 35 billion app downloads. But Android Market (renamed Google Play in March 2012) was catching up—it had 675,000 apps available and 25 billion app downloads.

SMARTPHONES: RECENT DEVELOPMENTS

In recent years, the rise of iOS and Android and the corresponding decline of the incumbents (Symbian and the BlackBerry OS) brought about important realignments in the industry. After Apple introduced an improved smartphone, the iPhone 3G, in mid-2008, Nokia, which owned 48 percent of Symbian, announced that it would buy the remaining 52 percent from the other stakeholders and would then set up the Symbian Foundation to "unify" and "open source" the Symbian operating system for smartphones.[19]

The Symbian Foundation—whose founding members included Nokia, Sony Ericsson, Motorola, NTT DOCOMO, AT&T, LG Electronics, Samsung Electronics, Texas Instruments STMicroelectronics, and Vodafone—was an attempt by some of the key industry players to stop the decline of what had been the leading mobile operating system in the world. The attempt was unsuccessful and by late 2010, the Foundation had become purely a licensing body.

Although Nokia continued supporting the development of the Symbian operating system in theory, in practice it searched for alternatives to remain competitive in the changing smartphone market. In February 2011, Nokia announced a mobile phone partnership with Microsoft. The agreement specified that Nokia would use Microsoft's Windows 7 as the primary operating system on its mobile phones and announced the partners' intent to establish a third ecosystem that encompassed app developers and network operators. Nokia chose to form an alliance with Microsoft, as opposed to adopting Android as its mobile operating system, because it feared it would be difficult to differentiate its brand in the Android ecosystem. It chose to be the key handset maker on the Windows platform rather than being one among many on the Android platform, even though the installed base of Microsoft's mobile platform did not compare with that of Google's.

RIM, the other incumbent in decline, tried a different strategy to stay competitive. It developed a new operating system, BlackBerry 10, and unveiled it in early 2013 at the same time that it renamed the company itself BlackBerry.

Figure 11.1 tracks worldwide market shares for mobile operating systems between 2007 and 2012. Although Symbian continued to grow up to 2010,

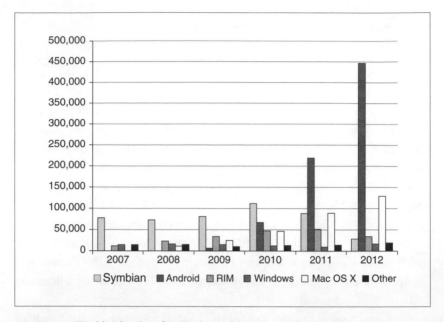

Figure 11.1. Worldwide sales of smartphones by operating system, 2007–2012. Units in thousands.

Source: M. Campbell-Kelly, D. Garcia-Swartz, R. Lam, and Y. Yang, "Economic and Business Perspectives on Smartphones as Multi-Sided Platforms," *Telecommunications Policy* (2015, forthcoming) and the sources cited therein.

its share of the rapidly growing market was in decline. By 2012, it had been completely eclipsed by iOS and Android.

TABLET COMPUTERS

Current-generation tablet computers are portable computing devices that evolved from the user experience and technologies of smartphones, equipped with larger screens and stripped of their telephony functions. Although the introduction of Apple's iPad in April 2010 changed the tablet market in a radical way, the concept of the tablet computer was developed much earlier. In the 1970s and 1980s, there were several attempts by Xerox, Palm, Microsoft, Apple and others to develop a handheld computer in tablet form. These efforts were unsuccessful commercially, but the technologies developed subsequently evolved into smartphones and then tablet computers.[20]

The earliest design for a tablet-style computer came from a Xerox's PARC research group led by the computer scientist Alan Kay, which set out to develop a portable computing device called the Dynabook in the early 1970s. Chuck Thacker and Butler Lampson, the two PARC engineers who worked with Kay on the project, built the Alto desktop computer, the closest they were able to get to the Dynabook concept with the technology then available. Xerox subsequently launched desktop computer products (the Star and model 810) based on the Alto in the early 1980s, but they were unsuccessful due to their high price, as discussed in Chapter 7. Apple later adopted Xerox PARC's ideas for its Macintosh computer.

In 1987, Apple engineer Steve Sakoman, who had helped lead the teams responsible for the development of various Macintosh models, started working on an Apple tablet computer, the Newton.[21] The first version of the Newton, called MessagePad, did not reach the market until mid-1993. Handwriting recognition, which was supposed to be one of its key features, worked imperfectly at best. Between 1993 and 1997, Apple introduced eight different Newton models, mostly under the MessagePad name, with modest results. By early 1998, when the project was discontinued, the firm had reportedly invested half a billion dollars into its development and marketing, achieving an installed base of at most 300,000 devices at a time when the installed base of Windows CE handheld computers was about 500,000.

The same two engineers who built the Alto in the 1970s, Thacker and Lampson, headed a design team at Microsoft that, in the late 1990s and early 2000s, developed the company's Tablet PC device. Although the prototype looked promising, Microsoft's Tablet PC (and those made by other manufacturers) remained a niche product. By 2005, Tablet PCs accounted for 1.5 percent of portable PCs sold worldwide. Among the main reasons for the early tablet computers' limited success were their stylus-based, unfriendly interface (compared with the later touch screen) and the lack of tablet-specific software applications.

Just as there was a "before" and "after" the iPhone in the market for smartphones, there was a "before" and "after" the iPad in the market for tablet computers. Introduced in January 2010, the iPad was, according to the Apple news release, a "revolutionary device" designed for browsing the web, reading and sending e-mail, viewing pictures, watching videos, listening to music, playing games, and reading e-books.[22] Out of 16 million tablet computers shipped worldwide in 2010, 15 million were from Apple.[23]

Competition in the tablet market intensified in 2011, coming mainly from Android-based devices. Apple's share of the table market declined to almost 67 percent in 2011, and Android's share grew to almost 29 percent, with smaller players, such as BlackBerry, accounting for the rest. As this book was going to press, the market for tablet computers remained strongly contested, with Microsoft having introduced a hardware product, the Surface, in June 2012, as well as adding interface improvements to its Windows 8 operating system that make it suitable for tablet devices.

THE IMPACT OF THE COMMERCIAL INTERNET: TAKING STOCK

The period from 1995 to 2010 (and beyond) has been one of standards diversity. System/360 and its compatible successors still reign supreme in the world of mainframes, whereas the IBM PC standard still dominates the personal computer segment. Computers of various kinds have been connected with one another through a network of networks, the Internet, built around open standards. The arrival of the "mobile Internet" has brought to the forefront new standard battles, particularly between Apple's iOS and Google's Android.

Although the arrival of the commercial Internet brought about the demise neither of the mainframe nor of the personal computer, the rise of the mobile Internet in recent years is having a major impact on the computer scene. In early April 2013, news agencies reported that worldwide personal computer shipments in the first quarter of the year had declined by more than 10 percent relative to the same period in 2012, the greatest drop on record.[24] Analysts declared that a tipping point had been reached and that mobile computing was in the ascendant.

Whether a new era of computing—the "mobile Internet" computing cycle—has begun or not is debatable, but new trends in computing are certainly evident. Users are flocking to smaller and lighter computing devices that allow them to access the Internet from anywhere at any time; the mouse-driven and touch-pad user interfaces are giving way to the touchscreen; and "apps" created for smartphones and tablets increasingly compete with the web as channels for accessing Internet content.[25]

Mobile devices are both complements and substitutes for desktops and notebooks. Many computer users have acquired smartphones and tablets in addition to, and not as a replacement for, the devices they already own. More generally, smartphones and tablets have tended to replace desktops and note-books for content consumption—listening to music, viewing pictures, watching videos, playing games, and general Internet browsing—while traditional personal computers have held their own in content creation—creating and editing spreadsheets and documents, among other things. But since, according to some surveys, 75 percent of computer usage is content consumption and sharing, rather than content creation, the rise of smartphones and tablets will likely cannibalize personal computer usage, and has already started to do so.

CHAPTER TWELVE

Globalization

Globalization of the computer industry accelerated dramatically between 1995 and 2010. This globalization involved hardware, software, and services, but it was deeper, and happened earlier, in hardware than in software and services.

EVIDENCE OF GLOBALIZATION

Table 12.1 presents the top 10 computer hardware firms in the world in 2009, and Table 12.2 shows the top 20 in computer software and services. (Classifying an enterprise as a "hardware" or "software" firm is somewhat arbitrary, since many of the top IT companies are highly diversified; a firm is ranked by analysts according to the segment in which the company was generating the most revenues in any given year.) The tables show that many more non-U.S. companies made it to the top 10 in hardware than in software and services.[1]

Seven non-American companies were in the top 10 in the hardware segment in 2009, but only four made it to the top 10 in software and services in that year. (The case of Accenture is peculiar: it was born as the IT consulting arm of Arthur Andersen, incorporated originally in Bermuda, and changed its place of incorporation to Ireland in 2009.) Furthermore, despite the fact

Table 12.1.   Top 10 Computer Hardware Firms in 2009 (Revenues in USD Million)

Company	Country	Estimated hardware revenues	Total revenues
Hewlett-Packard	United States	74,675	114,552
Hon Hai Precision Industry	Taiwan	61,810	61,810
Dell	United States	43,697	52,902
Toshiba	Japan	41,502	72,112
Apple	United States	36,458	42,905
Quanta Computer	Taiwan	25,946	25,946
ASUSTek Computer	Taiwan	18,907	18,907
NEC	Japan	18,696	38,528
Acer	Taiwan	17,787	17,787
Compal Electronics	Taiwan	15,171	15,171

Source: OECD Information Technology Outlook 2010 (Paris: OECD, 2010), and annual reports for Hewlett-Packard, Dell, Apple, Toshiba, and NEC.

that a significant literature exists with a focus on the rise of Israel, Ireland, and India, not many companies from these countries were in the top 10 in either segment as of 2009. In computer hardware, there were none. In computer software and services, the Ireland-based Accenture was ranked fifth, whereas the two largest Indian software-services companies—Wipro and TCS—ranked at the bottom of the top 20 list. Amdocs, the largest Israeli software firm, ranked only thirtieth. The most striking fact about these rankings is the strong presence of Taiwanese companies in the upper echelons of the computer hardware segment.

The tables also reveal that by the end of the first decade of the twenty-first century, none of the European national champions were in the top spots of the international computer industry. In 1999, Fujitsu, which owned a majority stake in ICL since 1990, and Siemens, the German champion, founded the joint venture Fujitsu Siemens Computers. The venture absorbed almost all of ICL and Siemens-Nixdorf's computer hardware business combined, and it became an important player in the server, PC, and data storage markets. In 2009, Fujitsu acquired the Siemens stake in Fujitsu Siemens and the company became Fujitsu Technology Solutions, a subsidiary of Fujitsu Ltd. Thus, in practice, the computer operations of ICL, Siemens, and Nixdorf were subsumed under the Fujitsu Technology Solutions name. Although Fujitsu no longer features among the dominant hardware firms, it ranked third in software and services in 2009.

Table 12.2.   Top 20 Computer Software and Services Companies in 2009
(Revenues in USD Million)

Company	Country	Software and services revenues	Total revenues
IBM	United States	74,934	95,758
Microsoft	United States	50,820	58,573
Fujitsu	Japan	27,539	50,317
Oracle	United States	23,252	23,252
Accenture	Ireland	21,577	23,171
CSC	United States	16,740	16,740
SAP	Germany	15,235	15,295
EMC	United States	14,026	14,026
Hitachi	Japan	12,254	96,436
Lockheed Martin	United States	12,130	45,198
Capgemini	France	11,674	11,674
NTT Data	Japan	11,387	11,387
SAIC	United States	10,070	10,070
ACS	United States	6,523	6,523
Symantec	United States	6,150	6,150
Logica	United Kingdom	5,797	5,797
SunGard Data Systems	United States	5,345	5,508
Wipro	India	5,004	5,004
TCS	India	4,889	4,889
Sun Microsystems	United States	4,745	11,449

Source: "Top 500 in Software," *Software Magazine,* 2010; Fujitsu's data estimated from annual report.

Groupe Bull was the only one of the European national champions that managed to preserve the brand. As explained in Chapter 9, between 1995 and 1997, Groupe Bull was gradually privatized, with France Télécom and NEC becoming core shareholders and the state's stake reduced to about 17 percent. After going through a period of rapidly changing fortunes in the late 1990s, the company underwent a radical restructuring process in the early 2000s that ended up in recapitalization and full privatization in 2004.

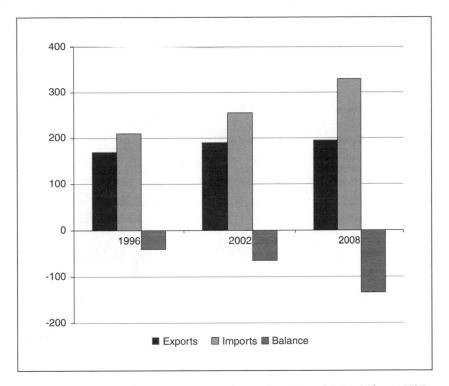

Figure 12.1. OECD trade in computer goods, 1996, 2002, and 2008. Value in USD billion.
Source: OECD Information Technology Outlook, 2010 (Paris: OECD, 2010), 104.

In any case, by 2009, Groupe Bull was not large enough to rank among the top firms in any industry segment.

International trade in computers increased significantly after 1995. Figure 12.1 presents the value of the Organization for Economic Co-operation and Development (OECD) trade in computer goods—including computers and peripheral equipment but excluding software products—in 1996, 2002, and 2008. (During this period, the OECD included more than 20 European countries plus Australia, Canada, Japan, Mexico, New Zealand, South Korea, and the United States.) Figure 12.2 presents the value of OECD trade in computer services in 1996 and 2008. As can be inferred from the figures, the OECD has consistently been an importer of computer goods and an exporter of computer services since 1995, and this has become increasingly true over time.

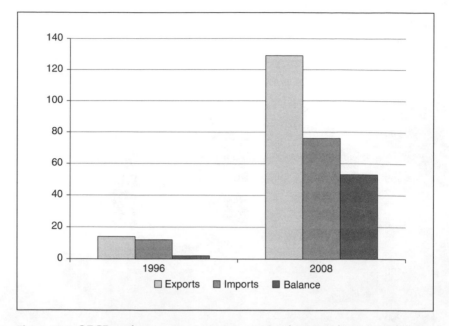

Figure 12.2. OECD trade in computer services, 1996 and 2008. Value in USD billion. *Source: OECD Information Technology Outlook, 2010* (Paris: OECD, 2010), 85.

Between 1996 and 2008, the total value of traded computer goods (excluding software products) increased from $380 billion to $525 billion, and the corresponding value for computer services rose from $26 billion to $205 billion. Although the value of traded computer goods exceeded the value of the services trade generally, computer services rose much faster than computer goods. These trends indicate growing globalization of the computer industry after 1995, but with the process happening earlier in computer hardware and with computer services catching up more recently.

GLOBALIZATION OF COMPUTER HARDWARE PRODUCTION

Behind the growth in international trade in computer goods and services lies a deeper process that has been taking place for several decades and has accelerated in recent years: the relocation of production away from traditional areas. Figure 12.3 summarizes the tectonic shifts that have occurred in the past 30 years in the international localization of computer hardware production.

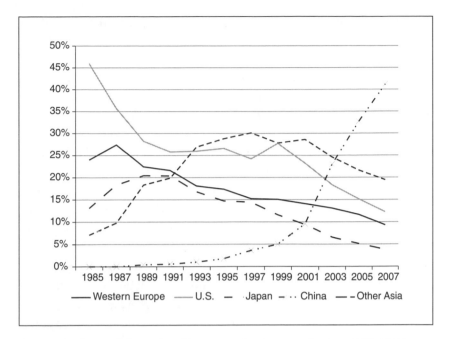

Figure 12.3. Regional share of world computer-hardware production, 1985–2007. Percentage of total value.

Notes: "Other Asia" includes Australia, Hong Kong, India, Indonesia, New Zealand, the Philippines, Singapore, South Korea, Taiwan, Thailand, and Vietnam. Shares at each point in time do not add up to exactly 100 because a few areas have been excluded.
Source: Reed Electronics Research, *Reed Yearbook of World Electronics Data*, 1985–2007.

In 1985, when personal computers began to penetrate the computer world, the United States was the international leader in the production of computer hardware, and Europe and Japan followed far behind. The Asian Tigers (Hong Kong, Singapore, South Korea, and Taiwan), which make up a good portion of "Other Asia" in the figure, had started to appear on the horizon but accounted for less than 10 percent of the total, while China had negligible output of computer hardware. By 1995, when the commercial Internet was beginning to expand, the share of the traditional powerhouses—Europe, the United States, and Japan—was declining at a steady pace, and the countries in the "Other Asia" region—mainly the Asian Tigers—already had the largest share of global production.

In the years that followed, the international distribution of production continued shifting. By 2007, Europe, the United States, and Japan (combined) accounted for only 25 percent of total world production. The share of the Asian countries other than China peaked in the late 1990s and declined consistently thereafter to less than 20 percent in 2007. That year, China accounted for a remarkable 41 percent of the world production of computer hardware. In just seven years, China's share went from less than 10 percent to more than 40 percent. This geographic relocation of production was facilitated by the modularity of the personal computer. As explained in Chapter 9, this made it possible for firms located in different parts of the world to enter the personal computer industry as component manufacturers.[2]

Modularity and international wage differentials led to vertical disintegration and internationalization. At first, component manufacturing migrated to Asian-Tiger countries, particularly Taiwan, and then migrated further to China and other countries, with final assembly often remaining in the United States and Mexico. Because the personal computer quickly became a commodity, companies competed not on product quality but on the effectiveness of their logistics and value-chain management more generally.[3]

Although the existing information on mainframe manufacturing is scarce and fragmented, it does not appear that the relocation of hardware production described here has affected mainframes in the same way as it has personal computers. When IBM introduced a new mainframe model, the zEnterprise EC12, in 2012, it became clear that the company intended to continue manufacturing mainframes mostly in the United States while at the same time globalizing its operations and workforce and shrinking its manufacturing business. Parts for IBM's mainframes are made at IBM's facilities in the United States—in Endicott and Fishkill, in the state of New York—and in Germany, and the final assembly is carried out in Poughkeepsie, New York, where the company inaugurated a $30 million plant in 2010.[4]

Understanding the globalization of personal computer hardware production requires that we examine the roles played by some of the new countries and their companies, which we do next by focusing on Taiwan, China, and Mexico.

As explained in Chapter 9, Taiwan became a player in the international computer industry in the 1980s, when small Taiwanese firms, taking advantage of international wage differentials, started producing motherboards for internationally branded personal computer firms. This so-called original equipment manufacturer (OEM) business model eventually came to pervade the Taiwanese personal computer industry. Economies of scale in production were achieved as the international market for personal computers expanded rapidly in the 1980s and early 1990s and volume orders flowed from the world industry leaders to the Taiwanese producers.

As the Taiwanese personal computer industry grew in size and complexity, a variety of business models developed.[5] Dozens of firms operated as component suppliers, selling their products—memory units, monitors, motherboards, connectors, and power supplies, for example—to Taiwanese original design manufacturers (ODMs) such as Quanta, Compal, Wistron, ASUSTek, Mitac, and Inventec. (The ODM business is like the OEM business, but an ODM also contributes a portion of the design for the product.) The ODMs thus became the key link between the component makers and the branded personal computer manufacturers such as Apple, Dell, Hewlett-Packard, and NEC, with the latter increasingly outsourcing not only assembly but also new product development to the ODMs.

Very few of the Taiwanese ODMs were able to develop their own, international brand. The ones that did—ASUSTek is one of the prime examples—were technically oriented but made consistent investments in branding and marketing. ASUSTek, later to become the world's largest motherboard maker, was formed in 1989 by four ex-Acer engineers. Under a new CEO, an ex-Acer employee who took the helm at ASUSTek in the early 1990s, the company developed into a highly technically oriented firm with a business culture that emphasized in-house R&D to an extent that was unusual among Taiwanese personal computer companies.

When Intel temporarily ramped up its own motherboard business in the mid-1990s, many of the Taiwanese manufacturers suffered, but ASUSTek (and a few other technically oriented motherboard makers) expanded to dominate the domestic and international market. By 2000, the big four Taiwanese makers, including ASUSTek, accounted for 60 percent of the country's shipments, and Taiwan as a whole accounted for 84 percent of the world market for motherboards.[6]

Another avenue for the rise of the Taiwanese ODMs was the growth in international shipments of portable computers (later known as laptops). After the first portable was introduced by Compaq in 1982 and demand for portables started growing, several manufacturers of personal computers—

including IBM, Apple, Toshiba, and Epson—jumped on the bandwagon and introduced their own products. This in turn created the conditions for several Taiwanese companies to enter the market as suppliers of components and as assemblers for companies such as Dell, Hewlett-Packard, and IBM.

By 1987, Taiwan had become the top manufacturer of pocket calculators in the world, and laptop manufacturing required competencies similar to those seen in calculator manufacturing—design integration and miniaturization. Taiwanese pocket calculator manufacturers, which up to that point had been OEMs for Japanese firms in the calculator business, saw in the laptop an opportunity to move into an adjacent market—and they took it. Laptops produced in Taiwan represented 40 percent of the global market by 1998 and 91 percent by 2009, with Quanta, Compal, Wistron, Inventec, ASUSTek, and Mitac among the market leaders.

The two Taiwanese companies that were most successful in developing an international brand, ASUSTek and Acer, faced an increasing tension between the OEM and the own-brand sides of their business. As explained in Chapter 9, Acer had built a solid reputation in the 1980s as an OEM/ODM for U.S.-based computer makers, while at the same time marketing its own, Acer-branded, IBM-compatible personal computers. Acer expanded into the international personal computer scene by focusing on the European market, where distributors were more receptive to Taiwanese-branded PCs than their American counterparts. Internal tensions at Acer grew in the 1990s because the OEM side of the business required excellence only in the manufacturing process, whereas the own-brand side of the business demanded substantial investments in the development of capabilities in branding, marketing, sales, distribution, and customer support, which in turn meant lower profit margins in the short run. By the late 1990s, it had become clear that Acer could not maintain both segments of the business together, not least because of client conflicts. In 2001, Acer decided to spin off the manufacturing business, which it did the following year by creating the Wistron Corporation.

Like Acer, ASUSTek focused on Europe initially to develop its branding and marketing capabilities, establishing close relationships with local distributors. By the mid-2000s, ASUSTek had become a major player in the world laptop market, shipping 3.8 million units in 2005, of which 2.3 million were manufactured for others firms to rebadge as their own brands. By this time, the company was shipping more own-brand laptops than Sony and Apple, the two largest ASUSTek clients on the OEM/ODM side of the business. ASUSTek ended up spinning off its manufacturing operations into a subsidiary, Pegatron, in early 2008, with ASUSTek retaining the brand and becoming essentially a marketing business.

Unlike ASUSTek and Acer, which developed their own brands, most Taiwanese OEM/ODMs remain almost unknown outside the country. Until recently, this included Hon Hai Precision Industry, also known as Foxconn, which was the second-largest computer hardware manufacturer in the world in 2009 after HP (see Table 12.1). Founded in Taipei in 1974, Hon Hai started out as an OEM for TV makers and expanded into personal computer components in the 1980s.[7] Orders for Foxconn's products grew as the international personal computer industry expanded. Rising production costs in Taiwan prompted Foxconn to open its first manufacturing facility in China in 1988. Over time, the company evolved from manufacturing components to building finished products in-house, and this enabled it to offer complete system manufacture on an OEM/ODM basis. By 2007, its customer list included Apple (for the iPhone and some iPod models), Dell and Hewlett-Packard (for desktop PCs and parts), Nokia and Motorola (for mobile phones and parts), and Sony and Nintendo (for videogame consoles). Although headquartered in Taiwan, the company had manufacturing facilities in China, the Czech Republic, Hungary, Mexico, Brazil, India, and Vietnam.

Computer manufacturing started playing an important role in Chinese economic policy in the second half of the 1980s, when the Seventh Development Plan—formally the "Seventh Five-Year Plan for National Economic and Social Development of the People's Republic of China"—identified the domestic electronics industry as crucial for the development of the entire economy. In the Ninth Development Plan (1996–2000), the Chinese government set out to increase the share of domestic components in computers assembled in China and to help two or three domestic personal computer companies achieve annual production capacities of no less than $1 billion. The government invited foreign computer makers to establish joint ventures with domestic firms and to effectuate technology transfers in exchange for production licenses and access to the highly attractive Chinese domestic market. Joint ventures were established between IBM, Compaq, Hewlett-Packard, Toshiba, NEC, and LG Electronics, on the one hand, and some of the local personal computer manufacturers such as Great Wall, Stone Group, Star Group, Legend, Founder, and Tontru, on the other.

Several of the domestic computer makers—including Great Wall, Legend, and Founder—benefited both from their alliances with foreign PC makers and from preferential government procurement policies, and grew to become important players in the Chinese domestic market. Foreign computer manufacturers set up production facilities in China in the 1990s and captured as much as 60 percent of the local market in the early years, but their market shares declined in the late 1990s as domestic producers engaged in price-cutting and became more competitive.

Taiwanese companies played an especially important role in the development of the Chinese computer industry. Originally, their entry into China was driven by an attempt to lower production costs, but starting in the mid-1990s, they ramped up investments in China and expanded the scale and scope of production to include personal computer manufacturing. By the year 2000, Taiwanese companies had most of their production located in China.

In the first decade of the twenty-first century, the role of China as the world's manufacturer of computers and peripherals grew at a breathtaking pace. Chinese exports of computer equipment rose almost by a factor of 10 between 2000 and 2008 (from $17.8 billion to $168.2 billion), and its trade surplus by a factor of almost 17 (from $7.6 billion to $127 billion). The counterpart of this was an increase in the OECD's trade deficit in computers from $66.7 billion in 2000 to $134 billion in 2008.[8]

Lenovo is the one Chinese computer company that has been successful in establishing an international brand. Previously trading as The Legend Group, it launched the first Legend PC in the Chinese market in 1990. By 1996, the year the company introduced its first own-brand laptop, Legend had become the leader in the Chinese personal computer market, and by the end of the decade it was the top PC vendor in the Asia-Pacific region. The rebranding from Legend to Lenovo took place in 2003. The following year, Lenovo announced that it would acquire IBM's PC division, a transaction completed in 2005.

By late 2012, Lenovo had become, with Hewlett-Packard, one of the top two personal computer makers in the world. It was the leading supplier in five of the top seven personal computer markets in the world, including Japan and Germany, and its mobile division had become a strong contender in the Chinese smartphone market.[9]

Mexico was another country that played an increasingly important role in the geographic restructuring of the international personal computer hardware industry.[10] Until the 1980s, Mexican economic policies were geared toward import substitution, with both domestic and foreign-owned companies building up production capacity to supply a heavily protected local market. The first economic policy measures centered on the computer industry were introduced in the 1980s, when the government formulated the so-called Programa de Cómputo, which shifted the focus from import substitution to export promotion and the development of local technological capabilities. The program limited foreign ownership to 49 percent in the production of personal computers and peripherals and required that a minimum quota of domestic parts and components be used in the assembly of personal computers and minicomputers.

In the 1980s, trade deficits in computer equipment became a concern for the Mexican government, which, contrary to the requirements of the Programa de Cómputo, ended up granting IBM the right to fully own its new plant in Guadalajara. Encouraged by the fact that IBM's exports from Mexico made an important contribution toward reducing the country's trade deficit in computer equipment, the government relaxed its import barriers in the late 1980s, enabling domestic firms to assemble Asian personal computers. The North American Free Trade Agreement linking Canada, Mexico, and the United States (NAFTA) liberalized the market further, with personal computer tariffs reduced to zero in 1998.

In the 1990s, with liberalization and NAFTA in full swing, Mexico became essentially a platform for foreign companies to perform final assembly of computer products for export to the American market. Both labor and logistics costs played a role. Unlike the consumer electronics industry, which tended to cluster along the Mexican-U.S. border, the computer industry in Mexico tended to locate in Guadalajara, in the central western section of the country, where wages were somewhat lower than further north.

The main computer companies locating there were foreign multinational corporations, including IBM, Hewlett-Packard, and Acer, and some Asian manufacturers of TV sets and computer monitors. Another breed of companies that also set foot in Mexico in the second half of the 1990s were the large so-called contract manufacturers, which supplied both components and assembled computers to the internationally branded PC companies on an OEM basis. Among the largest in this class were the California-based Solectron and the Singapore-based Flextronics. (Flextronics acquired Solectron in 2007.) They were attracted both by the presence of large customers such as IBM and by logistical cost advantages—proximity to the immense U.S. market more than compensated for somewhat higher wages in Mexico than in Asia. Although early on the industry focused on assembly, it later became more diversified.

GLOBALIZATION OF THE SOFTWARE PRODUCTS INDUSTRY

Globalization of the software-products industry has proceeded at a much slower pace than globalization of computer hardware. In 2009, for example, U.S. companies accounted for about 76 percent of the revenues generated by the top 10 computer software and services firms in the world.

Although American companies remained dominant in the international computer software scene after 1995, a few countries started playing a more influential role than they did in the past. Non-U.S. software-product industries tend to be quite heterogeneous, and none can be viewed as typical. Insofar as there is a unifying theme, it is historical path dependency. The industries that have developed have been shaped by preexisting capabilities and relationships. Here we discuss the software-product industries of Israel and Ireland, two of the most successful.[11] In both countries, the software industry is fragmented, with numerous relatively small firms successful in particular software niches, but there are no firms among the world's top 20 from either nation.

By the early 2000s, Israel was, after the United States and Canada, the country with the highest number of IT companies listed on the NASDAQ exchange. Israel's software-product companies pioneered many computer technologies that became market niches in their own right, including voice over Internet protocol (VoIP), encryption, antiviral protection, and firewalls.[12]

Israel's IT industry became a world success story for three main reasons. First, the country had from the beginning a significant defense sector and academic research system. Second, beginning in the early 1970s, the state implemented industrial policies geared toward creating new R&D-intensive products, with private firms (rather than the state) identified as the main agents in charge of conducting R&D. Third, the state favored a division of labor in which indigenous firms specialized in product R&D and multinational corporations acted as marketing conduits.

In 1974, a former chief of staff of the Israeli military was recruited to become the government's first full-time chief scientist. From this point on, the Office of the Chief Scientist (OCS) played a central role in formulating and implementing Israel's industrial policies. The other institution that helped develop the Israeli IT industry was the BIRD (Bi-national Industrial Research and Development) Foundation, formed in 1976 with the goal of fostering cooperation between Israeli and American firms in the joint development and marketing of new products.

The first product-oriented software companies were founded in the late 1970s and early 1980s. They served sophisticated customers, mainly in the defense establishment, and marketed products that addressed problems usually arising from the software development process itself. Critical to the growth of the early software companies was the support they received in the form of OCS grants.

This pattern continued during the 1980s, when several IT companies— including Gilat Satellite, Comverse, and Mercury—were formed in Israel with support from the OCS and the BIRD Foundation. Comverse focused originally on centralized voice and fax-messaging hardware systems and transitioned into software in the 1990s, when it expanded quickly because its voicemail software was used in mobile phones, a booming industry in that decade. Mercury Interactive was formed to develop a software-debugging tool, but in the second half of the 1990s shifted its development efforts toward testing and analyzing the performance of enterprise and Web-based applications.

The changes that took place in the telecommunications industry all over the world in the late 1980s and throughout the 1990s gave rise to opportunities for hardware and software firms that thrived in niche markets. Perhaps nothing exemplifies better the growth of Israeli firms in niche telecom markets than the story of Amdocs, founded in 1982. The firm, originally called Aurec, started as a provider of automated telephone directory systems and later moved into billing and CRM systems for the telecom industry as well. By the early 2000s, it was a full-service software company catering to all the needs of the industry.

Security software was another niche in which Israeli companies thrived. As explained in Chapter 10, one of the main effects of the growth of the commercial Internet was the increasing demand for security software. The firewall, for example, is a piece of software that protects networks from unwanted intrusions and attacks. Although firewall technologies were tested in the United States in the late 1980s, the technology that eventually became dominant was developed in the context of Israeli military networks that predated the commercial Internet. Its inventor, Gil Shwed, founded Check Point in 1993 to commercialize its main product, FireWall-1, which started encountering strong demand among civilian customers after 1995. By early 1996, Check Point was the worldwide market leader in firewall software with a 40 percent share. In the first decade of the twenty-first century, the company expanded through acquisitions and by 2011 had more than $1 billion in annual revenues.[13]

By the end of 2003, the Irish software industry was made up of 900 firms, employed almost 24,000 people, and generated total revenues of about $18 billion, mostly from exports.[14]

Ireland's industrial policies were oriented by Department of Finance secretary T. K. Whitaker's *First Programme for Economic Expansion,* a pivotal document published in 1958. The main problem to be addressed by industrial policy was job creation, and the means for addressing it was attracting foreign direct investment. Over time, this translated into providing incentives to foreign (mainly American) multinational corporations to locate in Ireland and engage in manufacturing activities for export. The institutional vehicle for putting this policy into practice was the Industrial Development Authority (IDA).

This economic policy background explains why the Irish software industry has traditionally consisted of two sectors: foreign and domestic. The foreign segment, dominated by U.S.-based multinational corporations, has tended to focus on software logistics and localization—that is, the adaptation of software created in the United States to the needs of various European national markets. The domestic segment, made up of smaller companies, has concentrated on software-product development. Some of the domestically owned companies have become important international players in specific market niches.

Foreign software companies established three different types of operations in the country: some of them—including Microsoft, Oracle, Novell, Lotus, and Symantec—specialized in manufacturing, distributing, and localizing software packages; others, such as Amdahl DMR Ireland, IBM, EDS Ireland, and Accenture, supplied systems integration and software services; and a third group of companies—including Ericsson, Alcatel, Siemens, Lucent Technologies, Motorola, and Compaq—set up dedicated software development centers. By 1992, 15 of the world's top 40 software companies had operations in Ireland.

The first indigenous software companies in Ireland were founded in the 1960s and 1970s, as the multinational corporations were starting to move into the country. In the 1970s and early 1980s, some of the large computer manufacturers—including DEC, IBM, and ICL—started offering their hardware with software packages created by Irish software companies in bundled deals. The banking software specialist Kindle Banking Systems, for example, was formed in 1981 to create financial systems for ICL hardware and developed a reputation in the international market. In the mid-1980s, many Irish software companies made the transition from software consulting to software products. Insight Software and Real-Time Software (RTS), for example, developed products that worked on Maapics, the main minicomputer-based IBM software suite for manufacturing facilities.

The early development of the software industry in Ireland was thus fundamentally different from that in Israel. The first Israeli-based software companies were established within a system of innovation where R&D was a priority, and thus many of them focused on developing software tools, while the early software firms in Ireland created products for specific industries, including finance, insurance, and manufacturing control. Irish software companies that concentrated on developing software tools started appearing only in the 1990s.

A further stimulus to the growth of the Irish software industry in the 1990s came from the connections between Irish educational institutions and the European Union. From the late 1980s on, and with greater intensity in the 1990s, Irish colleges and universities—and Trinity College, University of Dublin (TCD), especially—started participating in research programs funded by the European Union. Trinity's Computer Science Department became one of the largest beneficiaries in Europe of ESPRIT grants for computer science. The most important software company to come out of TCD was Iona, a company founded to market products implementing an internationally recognized software standard named CORBA. (CORBA enables pieces of software written in multiple languages and for diverse computer platforms to interoperate with one another.)[15]

The domestic sector of the Irish software industry reached a high point in the late 1990s, when six Irish software companies listed on NASDAQ. In the early 2000s, following the dot-com bust, the domestic segment of the industry declined, with employment, revenues, and exports deteriorating. While the Irish indigenous software companies retreated, however, the multinational corporations in Ireland expanded, extending their R&D activities by acquiring Irish IT firms and by setting up their own in-house R&D facilities in the country.

GLOBALIZATION OF COMPUTER SERVICES

The globalization of software services has received attention in the trade and academic press because of the rise to prominence of a number of Indian companies. The evidence shows, however, that, just as in the case of software, globalization in services has proceeded much more slowly than in hardware. None of the Indian companies often cited as examples of globalization, such as Wipro and TCS, were among the top 10 in 2009. In that year, the top computer-services company in the world, IBM, had computer-services revenues of about $55 billion, more than 10 times as much as Wipro, the largest of the major Indian computer-services firms.[16]

Very little IT activity existed in India before the 1970s. Founded in 1968 to serve the in-house data processing needs of the Tata Group, the largest industrial group in the country, Tata Consulting Services (TCS) was the pioneer firm in the Indian software industry. It started offering electronic data-processing services to outside customers in 1969.

The following year, TCS became Burroughs's exclusive sales agent for India. The Foreign Exchange Regulation Act of 1973 (FERA-1973) forced foreign firms to operate in India only as minority partners in joint ventures. Although the Burroughs-TCS relationship continued, IBM chose to leave the country in 1978. A few companies were established in the mid-1970s under the FERA-1973 model, including a joint venture between American minicomputer maker Wang and a group of former TCS employees.

India's software-services exports started in 1974, fueled by international wage differentials—in that year Burroughs asked TCS to install its systems software at the offices of its American customers. Other domestic companies copied the TCS example, and thus the "body-shopping" model emerged—Indian programmers were "exported" for assignments overseas mostly in system installation and maintenance. By 1980, the industry consisted of 21 firms and generated $4 million in export revenues, 63 percent of which was accounted for by TCS and a sister company, Tata Infotech.[17]

Tata Burroughs Ltd. (later known as Tata Unisys Ltd.) provides an example of how the body-shopping model operated. In the late 1970s, Burroughs (later Unisys) and Tata formed a company named Tata Burroughs Ltd. that allowed the American company to "steal" business from IBM. Burroughs (Unisys) computer sales representatives went to potential customer sites anywhere in the world where IBM mainframes were installed and offered to convert all the existing IBM software to run on Unisys hardware at no cost to the customer. Taking advantage of the opportunity to rely on low-cost programming services from Tata Unisys Ltd., the salespeople also offered to create new applications software at two-thirds the market rate. For Tata Unisys Ltd., this was a two-edged sword—although it received a steady flow of business from Unisys's clients internationally, it also became heavily dependent on the ups and downs of the Unisys computer business.

In the mid-1980s, a combination of policies and industry developments provided a boost to the incipient Indian software-services industry. In 1984, the government introduced a series of liberalization policy measures related to IT. The New Computer Policy (NCP-1984) reduced import duties on computer hardware and software, recognized the software business as an "industry" (which made it eligible for loans from commercial banks), "de-licensed" it (which meant that permits were no longer required to enter the industry), and allowed for the operation of wholly foreign-owned firms developing software for export. Electronics export processing zones—with subsidized rental rates for office space and guaranteed power and water—started including software firms as well. In 1985, all export revenues from these zones were deemed exempt from income tax. These incentives helped develop an Indian IT industry geared toward catering to the foreign demand for software services.

These policy measures were introduced around the same time that developments in software architectures enabled projects to be more readily divided into discrete programming tasks, and improvements in telecoms enabled them to be done remotely. Indian programmers were now able to work on discrete portions of huge projects without leaving their home country. In the mid-1980s, several American multinational corporations opened wholly owned subsidiaries in India to carry out software development. Texas Instruments was the first, and HP and DEC followed. A few years later, international banking institutions with Indian operations and call centers, such as Citibank, started producing custom software in India as well. The Indian software industry matured after 1985, as the trend toward software off-shoring intensified. The number of software firms in India rose from 35 before the reforms of the mid-1980s to 700 in 1990.[18]

Another major reform period began in 1991. Recognizing that the domestic software-services industry required inputs from abroad, the government reduced import tariffs on software and hardware, which had risen again since the earlier reforms. The telecommunications infrastructure became more liberalized starting in 1995, and a venture-capital industry emerged. Indian firms were also allowed to spend their export earnings on opening offices abroad, which helped Indian software companies in a number of ways: they obtained access to midsized customers and were able to better serve large clients needing on-site support.

In 1990, there was only one Indian-owned company (TCS) among the top eight software exporters in the country. The rest were either subsidiaries of, or joint ventures with, foreign multinational corporations. By 2000, however, seven of the top eight software exporters were domestic firms—TCS, Infosys, Wipro, Satyam, HCL, Silverline, and NIIT. Apart from TCS, which was still privately owned by the Tata Group, the rest were publicly held companies, and four of them (Infosys, Wipro, Satyam, and Silverline) traded on both Indian and American stock exchanges.[19]

The first decade of the twenty-first century witnessed a process by which the large Indian software-services companies, such as TCS, Infosys, and Wipro, moved up the layers of the software industry, from the bottom layers requiring the least sophistication (such as system maintenance and business process outsourcing) to those requiring the most competence (such as IT systems design and systems integration). Thus, an integrated software-services business model developed in which the top Indian firms started competing across the board with some of the industry's world leaders such as IBM and EDS.

Conclusions

I n our analysis of the computer industry, we have tracked a number of themes: technological change, computers as systems, the rise and fall of standards, the confrontation between proprietary and open standards, the international dimensions of the industry, and the coexistence of persistence and change.

TECHNOLOGICAL CHANGE

Above all, the history of the computer industry is the history of how different companies managed to harness the power of technological change to become market leaders.

In the mid-1950s, IBM exploited the knowledge of ferrite-core memory acquired during the SAGE project to steal the leadership position from Remington Rand in the American mainframe market. Later in the decade, it used the knowledge of semiconductor technology amassed during the STRETCH supercomputer project to consolidate its dominance of the market for second-generation (discrete transistor) data-processing computers. In the mid-1960s, it used its Solid Logic Technology, an early form of integrated-circuit technology, in the market-changing System/360. In the late 1960s and early 1970s, it introduced System/370 models that used true integrated circuits and semiconductor memory. IBM did not invent these technologies but rather perfected them and often found a way to implement them in computers earlier than its competitors.

Intel, established in 1968, provides another example of the role of technological change in the history of the computer industry. Robert Noyce, one of Intel's founders, was the coinventor of the integrated circuit, and Ted Hoff was an Intel employee when, in 1971, he invented the microprocessor, the so-called "computer on a chip." From then on, Intel's technological advances made possible the development of a new segment of the computer industry—personal computers that would soon weaken the dominant role of the mainframe in corporate IT.

Across the industry, technological change shaped the evolution of the industry in two important ways. First, the price of computation fell dramatically from year to year. Second, entry into new computer segments became relatively easier over time—there were a few mainframe manufacturers in the 1950s and 1960s, dozens of minicomputer vendors in the 1970s, and hundreds of personal computer makers in the 1980s and 1990s.

COMPUTERS AS SYSTEMS

Computers are systems—that is, bundles of components (hardware, software, and services). The history of the computer industry is also the narrative of how different players have competed in the process of supplying different components for the system.

Early on, mainframe manufacturers supplied most components themselves. System/360 was, in the mid-1960s, the leading example of this vertically integrated model. By the time IBM introduced System/360, however, there were already signs that the industry had started to specialize and fragment. Independent software houses were supplying corporate software products, while independent manufacturers of peripherals were competing strongly with IBM.

Under a looming antitrust investigation, IBM facilitated the rise of third-party suppliers of system components by unbundling software and services from hardware, a process that started in the late 1960s and deepened in the late 1970s, when IBM unbundled operating-system software. In any case, IBM (and other mainframe manufacturers) did not readily cede the various markets for complements to third-party vendors—competition between IBM and specialist manufacturers of peripherals for mainframes, for example, was intense in the 1960s and 1970s.

Vertical disintegration *did* happen in the industry in the 1980s, as IBM outsourced the key components of its personal computer from third-party vendors. The process continued in the following decades with the key personal computer vendors outsourcing the manufacturing of most, if not all, components first to Taiwanese and later to Chinese companies.

At the same time that the industry was fragmenting and specializing, the revenue-generating locus of the computer system migrated from hardware to software and services. The shift in focus meant that companies that had set out as hardware firms but were not able to adapt to a new world centered on software and services saw their role in the industry diminished. This was exemplified by IBM's fall from grace in the early 1990s, and its subsequent renaissance only when it wholeheartedly embraced the new paradigm.

THE RISE AND FALL OF STANDARDS

Computer standards are technical specifications that dictate how the components of a technological system interoperate with one another. A major theme of the history of the computer industry is the rise and fall of standards. No standard dominated the period from 1950 to 1965. However, when IBM introduced the 1401 in 1959, Honeywell perceived an emerging de facto standard and introduced its model 200, a machine that was "compatible" with the 1401 but had superior price-performance. This strategy anticipated those later observed toward System/360 and the IBM PC.

The next two periods of approximately 15 years were the era of the System/360 standard (1965–1980) and the era of the IBM PC standard (1980–1995). IBM profited from these two standards very differently. It owned the System/360 standard and was rewarded handsomely by that ownership; by contrast, the company did not own the IBM PC standard and thus failed to profit proportionally. The beneficiaries of the latter standard were Microsoft, which owned the DOS and Windows operating systems, and Intel, which owned the microprocessor technology.

The standards generated reactions among competitors that hinged on one crucial decision—whether to compete with IBM by offering computers compatible or incompatible with the standard of the day. They also generated reactions among the creators of complementary products: the makers of software and peripherals, for example, quickly reoriented their strategies toward creating products that conformed to the prevailing standard. Customers also invested in the standard, which gave rise to switching costs and inertia. And, finally, non-U.S. governments reacted to the first standard (System/360) because they perceived it would lead to the American domination of domestic computer markets all over the world.

Once established, computer standards are extremely persistent. The System/360 standard lived on in the System/370 and System/390 computers, and it survives in today's mainframes. The IBM PC standard remains dominant in personal computers. As segments of the industry declined in importance, however, the related standards came to play roles of lesser significance and visibility in the overall computer industry. This happened when personal computers began to displace mainframes and minicomputers, and is happening now as smartphones and tablets are displacing personal computers.

THE BATTLE BETWEEN PROPRIETARY AND OPEN STANDARDS

Rivalry in computer standards entered a new era with the battle between open and proprietary standards in the 1980s. The first open standard of significance was the UNIX operating system. UNIX came to play an important role in the industry at a time when client-server computing had started to displace mainframe-based computing in corporate environments.

The rising importance of UNIX, and open standards more generally, weakened the competitive position of companies that had grown by taking advantage of their own proprietary standards, from Nixdorf in Germany to Apollo in the United States and IBM all over the world. Open standards led to a world in which customers no longer needed to be tied to a single vendor— they could buy components from different suppliers and combine them into well-functioning systems. In combination with the growth of client-server computing, open standards undermined IBM's dominance of the industry in the early 1990s. IBM was forced to drastically cut the price of its mainframes in order to survive.

The current battle between Apple's iOS and Google's Android in smartphones is another example of the proprietary-versus-open standard confrontation. With its iOS platform, Apple implemented the strategy it used in the personal computer market—a closed, proprietary system which enabled it to capture all of the hardware revenues and a high proportion of software and service sales. Google, on the other extreme, has implemented an open standard licensed for free to all comers and with a focus on services rather than hardware—Google does not make money from licensing the software but rather from ads shown on the mobile Internet platform. Proprietary standards confer the maximum degree of control. Open standards provide less control over the evolution of the standard and often lead to fragmentation but also facilitate adoption, as Google's Android strategy suggests.[1]

THE INTERNATIONAL DIMENSIONS OF THE COMPUTER INDUSTRY

Contrary to what is sometimes supposed, the computer industry has had an international flavor from its very beginnings. The key computer ideas in the 1940s and 1950s were developed not only in the United States but also in what has been called a transatlantic community that included several Western European countries.[2]

The global dimensions of the industry evolved both on the demand and the supply sides. On the demand side, the non-U.S. installed base of computers became increasingly important as time went by. On the supply side, a number of non-U.S. companies had achieved reasonably large shares of their domestic markets by the late 1970s. This was especially true in Japan, where the government intervened early and consistently to support the domestic computer vendors.

Although Japanese computer manufacturers were well positioned to compete globally in the late 1970s, the market changed with the advent of microcomputers and personal computers. The modularity of the personal computer, combined with international wage differentials and targeted government support, allowed the Asian Tigers—Taiwan especially—to play a much greater role in the international computer industry than did the Japanese in the 1980s and 1990s. Toshiba, a company that had played a minor role in the mainframe era, was the only Japanese company that found success in a niche of the global personal computer industry (primarily in laptop computers).

During the 1990s and 2000s, computer hardware production shifted from the Asian Tigers to China, while new international players appeared in software (such as Israel and Ireland) and in computer services (notably India).

Globalization of the computer industry, however, occurred much faster in hardware than in any other sector of the industry. Although much has been written about the Indian vendors of software and services, as of 2010, none of them could rival IBM. In fact, in 2011, IBM alone generated more revenues from software and services than the Indian software and services industry in its totality.

PERSISTENCE AND CHANGE

There is, finally, a paradox at the heart of the history of the international computer industry—the coexistence of persistence and change. A superficial interpretation of the industry's history might conclude that all is transient—transitions have occurred from mainframes to minicomputers, then to client-server systems, to personal computers, and most recently to smartphones and tablet computers; the core of the industry has shifted from hardware to software and services; and the location of hardware production has moved from West to East.

A deeper look, however, reveals an underlying persistence in the industry—the persistence of both standards and companies. The persistence of standards is unsurprising, since by their nature standards generate switching costs and therefore inertia.

The persistence of companies at the top of the industry is more surprising, since in such a dynamic industry we would not expect companies to occupy leading positions for long. The secret to the persistence of companies is, in an overworked but fundamentally true phrase of our era, constant reinvention. Only companies that have responded to rapidly evolving technologies and markets have been able to survive and thrive. No one can predict the future of the industry. If history is any guide, however, it is likely that information technologies will continue to evolve and surprise us and to catalyze new global players, some of which will join that elite corps of enterprises that have prospered over many decades.

Notes

INTRODUCTION

1. To our knowledge, one other business history of the computer industry has been published in recent years—the excellent book by J. Yost, *The Computer Industry* (Westport, CT: Greenwood Press, 2005). There are, however, important differences between Yost's book and ours. First, his book provides considerably more detail on the history of individual companies than we do, whereas we provide more abundant statistical information on industry-level developments. Second, his book focuses on the United States only, whereas we cover the evolution of the industry in several other countries. Third, his book does not cover the most recent industry developments, but we do. For all these reasons, his book and our book are complements rather than substitutes.

2. Two insightful analyses of the evolution of the computer industry from an economic perspective are T. Bresnahan and S. Greenstein, "Technological Competition and the Structure of the Computer Industry," *Journal of Industrial Economics* 47, no. 1 (March 1999), and T. Bresnahan and F. Malerba, "Industrial Dynamics and the Evolution of Firms' and Nations' Competitive Capabilities in the World Computer Industry," in *Sources of Industrial Leadership: Studies of Seven Industries,* ed. D. Mowery and R. Nelson (Cambridge: Cambridge University Press, 1999).

3. An early discussion of standards in high-technology industries can be found in P. David and S. Greenstein, "The Economics of Compatibility Standards: An Introduction to Recent Research," *Economics of Innovation and New Technology* 1

(1990). The recent classic by C. Shapiro and H. Varian, *Information Rules: A Strategic Guide to the Network Economy* (Boston: Harvard Business School Press, 1998) examines many of the key economic issues that characterize high-technology industries, including the computer industry, in an exceedingly accessible way. A more technical analysis can be found in J. Farrell and P. Klemperer, "Coordination and Lock-In: Competition with Switching Costs and Network Effects," in *Handbook of Industrial Organization,* vol. 3, ed. M. Armstrong and R. Porter (Amsterdam: North Holland, 2007).

4. The article by Martin Campbell-Kelly and Daniel Garcia-Swartz, "Persistence and Change at the Top of the IT Sector," *International Journal of the Economics of Business* 16, no. 1 (February 2009), uses the "Datamation 100" index to track the main quantitative trends among the leading firms in the computer industry between the mid-1970s and the mid-1990s.

1. THE MAINFRAME COMPUTER INDUSTRY

1. For historical background on the U.S. economy during the period covered in this book, see S. Engerman and R. Gallman, eds., *The Cambridge Economic History of the United States,* vol. 3, *The Twentieth Century* (Cambridge: Cambridge University Press, 2000), especially the chapters on macro-economic growth by M. Abramovitz and P. David, on technological change by D. Mowery and N. Rosenberg, and on the corporate economy by L. Galambos. For background on the economic history of the European countries covered in this book, see B. Eichengreen, *The European Economy since 1945* (Princeton, NJ: Princeton University Press, 2007), and S. Broadberry and K. O'Rourke, eds., *The Cambridge Economic History of Modern Europe,* vol. 2, *1870 to Present* (Cambridge: Cambridge University Press, 2010), especially the chapters in Part III. For the economic history of the East Asian countries covered in this book, see especially D. Perkins, *East Asian Development: Foundations and Strategies* (Cambridge, MA: Harvard University Press, 2013).

2. Information on monthly rental costs for a variety of computer models introduced in the 1950s and 1960s is available in M. Phister, *Data Processing Technology and Economics* (Bedford, MA: Digital Press, 1979), 338–357. On the total cost of operating a computer system in the early years of the industry, see Phister, *Data Processing,* 146ff.

3. On ERA and EMCC, see especially A. L. Norberg, *Computers and Commerce: A Study of Technology and Management at Eckert-Mauchly Computer Company, Engineering Research Associates, and Remington Rand, 1946–1957* (Cambridge, MA: MIT Press, 2005). On ERA, see also E. Tomash, "The Start of an ERA: Engineering Research Associates, Inc., 1946–1955," in *A History of Computing in the Twentieth Century,* ed. N. Metropolis, J. Howlett, and G. C. Rota (New York: Academic Press, 1980), 485–495. A key reference on ERA, and on computer-industry developments in Minnesota more generally, is the excellent recent book by T. Misa, *Digital State:*

The Story of Minnesota's Computing Industry (Minneapolis: University of Minnesota Press, 2013).

4. F. Fisher, J. McKie, and R. Mancke, *IBM and the U.S. Data Processing Industry* (New York: Praeger, 1983), 9–10.

5. For details on the Southern California aerospace industry and its connections with the computer industry in the early years, see especially P. Ceruzzi, *Beyond the Limits: Flight Enters the Computer Age* (Cambridge, MA: MIT Press, 1989).

6. Useful sources on IBM's early forays into computing include C. Bashe, L. Johnson, J. Palmer, and E. Pugh, *IBM's Early Computers* (Cambridge, MA: MIT Press, 1986); E. Pugh, *Memories That Shaped an Industry: Decisions Leading to IBM System/360* (Cambridge, MA: MIT Press, 1984); and E. Pugh, *Building IBM: Shaping an Industry and Its Technology* (Cambridge, MA: MIT Press, 1996). R. DeLamarter, *Big Blue: IBM's Use and Abuse of Power* (New York: Dodd, Mead & Company, 1986) offers a critical perspective on IBM's early computing activities. In our analysis of the computer industry from 1950 to 1965, we also rely heavily on Fisher et al., *IBM and the U.S. Data Processing Industry;* K. Flamm, *Creating the Computer* (Washington, DC: The Brookings Institution, 1988); K. Fishman, *The Computer Establishment* (New York: Harper & Row, 1981); and S. Rosen, "Electronic Computers: A Historical Survey," *Computer Surveys* 1, no. 1 (March 1969): 7–36. For useful analyses of specific dimensions of the IBM experience with computers, see also S. Usselman, "Unbundling IBM: Antitrust and the Incentives to Innovation in American Computing," in *The Challenge of Remaining Innovative,* ed. S. Clarke, N. Lamoreaux, and S. Usselman (Stanford, CA: Stanford University Press, 2009), and S. Usselman, "Learning the Hard Way: IBM and the Sources of Innovation in Early Computing," in *Financing Innovation in the United States, 1870 to the Present,* ed. N. Lamoreaux and K. Sokoloff (Cambridge, MA: MIT Press, 2009).

7. M. Campbell-Kelly, *ICL: A Business and Technical History* (Oxford: Oxford University Press, 1990), 66.

8. J. Cortada, *Before the Computer: IBM, NCR, Burroughs, and Remington Rand and the Industry They Created, 1865–1956* (Princeton, NJ: Princeton University Press, 1993), 225.

9. Pugh, *Building IBM,* 155.

10. E. Van Deusen, "The Two-Plus-Two of Sperry Rand," *Fortune,* August 1955, 128, and Fisher et al., *IBM and the U.S. Data Processing Industry,* 8–9.

11. For the price-performance comparisons in this chapter, see Phister, *Data Processing,* 338–357, and especially K. Knight, "Changes in Computer Performance," *Datamation,* September 1966, Table 1.

12. Fisher et al., *IBM and the U.S. Data Processing Industry,* 70.

13. Fishman, *The Computer Establishment,* 162–163.

14. For a history of RCA, including its computer forays, see especially R. Sobel, *RCA* (New York: Stein and Day, 1986). On the origins of RCA, see also L. Bergreen,

Look Now, Pay Later: The Rise of Network Broadcasting (Garden City, NY: Doubleday, 1980), especially chaps. 1–4. Further, the volume edited by N. Metropolis et al., *A History of Computing in the Twentieth Century*, contains essays on early computer developments at several companies, including IBM and RCA.

15. Fisher et al., *IBM and the U.S. Data Processing Industry*, 71–72.

16. The number of installations comes from the "Roster of College and University Computer Facilities," *Computers and Automation*, November 1970. The number of institutions of higher education in the United States comes from the Census Bureau, *Statistical Abstract of the United States, 1992* (Washington, DC: U.S. Bureau of the Census, 1992), 165.

17. Phister, *Data Processing*, 444, 447.

18. H. Berkman, "The Economics of Automatic Data Processing in Public Administration in the U.S.A.," in *Economics of Automatic Data Processing*, ed. A. Frielink (Amsterdam: North-Holland, 1965), 311–312.

19. J. Cortada, *Information Technology as Business History* (Westport, CT: Greenwood Press, 1996), 51, and Phister, *Data Processing*, 243–245.

20. F. Bello, "The War of the Computers," *Fortune*, October 1959, 130–131.

21. A census of computer installations by size of business plant for 1971 can be found in Phister, *Data Processing*, 447.

2. PRODUCT DIFFERENTIATION, SOFTWARE, AND SERVICES

1 See, for example, B. Sheppard, "Description of Digital Computers," *Computers and Automation*, June 1961, 99ff.

2. N. Schneidewind, "The Practice of Computer Selection," *Datamation*, February 1967, 22–25.

3. E. Pugh, *Building IBM: Shaping an Industry and Its Technology* (Cambridge, MA: MIT Press, 1996), 178–182.

4. F. Fisher, J. McKie, and R. Mancke, *IBM and the U.S. Data Processing Industry* (New York: Praeger, 1983), 17.

5. For the price-performance comparisons in this chapter, see K. Knight, "Changes in Computer Performance," *Datamation*, September 1966, Table 1. For the number of installations, see Fisher et al., *IBM and the U.S. Data Processing Industry*, 43–44.

6. Pugh, *Building IBM*, 266.

7. Two useful books about CDC are J. C. Worthy, *William C. Norris: Portrait of a Maverick* (Cambridge, MA: Ballinger, 1987), and R. Price, *The Eye for Innovation* (New Haven, CT: Yale University Press, 1995). T. Misa also covers CDC in chapter 4 of his book *Digital State: The Story of Minnesota's Computing Industry* (Minneapolis: University of Minnesota Press, 2013).

8. Fisher et al., *IBM and the U.S. Data Processing Industry*, 93. See also T. Wise, "Control Data's Magnificent Fumble," *Fortune*, April 1966.

9. Useful sources on DEC include J. Parker Pearson, *Digital at Work* (Bedford, MA: Digital Press, 1992); G. Rifkin and G. Harrar, *The Ultimate Entrepreneur: The Story of Ken Olsen and Digital Equipment Corporation* (Chicago: Contemporary Books, 1988); and E. Schein et al., *DEC Is Dead, Long Live DEC: The Lasting Legacy of Digital Equipment Corporation* (San Francisco: Berrett-Koehler, 2003).

10. Fisher et al., *IBM and the U.S. Data Processing Industry,* 55.

11. C. Bashe, L. Johnson, J. Palmer, and E. Pugh, *IBM's Early Computers* (Cambridge, MA: MIT Press, 1986), 323–333.

12. The article by M. Campbell-Kelly and D. Garcia-Swartz, "Pragmatism, Not Ideology: Historical Perspectives on IBM's Adoption of Open-Source Software," *Information Economics and Policy* 21, no. 3 (August 2009): 229–244, tracks IBM's changing approaches to the creation and marketing of software between the 1950s and the 1990s.

13. See J. Yates, "Application Software for Insurance in the 1960s and Early 1970s," *Business and Economic History* 24 (1995): 123–134, and J. Yates, *Structuring the Information Age: Life Insurance and Technology in the Twentieth Century* (Baltimore, MD: Johns Hopkins University Press, 2005).

14. An excellent account of IBM's SHARE is in A. Akera, "Voluntarism and the Fruits of Collaboration: The IBM User Group SHARE," *Technology and Culture* 42, no. 4 (2001): 710–736.

15. P. Armer, "SHARE—A Eulogy to Cooperative Effort," *Annals of the History of Computing* 2 (April 1980): 122–129.

16. M. Phister, *Data Processing Technology and Economics* (Bedford, MA: Digital Press, 1979), 277.

17. Company histories for some of the first software firms can be found in E. Kubie, "Recollections of the First Software Company," *IEEE Annals of the History of Computing* 16, no. 2 (1994); M. Goetz, "Memoirs of a Software Pioneer, Part 1," *IEEE Annals of the History of Computing* 24, no. 1 (2002); and W. Bauer, "Informatics: An Early Software Company," *IEEE Annals of the History of Computing* 18, no. 2 (1996).

18. Computer Sciences Corporation, *The CSC Story,* 3, http://assets1.csc.com /nordic/downloads/15321_2.pdf, accessed July 3, 2013.

19. Edward Kanarkowski, *ADP 50th Anniversary, 1949–1999* (Roseland, NJ: ADP, 1999).

20. On the early years of EDS, see especially D. Levin, *Irreconcilable Differences— Ross Perot versus General Motors* (Boston: Little, Brown and Company, 1989).

21. Phister, *Data Processing,* 253.

22. To our knowledge, several of the hypotheses presented here on why IBM became the leading firm in the computer industry were first suggested by S. Usselman, "IBM and Its Imitators: Organizational Capabilities and the Emergence of the International Computer Industry," *Business and Economic History* 22, no. 2 (Winter 1993).

3. THE INTERNATIONAL COMPUTER INDUSTRY

1. Two books that provide comparative perspectives on international developments in the early computer industry are K. Flamm, *Targeting the Computer: Government Support and International Competition* (Washington, DC: The Brookings Institution, 1987), and P. Gannon, *Trojan Horses and National Champions* (London: Apt-Amatic, 1997). Two old but still useful sources of information and analysis on the European computer industry are OECD, *Electronic Computers: Gaps in Technology* (Paris: OECD, 1969), and C. Freeman, "Research and Development in Electronic Capital Goods," *National Institute Economic Review* 34 (November 1965). J. Connolly, "History of Computing in Europe" (IBM World Trade Corporation, unpublished, 1967), presents a detailed chronology of computer events in Europe and other regions of the world. There were computer developments in countries not covered in this book; see J. Cortada, *The Digital Flood* (Oxford: Oxford University Press, 2012), especially chap. 4 on Italy, the Netherlands, and Sweden, and chap. 6 on the Eastern European countries. For a collection of essays on the evolution of the software industry in the United States, Western Europe, Japan, and Russia, see *The International Computer Software Industry*, ed. D. Mowery (Oxford: Oxford University Press, 1996).

2. The key references on computer developments in Britain are M. Campbell-Kelly, *ICL: A Business and Technical History* (Oxford: Oxford University Press, 1990), and M. Campbell-Kelly, "ICL and the American Challenge: British Government Policies for the Computer Industry," in *Technological Competitiveness: Contemporary and Historical Perspectives on the Electrical, Electronics, and Computer Industry*, ed. W. Aspray (New York: IEEE Press, 1993). The history of Elliot-Automation is covered by S. H. Lavington's *Moving Targets: Elliott-Automation and the Dawn of the Computer Age in Britain, 1947–67* (London: Springer, 2011). Other useful sources include J. Hendry, *Innovating for Failure* (Cambridge, MA: MIT Press, 1989); S. Lavington, *British Early Computers* (Bedford, MA: Digital Press, 1980); and G. Ferry, *A Computer Called LEO* (London: Fourth Estate, 2004). P. Stoneman, *Technological Diffusion and the Computer Revolution: The UK Experience* (Cambridge: Cambridge University Press, 1976) presents a wealth of quantitative evidence on early computer developments in the United Kingdom.

3. M. Phister, *Data Processing Technology and Economics* (Bedford, MA: Digital Press, 1979), 289.

4. The essential sources on the computer industry in France are J. P. Brulé, *L'Informatique malade de l'État* (Paris: Belles Lettres, 1993); J. Quatrepoint, J. Jublin, and D. Arnaud, *French ordinateurs: de l'affaire Bull á l'assassinat du Plan Calcul* (Paris: Moreau, 1976); and various articles by P. Mounier-Kuhn, including "Un exportateur dynamique mais vulnérable: les machines Bull (1948–1964)," *Histoire, économie et société* 4 (1995); "Bull: A Worldwide Company Born in France," *IEEE Annals of the His-*

tory of Computing 11 (1989); and "History of Computing in France: A Brief Sketch," mimeo., n.d. The book by P. Mounier-Kuhn, *L'Informatique en France* (Paris: Presses de l'Université Paris–Sorbonne, 2010) is useful as well.

5. Mounier-Kuhn, "Bull," 288.

6. Mounier-Kuhn, "History of Computing in France," 9, and "Bull," 288–289.

7. Phister, *Data Processing,* 289.

8. To our knowledge, there is no single volume that covers the evolution of the German computer industry. We have relied on S. von Weiher and H. Goetzeler, *Weg und Wirken der Siemens-Werke im Fortschritt der Elektrotechnik, 1847–1972* (München: Bruckmann, 1972), and B. Plettner, *Abenteuer Elektrotechnik: Siemens und die Entwicklung der Elektrotechnik seit 1945* (München: Piper, 1994).

9. Plettner, *Abenteuer Electrotechnik,* 244; Gannon, *Trojan Horses and National Champions,* 137; and Phister, *Data Processing,* 289.

10. For the Japanese computer industry, we have relied on M. Anchordoguy, *Computers Inc.: Japan's Challenge to IBM* (Cambridge, MA: Harvard University Press, 1989); R. Sobel, *IBM vs. Japan: The Struggle for the Future* (New York: Stein and Day, 1986); and M. Fransman, *The Market and Beyond: Information Technology in Japan* (Cambridge: Cambridge University Press, 1990). M. Fransman, *Japan's Computer and Communications Industry* (Oxford: Oxford University Press, 1995) is full of insights as well.

11. Fransman, *The Market and Beyond,* 25, and Anchordoguy, *Computers Inc.,* 22.

12. Anchordoguy, *Computers Inc.,* 24.

13. Anchordoguy, *Computers Inc.,* 36ff, Appendix A, and Appendix B.

14. For all the JECC-related statistics, see Anchordoguy, *Computers Inc.,* chap. 3.

15. Phister, *Data Processing,* 289, and Anchordoguy, *Computers Inc.,* 67.

16. Phister, *Data Processing,* 289.

17. A. Maddison, *Contours of the World Economy, 1–2030 AD: Essays in Macro-Economic History* (Oxford: Oxford University Press, 2007), 376 (table A1) and 382 (table A7).

4. IBM'S SYSTEM/360 IN THE AMERICAN MARKET

1. "Monthly Computer Census," *Computers and Automation,* January 1963.

2. M. Phister, *Data Processing Technology and Economics* (Bedford, MA: Digital Press, 1979), 310.

3. W. Sharpe, *The Economics of Computers* (New York: Columbia University Press, 1969), 81–93, 217–223.

4. J. Haanstra et al., "Processor Products—Final Report of SPREAD Task Group, December 28, 1961," *IEEE Annals of the History of Computing* 5, no. 1 (January 1983): 7. On System/360, see also T. Wise, "IBM's $5,000,000,000 Gamble," *Fortune,*

September 1966, and "The Rocky Road to the Marketplace," *Fortune,* October 1966. For an analysis of System/360 from the perspective of design and modularity, see C. Baldwin and K. Clark, *Design Rules,* vol. 1, *The Power of Modularity* (Cambridge, MA: MIT Press, 2000).

5. Wise, "IBM's $5,000,000,000 Gamble," 120.

6. F. Fisher, J. McKie, and R. Mancke, *IBM and the U.S. Data Processing Industry* (New York: Praeger, 1983), 143–148.

7. G. Bylinsky, "The Computer's Little Helpers Create a Brawling Business," *Fortune,* June 1970, 85.

8. G. Burck, "The Computer Industry's Great Expectations," *Fortune,* August 1968, 145.

9. Bylinsky, "The Computer's Little Helpers," 86; see also K. Fishman, *The Computer Establishment* (New York: Harper & Row, 1981), 233–234.

10. Fisher et al., *IBM and the U.S. Data Processing Industry,* 292–295.

11. Telex Corp. v. International Business Machines Corp., 510 F.2d 894 (10th Cir. 1975), ¶¶ 42–73, and also Greyhound Computer Corp., Inc., v. International Business Machines Corp., 559 F.2d 488 (1977), ¶ 34.

12. L. Beman, "I.B.M.'s Travails in Lilliput," *Fortune,* November 1973, 258.

13. Fisher et al., *IBM and the U.S. Data Processing Industry,* 313–314.

14. Greyhound v. IBM, ¶¶ 38–39, and Beman, "I.B.M.'s Travails in Lilliput," 150, 152.

15. M. Campbell-Kelly, M. Danilevsky, D. Garcia-Swartz, and S. Pederson, "Clustering in the Creative Industries: Insights from the Origins of Computer Software," *Industry and Innovation* 17, no. 3 (June 2010): 312.

16. Computer Sciences Corporation, "The 1960s: Risk-Takers and Visionaries in a New World of Computers," in *The CSC Story,* http://assets1.csc.com/nordic/down loads/15321_2.pdf, accessed July 3, 2013.

17. M. Goetz, "Memoirs of a Software Pioneer, Part 1," *IEEE Annals of the History of Computing* 24, no. 1 (2002), 49–53.

18. M. Campbell-Kelly, *From Airline Reservations to Sonic the Hedgehog: A History of the Software Industry* (Cambridge, MA: MIT Press, 2003), 104–109.

19. Edward Kanarkowski, *ADP 50th Anniversary 1949–1999* (Roseland, NJ: ADP, 1999), 18.

20. "Electronic Data Systems Corporation," *International Directory of Company Histories,* vol. 28, ed. Jay Pederson (Detroit: St. James Press, 1999), 112–116.

21. GE Information Services, "Twenty Years of Excellence: Special Edition Commemorating the 20th Anniversary of General Electric Information Services Company," *Spectrum,* December 1985, 3–9; and M. Campbell-Kelly and D. Garcia-Swartz, "Economic Perspectives on the History of the Computer Time-Sharing Industry, 1965–1985," *IEEE Annals of the History of Computing* (January-March 2008), 20ff.

5. IBM'S SYSTEM/370 IN THE AMERICAN MARKET

1 On IBM's bundling and unbundling decisions, see B. Grad, "A Personal Recollection: IBM's Unbundling of Software and Services," *IEEE Annals of the History of Computing* 24, no. 1 (January–March 2002).

2. K. Fishman, *The Computer Establishment* (New York: Harper & Row, 1981), 379. On the impact of the lawsuit on IBM, see also L. Gerstner, Jr., *Who Says Elephants Can't Dance?* (New York: HarperCollins, 2003), 118.

3. On the history of semiconductor technology, see especially E. Braun and S. Macdonald, *Revolution in Miniature: The History and Impact of Semiconductor Electronics* (Cambridge: Cambridge University Press, 1978), and T. Forester, ed., *The Microelectronics Revolution: The Complete Guide to the New Technology and Its Impact on Society* (Cambridge, MA: MIT Press, 1981).

4. For a useful article on System/370, see G. Bylinsky, "Vincent Learson Didn't Plan It That Way, but I.B.M.'s Toughest Competitor Is—I.B.M.," *Fortune,* March 1972.

5. On the Future System, see E. Pugh, L. Johnson, and J. Palmer, *IBM's 360 and Early 370 Systems* (Cambridge, MA: MIT Press, 1991), 538–553, and C. Ferguson and C. Morris, *Computer Wars: How the West Can Win in a Post-IBM World* (New York: Times Books/Random House, 1993), chap. 3.

6. M. Phister, *Data Processing Technology and Economics* (Bedford, MA: Digital Press, 1979), 630–631.

7. An insightful discussion of the IBM 4300 mainframes can be found in B. Uttal, "How the 4300 Fits I.B.M.'s New Strategy," *Fortune,* July 1979.

8. Fishman, *The Computer Establishment,* 155.

9. Details on the exit of GE and RCA from mainframe production can be found in G. Bylinsky, "Happily Married in Computers," *Fortune,* April 1973; A. Demaree, "RCA after the Bath," *Fortune,* September 1972; and G. Bylinsky, "UNIVAC's Buy of the Century," *Fortune,* April 1973.

10. B. Uttal, "Gene Amdahl Takes Aim at I.B.M.," *Fortune,* September 1977, examines Amdahl Corporation's competitive strategy. Additional details can be found in J. Rodengen, *The Legend of Amdahl* (Fort Lauderdale: Write Stuff Syndicate, 2000).

11. Uttal, "Gene Amdahl Takes Aim at I.B.M.," 110–112.

12. Fishman, *The Computer Establishment,* 243–245.

13. M. Campbell-Kelly, *ICL: A Business and Technical History* (Oxford: Oxford University Press, 1990), 313–316.

14. Minicomputers are discussed in C. G. Bell, "The Mini and Micro Industries," *Computer* 17, no. 10 (October 1984), and F. Coury, ed., *A Practical Guide to Minicomputer Applications* (New York, IEEE Press, 1972).

15. On Data General, see especially B. Uttal, "The Gentlemen and the Upstarts Meet in a Great Mini Battle," *Fortune,* April 23, 1979, and T. Kidder, *The Soul of a New Machine* (New York: Back Bay, 2000).

16. D. Packard, *The HP Way* (New York: HarperCollins, 1995), 101–106.

17. A key reference on IBM's small business systems is R. Taylor, "Low-End General Purpose Systems," *IBM Journal of Research and Development* 25, no. 5 (September 1981).

18. Phister, *Data Processing,* 616.

19. Fishman, *The Computer Establishment,* 207–208.

20. B. Elzen and D. MacKenzie, "From Megaflops to Total Solutions: The Changing Dynamics of Competitiveness in Supercomputing," in *Technological Competitiveness: Contemporary and Historical Perspectives on the Electrical, Electronics, and Computer Industries,* ed. W. Aspray (New York: IEEE Press, 1993), 126–133.

21. Fishman, *The Computer Establishment,* 208.

22. M. Campbell-Kelly, *From Airline Reservations to Sonic the Hedgehog* (Cambridge, MA: MIT Press, 2003), chap. 5.

23. Computer Sciences Corporation, "The 1970s: Timesharing Reshapes CSC," in *The CSC Story,* http://assets1.csc.com/nordic/downloads/15321_2.pdf, accessed July 3, 2013.

24. Calculations by the authors on the basis of "The Datamation 100: The Top 100 U.S. Companies in the DP Industry," *Datamation,* July 1980, 87ff.

25. Fishman, *The Computer Establishment,* 243.

6. INTERNATIONAL REACTIONS TO SYSTEM/360 AND SYSTEM/370

1. In addition to the sources cited in Chapter 3, here we have also relied on R. Coopey, "Empire and Technology: Information Technology Policy in Postwar Britain and France," in *Information Technology Policy: An International History,* ed. R. Coopey (Oxford: Oxford University Press, 2004); N. Jéquier, "Computers," in *Big Business and the State: Changing Relations in Western Europe,* ed. R. Vernon (Cambridge, MA: Harvard University Press, 1974); P. Mounier-Kuhn, "Le Plan Calcul, Bull et l'industrie des composants: les contradictions d'une stratégie," *Revue historique* 290, no. 1 (1995); and a series of articles in the German trade magazine *Computerwoche* (listed in various endnotes below).

2. M. Campbell-Kelly, "ICL and the American Challenge: British Government Policies for the Computer Industry," in *Technological Competitiveness: Contemporary and Historical Perspectives on the Electrical, Electronics, and Computer Industry,* ed. W. Aspray (New York: IEEE Press, 1993), 111–112.

3. M. Campbell-Kelly, *ICL: A Business and Technical History* (Oxford: Oxford University Press, 1990), 250.

4. P. Gannon, *Trojan Horses and National Champions* (London: Apt-Amatic, 1997), 152.

5. A short but detailed history of Bull and CII in the 1960s and 1970s can be found in "Bulls Erbe: Die verschlungenen Wege eines europäischen Computer-

konzerns," *Computerwoche,* October 17, 1986, http://www.computerwoche.de/a/die
-verschlungenen-wege-eines-europaeischen-computerkonzerns,1166464.

6. J. P. Brulé, *L'Informatique malade de l'État* (Paris: Belles Lettres, 1993), 105.

7. For various estimates of the cost of the first plan, see Mounier-Kuhn, "Le Plan
Calcul, Bull et l'industrie des composants," 8–9; Brulé, *L'Informatique malade de l'État,*
337; and Campbell-Kelly, *ICL,* 300.

8. Brulé, *L'Informatique malade de l'État,* 324, and Mounier-Kuhn, "Le Plan
Calcul, Bull et l'industrie des composants," 9.

9. Gannon, *Trojan Horses and National Champions,* 154.

10. K. Flamm, *Creating the Computer* (Washington, DC: The Brookings Institution, 1988), 162.

11. For a short but detailed summary of Siemens's involvement with computers,
see "Mischkonzerne wie RCA, GE, Philips und Honeywell warfen das Handtuch:
Menetekel für Siemens/Nixdorf: Nach Fusionen ging es oft bergab," *Computerwoche,*
January 19, 1990, http://www.computerwoche.de/a/menetekel-fuer-siemens-nixdorf
-nach-fusionen-ging-es-oft-bergab,1143942.

12. Campbell-Kelly, *ICL,* 300.

13. A. Harman, *The International Computer Industry* (Cambridge, MA: Harvard
University Press, 1971), 31, and Flamm, *Creating the Computer,* 164.

14. M. Amedick and U. Hashagen, "Nixdorf, Heinz," in *Encyclopedia of Computer
Science,* ed. A. Ralston, E. Reilly, and D. Hemmendinger, 4th ed. (London: Nature
Publishing Group, 2000), 1239–1241.

15. M. Fransman, *The Market and Beyond: Information Technology in Japan* (Cambridge: Cambridge University Press, 1990), 30–31.

16. M. Anchordoguy, *Computers Inc.: Japan's Challenge to IBM* (Cambridge, MA:
Harvard University Press, 1989), 36 and Appendix A.

17. M. Phister, *Data Processing Technology and Economics* (Bedford: Digital Press,
1979), 289, and Anchordoguy, *Computers Inc.,* 34.

18. An interesting reference on Olivetti's early forays into computer design and
manufacturing is P. G. Perotto, *Programma 101—L'invenzione del personal computer:
una storia appassionante mai raccontata* (Milan: Sperling & Kupfer, 1995). An analysis of the development of high-technology industries in Italy, including the computer
industry, can be found in C. Bussolati, F. Malerba, and S. Torrisi, *"L'evoluzione del
sistema industriale italiano e l'alta tecnologia," Liuc Papers,* no. 25, Serie Economia e
Impresa (November-December 1995).

19. On the Dutch computer industry, see especially D. de Wit, "The Construction of the Dutch Computer Industry: The Organisational Shaping of Technology,"
Business History 39, no. 3 (1997): 81–104.

20. For details on Unidata, see especially E. Kranakis, "Politics, Business, and
European Information Technology Policy: From the Treaty of Rome to Unidata, 1958–
1975," in *Information Technology Policy: An International History,* ed. R. Coopey

(Oxford: Oxford University Press, 2004). See also S. Hilger, "The European Enterprise as a 'Fortress'—The Rise and Fall of Unidata between Common European Market and International Competition in the Early 1970s," in *The European Enterprise: Historical Investigation into a Future Species,* ed. H. Schröter (Berlin: Springer Verlag, 2008), 141–154.

21. Brulé, *L'Informatique malade de l'État,* 133.

22. Ibid., 139.

23. Campbell-Kelly, *ICL,* 300.

24. See, for example, "Siemens: Wir bleiben IBM-kompatibel, Unbundling kommt," *Computerwoche,* May 9, 1975, http://www.computerwoche.de/a/siemens-wir-bleiben-ibm-kompatibel-unbundling-kommt,1204234; "Großoffensive von Siemens," *Computerwoche,* October 27, 1978, http://www.computerwoche.de/a/grossoffensive-von-siemens,1197268; and "Mischkonzerne wie RCA, GE, Philips und Honeywell warfen das Handtuch: Menetekel für Siemens/Nixdorf," *Computerwoche.*

25. A. Pantages, N. Foy, and A. Lloyd, "Western Europe's Computer Industry," *Datamation,* September 1976, 75.

26. Campbell-Kelly, *ICL,* 300.

27. F. Halpern, "Current Trends in the European Computer Market," *Datamation,* September 1980, 157.

28. Campbell-Kelly, *ICL,* 304–305.

29. Campbell-Kelly, "ICL and the American Challenge," 113–114.

30. Anchordoguy, *Computers Inc.,* 102, 137.

31. Ibid., 34–35.

32. Halpern, "Current Trends in the European Computer Market," 157–158; U.S. Congress, Office of Technology Assessment, *International Competitiveness in Electronics: Summary* (Washington, DC: U.S. Congress, Office of Technology Assessment, November 1983), 153.

33. E. Yasaki and A. Pantages, "Japan's Computer Industry," *Datamation,* September 1976, 93.

7. MICROCOMPUTERS AND PERSONAL COMPUTERS IN THE AMERICAN MARKET

1. In this chapter, we draw heavily from P. Freiberger and M. Swaine, *Fire in the Valley,* 2nd ed. (New York: McGraw-Hill, 2000), and J. Steffens, *Newgames—Strategic Competition in the PC Revolution* (Oxford: Pergamon Press, 1994). We also found useful R. N. Langlois, "External Economies and Economic Progress: The Case of the Microcomputer Industry," *Business History Review* 66, no. 1 (1992), 1–50. On the evolution of microcomputer software, we have drawn fundamentally from M. Campbell-Kelly, *From Airline Reservations to Sonic the Hedgehog* (Cambridge, MA: MIT Press, 2003) and R. Fertig, *The Software Revolution: Trends, Players, Market Dynamics in Personal Computer Software* (New York: North-Holland, 1985).

2. For details on the evolution of what eventually became known as Silicon Valley, see especially C. Lécuyer, *Making Silicon Valley: Innovation and the Growth of High Tech, 1930–1970* (Cambridge, MA: MIT Press, 2006).

3. Intel, "Microprocessor Quick Reference Guide," http://www.intel.com/press room/kits/quickreffam.htm, accessed July 8, 2013. See also Steffens, *Newgames,* 60–63.

4. Freiberger and Swaine, *Fire in the Valley,* 48.

5. An important reference on the history of Microsoft is D. Ichbiah and S. Knepper, *The Making of Microsoft* (Rocklin, CA: Prima Publishing, 1993).

6. On the history of Apple, see especially O. Linzmayer, *Apple Confidential 2.0* (San Francisco, CA: No Starch Press, 2004), and S. Levy, *Insanely Great* (New York: Penguin Books, 2000).

7. For a business history of Commodore, see B. Bagnall, *Commodore: A Company on the Edge* (Winnipeg: Variant Press, 2010).

8. Ichbiah and Knepper, *The Making of Microsoft,* chaps. 3–5.

9. On the history of spreadsheet software see M. Campbell-Kelly, "The Rise and Rise of the Spreadsheet," in *The History of Mathematical Tables: From Sumer to Spreadsheets,* ed. M. Campbell-Kelly, M. Croarken, R. Flood, and E. Robson (Oxford: Oxford University Press, 2003), 322–347.

10. For a recent business history of Intel see M. Malone, *The Intel Trinity* (New York: HarperCollins, 2014).

11. Steffens, *Newgames,* 178.

12. Ibid., 183–184.

13. "The Datamation 100," *Datamation,* June 15, 1991, 22.

14. See especially M. Dell and C. Fredman, *Direct from Dell: Strategies That Revolutionized an Industry* (New York: HarperCollins, 2000).

15. "What Price Glory?," *The Economist,* August 24, 1991.

16. "A Star Is Fallen," *The Economist,* May 25, 1991, and "The Texas Computer Massacre," *The Economist,* July 2, 1994.

17. Campbell-Kelly, *From Airline Reservations to Sonic the Hedgehog,* 250.

18. Ibid., 222. All the market share figures in this section are taken from this source.

19. B. Aboba, *The Online User's Encyclopedia: Bulletin Boards and Beyond* (Reading, MA: Addison-Wesley, 1993), 59.

20. For more information on the competitive interactions among the consumer online networks in the 1980s and early 1990s, see M. Campbell-Kelly, D. Garcia-Swartz, and A. Layne-Farrar, "The Evolution of Network Industries: Lessons from the Conquest of the Online Frontier, 1979–1995," *Industry and Innovation* 15, no. 4 (2008): 435–455.

21. R. Levering, M. Katz, and M. Moskowitz, *The Computer Entrepreneurs* (New York: New American Library, 1984), 414–420. Detailed information on the evolution of market shares for the consumer online networks can be found in M. Campbell-Kelly

and D. Garcia-Swartz, "The History of the Internet: The Missing Narratives," *Journal of Information Technology* 28 (2013): 18–33.

8. BEYOND PERSONAL COMPUTERS IN THE AMERICAN MARKET

1. "Tweaking Big Blue's Beard," *The Economist,* October 28, 1989. Unless otherwise noted, mainframe computer market shares in this section are taken from this source.

2. "Bunching Up against IBM," *The Economist,* May 10, 1986; "The Bunch Is Dead, Long Live the Pack," *The Economist,* November 15, 1986; and "One Merger That Didn't Work," *The Economist,* January 19, 1991.

3. K. Juliussen and E. Juliussen, *The Computer Industry Almanac 1990* (New York: Brady, 1989), 3.5.

4. These assertions are based on computations by the authors from information derived from "The Datamation 100" for 1981–1991; see the *Datamation* issues for December 1, 1981; June 1, 1982; June 1, 1983; June 1, 1984; June 1, 1985; June 15, 1986; June 15, 1987; June 15, 1988; June 15, 1989; June 15, 1990; and June 15, 1991.

5. Juliussen and Juliussen, *The Computer Industry Almanac 1990,* 3.5 and 3.6.

6. A useful monograph on the AS/400 is R. Bauer et al., *The Silverlake Project: Transformation at IBM* (Oxford: Oxford University Press, 1992).

7. F. Guterl, "Mainframes Are Breaking Out of the Glass House," *Datamation,* June 15, 1995, 35–36.

8. P. Ceruzzi, *A History of Modern Computing* (Cambridge, MA: MIT Press, 2002), 281.

9. M. Campbell-Kelly and D. Garcia-Swartz, "Pragmatism, Not Ideology: Historical Perspectives on IBM's Adoption of Open-Source Software," *Information Economics and Policy* 21, no. 3 (August 2009): 229–244.

10. "The Datamation 100," *Datamation,* June 15, 1987, 31; "The Datamation 100," *Datamation,* June 15, 1993, 22; M. Campbell-Kelly, *From Airline Reservations to Sonic the Hedgehog* (Cambridge, MA: MIT Press, 2003), 173–174.

11. Campbell-Kelly, *From Airline Reservations to Sonic the Hedgehog,* 175–177.

12. "The Birth of a New Species," *The Economist,* May 25, 1996.

13. Ibid. On relational database software, see also M. Campbell-Kelly, "The RDBMS Industry: A Northern California Perspective," *IEEE Annals of the History of Computing* 34, no. 4 (October-December 2012).

14. For details on SAP, see G. Meissner, *SAP: Inside the Secret Software Power* (New York: McGraw-Hill, 2000).

15. Campbell-Kelly, *From Airline Reservations to Sonic the Hedgehog,* 196.

16. Automatic Data Processing, *ADP 1994 Annual Report,* http://investors.adp .com/secfiling.cfm?filingid=912057-94-2935&cik=8670, accessed November 11, 2014.

17. Computer Sciences Corporation, "The 1990s: CSC Leads the Outsourcing Revolution," in *The CSC Story,* http://assets1.csc.com/nordic/downloads/15321_2.pdf, accessed July 3, 2013.

18. "It Is Better to Bid Than to Fold in Takeover Poker," *The Economist,* October 6, 1984; "Getting Hot under the White Collar," *The Economist,* January 5, 1985; "The World on the Line," *The Economist,* November 23, 1985.

19. "Networks' Net Profits," *The Economist,* March 10, 1990.

9. INTERNATIONAL DEVELOPMENTS

1. For the evolution of the computer industry in Europe during this period, we have drawn extensively from P. Gannon, *Trojan Horses and National Champions* (London: Apt-Amatic, 1997).

2. "Britisch-japanisches Kooperationsabkommen bestätigt: ICL-Fujitsu-Ehe verunsichert Siemens," *Computerwoche,* October 16, 1981, http://www.computerwoche .de/a/icl-fujitsu-ehe-verunsichert-siemens,1187644.

3. "Europas Computerindustrie kurz vor dem Ausverkauf: Fujitsu/ICL-Deal ist nür die Spitze des Eisberges," *Computerwoche,* August 10, 1990, http://www.comput erwoche.de/a/fujitsu-icl-deal-ist-nur-die-spitze-des-eisberges,1147049; "Chumps v. Champs," *The Economist,* October 6, 1990; and "Japan's Lou Gerstner," *The Economist,* November 23, 1996.

4. "Von drei Jessi-Projekten ausgeschlossen, aber Esprit entscheidet über ICLs Teilnahme von Fall zu Fall," *Computerwoche,* April 19, 1991, http://www.computerwoche .de/a/esprit-entscheidet-ueber-icls-teilnahme-von-fall-zu-fall,1139538, and "Europäische Elektronik-Lobby verbannt ICL vom runden Tisch," *Computerwoche,* February 15, 1991, http://www.computerwoche.de/a/europaeische-elektronik-lobby-verbannt-icl-vom-runden-tisch,1138477.

5. P. Brulé, *L'Informatique malade de l'État* (Paris: Les Belles Lettres, 1993), especially chaps. 15 and 16.

6. S. Kerr, "Are Three Heads Better Than One?," *Datamation,* January 15, 1987, 19–23, and Brulé, *L'Informatique malade de l'État,* 258.

7. Gannon, *Trojan Horses and National Champions,* 62–63.

8. "Nixed," *The Economist,* January 13, 1990.

9. The key reference for personal computer developments in Europe during this period is J. Steffens, *Newgames* (Oxford: Pergamon Press, 1994), especially chap. 7.

10. See, for example, "A Couple of Cheers from Europe," *The Economist,* February 23, 1985, and "Watching the Market," *The Economist,* October 26, 1985.

11. The essential reference for computer developments in Asia is J. Dedrick and K. Kraemer, *Asia's Computer Challenge* (Oxford: Oxford University Press, 1998), from which we draw extensively.

12. "Japan's Less-Than-Invincible Computer Makers," *The Economist,* January 11, 1992.

13. Dedrick and Kraemer, *Asia's Computer Challenge,* 83. Our analysis of the evolution of the personal computer industry in Japan, including market shares, draws from this source as well as from M. Fransman, *Japan's Computer and Communications Industry* (Oxford: Oxford University Press, 1995), chap. 4.

14. Steffens, *Newgames,* 238–239, 296–297, and 300–301.

15. On South Korea's industrialization, see A. Amsden, *Asia's Next Giant* (Oxford: Oxford University Press, 1989). For general background on the economic history of South Korea, see especially B. Eichengreen, D. Perkins, and K. Shin, *From Miracle to Maturity: The Growth of the Korean Economy* (Cambridge, MA: Harvard University Asia Center, 2012).

16. Dedrick and Kraemer, *Asia's Computer Challenge,* 122–126.

17. On Taiwan's computer industry, see, for example, "Inside the Box," *The Economist,* July 9, 1994. For general background on the Taiwanese economy, see especially L. Hsueh, C. Hsu, and D. Perkins, *Industrialization and the State: The Changing Role of Government in Taiwan's Economy, 1945–1998* (Cambridge, MA: Harvard Institute for International Development, 2001).

18. "The Various Games of Go," *The Economist,* November 16, 1991.

19. "The Datamation 100," *Datamation,* June 15, 1996, 45.

20. On the evolution of industrial policy in Singapore, see R. van Elkan, "Singapore's Development Strategy," in *Singapore: A Case Study in Rapid Development,* ed. K. Bercuson (Washington, DC: International Monetary Fund, 1995).

21. "Big Noise, Big Profits," *The Economist,* August 14, 1993, and "Breathless," *The Economist,* June 11, 1994.

22. For details, see especially L. Gerstner, Jr., *Who Says Elephants Can't Dance?* (New York: HarperCollins, 2003).

23. Ibid., especially chaps. 4 and 12–19.

24. *IBM 1995 Annual Report,* especially 36–41, ftp://public.dhe.ibm.com/annualreport/1995/ibm1995.pdf, accessed November 11, 2014.

10. SOFTWARE AND SERVICES

1. On the evolution of the Internet, see especially J. Abbate, *Inventing the Internet* (Cambridge, MA: MIT Press, 1999), and M. Campbell-Kelly and D. Garcia-Swartz, "The History of the Internet: The Missing Narratives," *Journal of Information Technology* 28 (2013): 18–33. See also K. Hafner and M. Lyon, *Where Wizards Stay Up Late* (New York: Simon and Schuster, 1996), and P. Salus, *Casting the Net* (Reading, MA: Addison-Wesley, 1995).

2. See T. Berners-Lee, *Weaving the Web: The Past, Present, and Future of the World Wide Web by Its Inventor* (London: Harper Paperbacks, 1999).

3. In this chapter, we draw extensively from M. Campbell-Kelly and D. Garcia-Swartz, "From Products to Services: The Software Industry in the Internet Era," *Business History Review* 81, no. 4 (Winter 2007): 735–764.

4. On the ISPs, see especially S. Greenstein, "Innovation and the Evolution of Market Structure for Internet Access in the United States," in *The Internet and American Business,* ed. W. Aspray and P. Ceruzzi (Cambridge: MIT Press, 2008), 47–103.

5. L. Spurge, *MCI: Failure Is Not an Option* (Encino, CA: Spurge Ink!, 1998), 179–191, and A. Glossbrenner, *The Little Online Book* (Berkeley, CA: Peachpit Press, 1994), 110, 137.

6. On AOL, see especially K. Swisher, *aol.com* (New York: Random House, 1998).

7. M. Cusumano and D. Yoffie, *Competing on Internet Time: Lessons from Netscape and Its Battle with Microsoft* (New York: Touchstone, 1998), 96. We draw mostly from this source in our analysis of the Internet browser market.

8. For details, see especially *Microsoft, Antitrust and the New Economy: Selected Essays,* ed. D. Evans (Boston: Kluwer Academic Publishers, 2002).

9. S. Terdeman, "Web Authoring," *PC Magazine,* September 10, 1996, 115–117.

10. C. Ferguson, *High St@kes, No Prisoners: A Winner's Tale of Greed and Glory in the Internet Wars* (New York: Times Business, 1999).

11. Pamela Pfiffner, *Inside the Publishing Revolution: The Adobe Story* (Berkeley, CA: Adobe Press, 2002).

12. K. Angel, *Inside Yahoo!: Reinvention and the Road Ahead* (New York: Wiley, 2002), 12.

13. M. Mauldin, "Lycos: Design Choices in an Internet Search Service," *IEEE Expert* 12 (January-February 1997): 8–11.

14. T. Lenard and D. Britton, *The Digital Economy Fact Book,* 8th ed. (Washington, DC: The Progress and Freedom Foundation, 2006), 10, and D. Britton and S. Gonegal, *The Digital Economy Fact Book,* 9th ed. (Washington, DC: The Progress and Freedom Foundation, 2007), 12.

15. Angel, *Inside Yahoo!,* 124.

16. Ibid., 129–130.

17. d. boyd and N. Ellison, "Social Network Sites: Definition, History, and Scholarship," *Journal of Computer-Mediated Communication* 13, no. 1 (2007): 210–230.

18. F. Gillette, "The Rise and Inglorious Fall of MySpace," *Bloomberg Businessweek,* June 22, 2011.

19. The Facebook statistics are in the Registration Statement for Facebook, Inc., filed with the SEC on February 1, 2012, http://www.sec.gov/Archives/edgar/data/1326801/000119312512034517/d287954ds1.htm, accessed November 12, 2014.

20. On open-source software, see, among others, M. Campbell-Kelly and D. Garcia-Swartz, "The Move to the Middle: Convergence of the Open-Source and Proprietary Software Industry," *International Journal of the Economics of Business* 17, no. 2 (2010): 223–252.

21. R. Young and W. Goldman Rohm, *Under the Radar: How Red Hat Changed the Software Business—and Took Microsoft by Surprise* (Scottsdale, AZ: Coriolis, 1999), 35.

22. PricewaterhouseCoopers, *Technology Forecast 2002–2004,* vol. 2 (Menlo Park, CA: PricewaterhouseCoopers Global Technology Center, 2002), 214.

23. M. Egan with T. Mather, *The Executive Guide to Information Security: Threats, Challenges, and Solutions* (Indianapolis: Addison-Wesley Professional, 2005), 9.

24. "The 2005 Software 500," *Software Magazine,* September 2006.

25. The Intuit statistics are taken from the 1999, 2000, and 2005 *Annual Reports,* http://www.getfilings.com/o0000891618-99-004510.html (1999), http://http-down load.intuit.com/http.intuit/CMO/intuit/investors/annual_reports/2000_annual _report.pdf (2000), and http://web.intuit.com/about_intuit/investors/annuals/2005 _annual_report.pdf (2005), accessed November 12, 2014.

26. On software as a service, see M. Campbell-Kelly and D. Garcia-Swartz, "The Rise, Fall, and Resurrection of Software-as-a-Service: Historical Perspectives on the Computer Utility and Software for Lease on a Network," in *The Internet and American Business,* ed. W. Aspray and P. Ceruzzi (Cambridge: MIT Press, 2008), 201ff.

27. IDC, *Worldwide On-Demand Customer Relationship Management Applications: 2004 Vendor Analysis* (Framingham, MA: IDC, 2005), 21.

11. COMPUTER HARDWARE

1. The literature on mainframes in 1995–2010 is fragmented; see, among others, L. Fisher, "Mainframe Business, Though Faded, Is Still Far from Extinct," *New York Times,* May 18, 1998; "Back in Fashion," *The Economist,* January 14, 2010; "Old Dog, New Tricks," *The Economist,* September 6, 2012; and S. Lohr, "I.B.M. Mainframe Evolves to Serve the Digital World," *New York Times,* August 28, 2012.

2. See, for example, L. Gerstner, Jr., *Who Says Elephants Can't Dance?,* (New York: HarperCollins, 2003), 44–45.

3. "Back in Fashion," *The Economist.* January 14, 2010.

4. E. H. Schein et al., *DEC is Dead, Long Live DEC: The Lasting Legacy of Digital Equipment Corporation* (San Francisco: Berrett-Koehler, 2003), chap. 13.

5. M. Kanellos and I. Fried, "HP to Acquire Compaq for $25 Billion," *CNET News,* September 4, 2001.

6. E. Ogg, "HP to Acquire EDS for $13.9 billion," *CNET News,* May 13, 2008.

7. E. Montalbano, "Update: Oracle Agrees to Buy Sun for $7.4B," *Infoworld,* April 20, 2009.

8. See Pew Research Internet Project, Internet Use Over Time, http://www.pewin ternet.org/data-trend/internet-use/internet-use-over-time/, accessed November 12, 2014.

9. J. Curry and M. Kenney, "The Organizational and Geographic Configuration of the Personal Computer Value Chain," in *Locating Global Advantage: Industrial Dy-*

namics in the International Economy, ed. M. Kenney and R. Florida (Stanford, CA: Stanford University Press, 2004), 113–141. We draw extensively from this study in our analysis of the personal computer market after 1995.

10. In this section we draw frequently from M. Campbell-Kelly, D. Garcia-Swartz, R. Lam, and Y. Yang, "Economic and Business Perspectives on Smartphones as Multi-Sided Platforms," forthcoming in 2015 in *Telecommunications Policy.* In addition, two useful articles that present economic interpretations of the smartphone industry are J. West and M. Mace, "Browsing as the Killer App: Explaining the Rapid Success of the iPhone," *Telecommunications Policy* 34, no. 5 (2010): 270–286, and M. Kenney and B. Pon, "Structuring the Smartphone Industry: Is the Mobile Internet OS Platform the Key?," *Journal of Industry, Competition, and Trade* 11, no. 3 (2011): 239–261.

11. D. Jackson, "Palm-to-Palm Combat," *Time,* June 24, 2001.

12. C. Tilley, "The History of Microsoft Windows CE," http://www.hpcfactor .com/support/windowsce/, accessed December 4, 2013.

13. A. Orlowski, "Symbian, the Secret History: Dark Star," *The Register,* November 23, 2010.

14. R. McQueen, *BlackBerry: The Inside Story of Research in Motion* (Toronto: Key Porter Books, 2010), and A. Sweeney, *BlackBerry Planet: The Story of Research in Motion and the Little Device That Took the World by Storm* (Mississauga, Ontario: John Wiley & Sons Canada, 2009).

15. F. Vogelstein, "The Untold Story: How the iPhone Blew Up the Wireless Industry," *Wired,* January 9, 2008. For more details on the confrontation between Apple and Google, see F. Vogelstein, *Dogfight: How Apple and Google Went to War and Started a Revolution* (New York: Sarah Crichton Books, 2013).

16. See the official Apple press release titled "Apple Reinvents the Phone with iPhone," January 9, 2007, https://www.apple.com/pr/library/2007/01/09Apple -Reinvents-the-Phone-with-iPhone.html, accessed November 12, 2014.

17. J. Markoff, "I, Robot: The Man behind the Google Phone," *New York Times,* November 4, 2007, and D. Roth, "Google's Open Source Android OS Will Free the Wireless Web," *Wired,* June 23, 2008.

18. S. Olsen, "Advice for Apple iPhone Start-Ups," *CNET News,* March 6, 2008, and S. Olsen, "Apple, Google Vie for Hearts (and Wallets) of Developers," *CNET News,* March 31, 2008.

19. J. Skillings, "Nokia to Buy Symbian Outright, Launches App Effort," *CNET News,* June 24, 2008.

20. See especially J. Markoff, "Microsoft Brings In Top Talent to Pursue Old Goal: The Tablet," *New York Times,* August 30, 1999; and S. Levy, "Bill Gates Says, Take This Tablet," *Newsweek,* April 29, 2001.

21. O. Linzmayer, *Apple Confidential 2.0* (San Francisco: No Starch Press, 2004), 183–206.

22. See the official press release titled "Apple launches iPad," January 27, 2010, http://www.apple.com/pr/library/2010/01/27Apple-Launches-iPad.html, accessed November 12, 2014.

23. Morgan Stanley, "Tablet Demand and Disruption: Mobile Users Come of Age," February 14, 2011, 7, http://www.morganstanley.com/views/perspectives/tablets_demand.pdf, accessed July 10, 2013.

24. T. Ray, "PCs: Q1 Shipments Plunge 14%, Worst-Ever Drop, Says IDC," *Barron's,* April 10, 2013.

25. See, for example, C. Mims, "The Web is Dying; Apps are Killing It," *Wall Street Journal,* November 17, 2014, http://online.wsj.com/articles/the-web-is-dying -apps-are-killing-it-1416169934, accessed November 19, 2014.

12. GLOBALIZATION

1. Although the key source for Table 12.1 and Table 12.2 is the *OECD Information Technology Outlook 2010* (Paris: OECD, 2010), we also retrieved information from the following annual reports: HP 2009 Annual Report, http://h30261.www3.hp.com /phoenix.zhtml?c=71087&p=irol-reportsAnnual, accessed November 19, 2014; Dell 2010 Form 10-K, http://www.dell.com/learn/us/en/uscorp1/corporate-secure-en /documents-fy10_form10k_final.pdf, accessed November 19, 2014; Apple 2010 Form 10-K, http://www.dell.com/learn/us/en/uscorp1/corporate-secure-en/docu ments-fy10_form10k_final.pdf, accessed November 19, 2014; NEC 2010 Annual Report, http://www.nec.com/en/global/ir/pdf/annual/2010/ar2010-e.pdf, accessed November 19, 2014; Toshiba 2010 Annual Report, http://www.toshiba.co.jp/about/ir /en/finance/ar/ar2010.htm, accessed November 19, 2014; and Fujitsu 2010 Annual Report, http://www.fujitsu.com/downloads/IR/annual/2010/all.pdf, accessed November 19, 2014.

2. J. Curry and M. Kenney, "The Organizational and Geographic Configuration of the Personal Computer Value Chain," in *Locating Global Advantage: Industrial Dynamics in the International Economy,* ed. M. Kenney and R. Florida (Stanford, CA: Stanford University Press, 2004), 113–141.

3. There is some evidence that in recent years this migration process has continued, this time from China toward Myanmar, Laos, Thailand, Vietnam, and Cambodia. It is too early, however, for us to provide an evaluation of the extent to which these countries will truly become the "new China" as far as IT production is concerned. See, for example, L. Norton, "The New China," *Barron's,* November 17, 2014.

4. S. Lohr, "I.B.M. Mainframe Evolves to Serve the Digital World," *New York Times,* August 28, 2012.

5. W. Foster, Z. Cheng, J. Dedrick, and K. Kraemer, "Technology and Organizational Factors in the Notebook Industry Supply Chain" (Irvine: Personal Computer

Industry Center, University of California, 2006), http://escholarship.org/uc /item/36c6q2t9.

6. H. Yu and W. Shih, "Taiwan's PC Industry, 1976–2010: The Evolution of Organizational Capabilities," *Business History Review* 88, no. 2 (Summer 2014). We draw frequently from this article in our analysis of the evolution of the Taiwanese computer industry.

7. J. Dean, "The Forbidden City of Terry Gou," *Wall Street Journal,* August 11, 2007.

8. *OECD Information Technology Outlook, 2010* (Paris: OECD, 2010), chap. 2.

9. "From Guard Shack to Global Giant," *The Economist,* January 12, 2013. See also S. Montlake, "The Middle Way," *Forbes,* November 18, 2013, 62–64.

10. J. Dedrick, K. Kraemer, and J. Palacios, "Impacts of Liberalization and Economic Integration on Mexico's Computer Sector," *Information Society* 17, no. 2 (2001): 119–132. For more details, see also A. Borja, *El Estado y el desarrollo industrial: La política mexicana de cómputo en una perspectiva comparada* (Mexico DF: CIDE and Ediciones Miguel Ángel Porrua, 1995).

11. For a comprehensive discussion of the issues we address here, see also *Globalization and Offshoring of Software: A Report of the ACM Job Migration Task Force* (New York: Association for Computer Machinery, 2006).

12. In this section, we draw heavily from D. Breznitz, "The Israeli Software Industry," in *From Underdogs to Tigers: The Rise and Growth of the Software Industry in Brazil, China, India, Ireland, and Israel,* ed. A. Arora and A. Gambardella (Oxford: Oxford University Press, 2005), chap. 4; and C. de Fontenay and E. Carmel, "Israel's Silicon Wadi: The Forces behind Cluster Formation," in *Building High-Tech Clusters: Silicon Valley and Beyond,* ed. T. Bresnahan and A. Gambardella (Cambridge: Cambridge University Press, 2004), chap. 3.

13. Historical information on Check Point, including quantitative information, is available at the company's site at http://www.checkpoint.com/corporate/facts @a-glance/index.html, accessed July 11, 2013.

14. A. Sands, "The Irish Software Industry," in *From Underdogs to Tigers: The Rise and Growth of the Software Industry in Brazil, China, India, Ireland, and Israel,* ed. A. Arora and A. Gambardella (Oxford: Oxford University Press, 2005), 44. On the Irish software industry, see also A. Arora, A. Gambardella, and S. Torrisi, "In the Footsteps of Silicon Valley? Indian and Irish Software in the International Division of Labor," in *Building High-Tech Clusters: Silicon Valley and Beyond,* ed. T. Bresnahan and A. Gambardella (Cambridge: Cambridge University Press, 2004), chap. 4, and J. Sterne, *Adventures in Code: The Story of the Irish Software Industry* (Dublin: Liffey Press, 2004).

15. D. Breznitz, *Innovation and the State: Political Choice and Strategies for Growth in Israel, Taiwan, and Ireland* (New Haven, CT: Yale University Press, 2007), 173.

16. On the Indian software industry, see R. Heeks, *India's Software Industry: State Policy, Liberalisation, and Industrial Development* (New Delhi: Sage Publications, 1996); S. Athreye, "The Indian Software Industry," in *From Underdogs to Tigers: The Rise and Growth of the Software Industry in Brazil, China, India, Ireland, and Israel*, ed. A. Arora and A. Gambardella (Oxford: Oxford University Press, 2005), chap. 1; and especially R. Dossani, "Entrepreneurship: The Real Story behind Indian IT," in *Making IT—The Rise of Asia in High Tech*, ed. H. Rowen, M. Gong Hancock, and W. Miller (Stanford, CA: Stanford University Press, 2007). For quantitative information, see also NASSCOM, *The IT Industry in India 2004* (New Delhi: NASSCOM, 2004).

17. Dossani, "Entrepreneurship," 229. Most of the quantitative information on the evolution of the Indian software industry in this section comes from this source.

18. Ibid., 233.

19. Ibid., 235.

CONCLUSIONS

1. On the contrast between closed and open strategies in the history of the computer industry, see especially J. West, "How Open Is Open Enough? Melding Proprietary and Open Source Platform Strategies," *Research Policy* 32, no. 7 (2003): 1259–1285.

2. See J. Cortada, *The Digital Flood* (Oxford: Oxford University Press, 2012).

Index